Hong Kong, 1997

Hong Kong, 1997

The Politics of Transition

Enbao Wang

LYNNE
RIENNER
PUBLISHERS

BOULDER
LONDON

Published in the United States of America in 1995 by
Lynne Rienner Publishers, Inc.
1800 30th Street, Boulder, Colorado 80301

and in the United Kingdom by
Lynne Rienner Publishers, Inc.
3 Henrietta Street, Covent Garden, London WC2E 8LU

Library of Congress Cataloging-in-Publication Data
Wang, Enbao, 1953–
  Hong Kong, 1997 : the politics of transition / Enbao Wang.
      p.   cm.
  Includes bibliographical references and index.
  ISBN 1-55587-597-1 (hc: alk. paper)
  1. Hong Kong—Politics and government. 2. Hong Kong—Relations—
China. 3. China—Relations—Hong Kong. 4. China—Politics and
government—1976–   I. Title.
DS796.H757W36 1995
951.2505—dc20   95–12694
                                                                              CIP

British Cataloguing in Publication Data
A Cataloguing in Publication record for this book
is available from the British Library.

This book was typeset by Letra Libre, Boulder, Colorado.

Printed and bound in the United States of America

        The paper used in this publication meets the requirements
  ∞   of the American National Standard for Permanence of
        Paper for Printed Library Materials Z39.48-1984.

    5   4   3   2   1

Contents

China's Policy Toward the 1997 Issues:
  Challenges and Promises, 201
Conclusion, 204

Tables

Acknowledgments

From the time I chose the topic for my book until the final version that is now submitted to readers, I have greatly appreciated the assistance of the individuals whose help was vital for completion of the project. Though I cannot mention the names of each of those individuals, I do remember their efforts warmly. The following people, however, must be recognized for their significant involvement in my research.

This book grew out of research material I attained while writing my dissertation at the University of Alabama, and I would first like to thank my dissertation committee chair, Professor Barbara Chotiner. She read my drafts several times and left her corrections, comments, and suggestions on some thousand pages of my writings. In order to help amend my drafts, Professor Chotiner even sacrificed two of her summer vacations. Professor Carol Cassel read the whole of my first draft, corrected my English, and made important suggestions. I am deeply indebted to these two professors for their generous time spent with my manuscript. Without their guidance and assistance, I would not have been able to complete this project expeditiously.

Thanks also go to other members of my dissertation committee, Professors John O'Neal, Ronald Robel, and Terry Royed. Their quick response in reading the drafts and providing comments is greatly appreciated. Professor Steven Reed also made comments on my research.

In the course of research for this book, I have been ably aided by Professor Xiao Weiyun at Beijing University. My colleagues and friends Shaomin Huang, Marilyn Levine, Xia Li, Guangmao Nie, and Geri Waters offered various forms of assistance. I would also like to acknowledge Bin Yu for his valuable suggestions on the content of this book. In addition, Tom Buckly, Brad Lian, and Quddus Addison helped correct my English.

I am especially grateful to Martha Peacock, editor at Lynne Rienner Publishers, who helped me to choose the title of the book and offered substantial assistance in the publication process. Susan Hammond's excellent copyediting polished the final form of the manuscript.

Let it be noted, however, that the views of this book are entirely my own and I alone am responsible for those views and any errors in this book.

Finally, I would like to acknowledge the contributions of my wife, Bailing Liang, and my son, Liang Wang. Without their encouragement, understanding, and support, it would have been impossible to overcome so many difficulties in completing this endeavor. Because of their willingness to sacrifice, I was able to concentrate on my research.

Enbao Wang

Acronyms

ARATS   Association for Relations Across the Taiwan Straits
BDTCs   British Dependent Territories Citizens
BL   Basic Law
BLCC   Basic Law Consultative Committee
BLDC   Basic Law Drafting Committee
BPF   Business and Professionals Federation
CCP   Chinese Communist Party
CPPCC   Chinese People's Political Consultative Conference
CRC   Cooperative Resource Center
DABHK   Democratic Association for the Betterment of Hong Kong
DP   Democratic Party
EC   European Community
ETDZ   Economic and Technological Development Zone
Exco   Executive Council
FBIS   Foreign Broadcast Information Service
FEER   Far Eastern Economic Review
FTZ   Free Trade Zone
GATT   General Agreement on Tariffs and Trade
GNP   gross national product
HK   Hong Kong
ICCPR   International Covenant on Civil and Political Rights
ICESCR   International Covenant on Economic, Social, and Cultural Rights
IMF   International Monetary Fund
JLG   Joint Liaison Group
KMT   Kuomintang, or the Nationalists
LDF   Liberal Democratic Federation
Legco   Legislative Council
LP   Liberal Party
NCNA   New China News Agency, or Xinhua
NPC   National People's Congress
PLA   People's Liberation Army
PRC   People's Republic of China

PWC	Preliminary Working Committee
SAR	Special Administrative Region
SEZ	Special Economic Zone
SEF	Straits Exchange Foundation
UAE	United Arab Emirates
UDHK	United Democrats of Hong Kong

Introduction:
The Hong Kong Question

The world is watching Hong Kong: on July 1, 1997, Hong Kong, currently a British colony, will revert to Chinese sovereignty. Hong Kong is important to the world economy as a financial, trading, and transportation center. Hong Kong is the bridge between China and the West and between Asia and the rest of the world. Most large corporations have a branch in Hong Kong. After 1997, will the prosperity of Hong Kong, known as the "pearl of the East," be maintained? Will Hong Kong continue to be an ideal place to do business?

Hong Kong is greatly different from mainland China in terms of political, economic, and legal systems as well as way of life. With a free market economy allowing private ownership, Hong Kong is capitalist. Although Hong Kong has no democratic system, it is ruled under British common law. In contrast, mainland China is a socialist country ruled by the Communist Party. Will the transfer of sovereignty affect the standard of living of the six million people of Hong Kong? Will Hong Kong's capitalism be maintained?

Furthermore, why did the Chinese allow the British to rule Hong Kong for over 150 years but also decide to resume sovereignty over the region in 1997? How will China handle Hong Kong? What is China's policy toward Hong Kong after 1997? This book tries to answer these questions by examining China's policy toward Hong Kong and then attempts to predict what will happen after 1997.

China's policy toward Hong Kong can be simplified as "one country, two systems," meaning that after 1997, Hong Kong's current system will remain unchanged for fifty years while mainland China will continue to be socialist. This book predicts that it is likely that Hong Kong will remain capitalist and that "two systems" will indeed coexist in mainland China and Hong Kong after 1997; that Hong Kong's economy will continue to grow; and that Hong Kong will continue to be an important international trading, monetary, and transportation center.

I do not intend to create new theories in this book, but rather to examine, in light of existing concepts such as sovereignty, autonomy, and economic interdependence, the complicated issue of Hong Kong and Chinese policy. Instead of simply describing the development of China's policy toward Hong Kong, this study probes the reasons for which policies were made during successive phases—the Sino-British Joint Declaration of 1984, the Basic Law of 1990, and the policy in the transition period from 1984 to 1997.

This book argues that China's one country, two systems policy not only encompasses the difference between mainland China's socialism and the capitalism of Hong Kong, Macao, and Taiwan, but also involves many more issues such as sovereignty, autonomy, modernization, and national reunification. The policy also links China's domestic politics with international issues. Since the early 1980s when the one country, two systems policy was proposed, it has been greatly challenged, and will continue to encounter challenges when it is actually put into practice after 1997. However, as the one country, two systems concept is entirely new, it also carries intriguing promise and dimensions of probability, given trends in regional development. The formula may not be ideal, but it is pragmatic and useful for settling many of the complicated issues involving China's reunifications with Hong Kong, Macao, and Taiwan.

This book comprehensively examines Chinese policy toward Hong Kong, including: (1) the conditions under which China's decision to resume sovereignty and China's policy toward Hong Kong were made, (2) Chinese policy toward Hong Kong as stated in the Basic Law of the Hong Kong Special Administrative Region, and (3) the likelihood that China will implement this policy. In other words: why did China develop the policy of one country, two systems? What is China's Basic Law toward Hong Kong? How well is China prepared to implement that policy?

Chapters 1 and 2 attempt to answer the first question. Chapter 1 focuses on the reasons for China's decision to resume sovereignty over Hong Kong and practice one country, two systems, and demonstrates that policymakers in Beijing actually had limited choice on the issue of sovereignty. National forces and international trends determined not only that China would take Hong Kong back but also the way in which the restoration would be accomplished. Those national and international factors are the key to understanding China's policy toward Hong Kong. They include: the concept of sovereignty; Chinese nationalism; the traditional position of the People's Republic of China on British rule of Hong Kong; the demise of the British Empire after World War II; the emergence of Communist China as a military power; and the difference between the mainland's and Hong Kong's political, legal, and economic systems and ways of life. In addition, because China expected that Hong Kong would play a key role in its ambitious modernization programs, maintaining a prosperous Hong Kong was in China's interest. All these factors indicate that although the Chinese policy toward Hong Kong may not be ideal, it is a reasonable and pragmatic choice for Britain, China, and Hong Kong. Britain and Hong Kong's interests are served because Hong Kong's current economic and legal systems will be maintained after 1997. China had two goals in the settlement of the

Hong Kong question: to resume sovereignty, and to maintain a prosperous Hong Kong for China's modernization drive. The slogan one country, two systems expresses the interests of all three parties involved: People's Republic of China (PRC), Britain, and Hong Kong.

Chapter 2 demonstrates that the one country, two systems policy was not China's temporary concession to Great Britain but its long-term reunification policy. The one country, two systems policy was originally designed for Taiwan, which has had a hostile relationship with China since Taiwan's National Party rule in 1949. But when the Hong Kong question came onto Beijing's agenda in the early 1980s the Beijing authorities saw that both the Hong Kong issue and the Taiwan question could be resolved under the same principle. Logically, the Beijing regime wants to make the Hong Kong model of peaceful settlement through negotiation and economic cooperation attractive for Taiwan; therefore, Hong Kong's capitalism will be more assured because of the Taiwan issue.

Chapters 3–5 discuss the Basic Law of the Hong Kong Special Administrative Region (SAR). China's one country, two systems policy declared in the 1984 Sino-British Joint Declaration became the skeleton of the Basic Law drafted between 1985 and 1990. Both the declaration and the Basic Law are legal formulations of the Chinese policy toward Hong Kong; the difference between them is that the declaration is an international agreement while the Basic Law is China's internal law. Of the two, the Basic Law was the more controversial in Hong Kong.

In these chapters I do not discuss how the Basic Law was made, or how its drafters from the mainland and from Hong Kong disputed each article, each term, and even each word during the five-year drafting process. Several studies have already treated this matter.[1] Rather, this section focuses on the two most controversial issues: democratization of Hong Kong (Chapter 3), and the relationship between sovereign China and autonomous Hong Kong (Chapters 4 and 5). During the Basic Law drafting process, there was little dispute between Beijing and Hong Kong on the SAR's economic and legal systems because they were to remain unchanged after 1997. However, on the issue of democratization there were serious disputes between Beijing and Hong Kong, and among Hong Kong's residents themselves. The Beijing authorities and some Hong Kong citizens also had strong disagreements about how much autonomous power Hong Kong should possess. The controversy on this issue will continue to affect the relationship between Beijing and Hong Kong after 1997.

Chapter 3 discusses two questions: (1) how does the Basic Law accord with Hong Kong's current political system? and (2) whose interests are represented by the Basic Law? This chapter argues that the formation of the SAR's political system provided by the Basic Law was affected by several factors, among them the politics and government of the current British colonial rule (its constitution and practice) and the differences between liberals and conservatives of the colony over the matter. A more important factor, however, was

Beijing's position on Hong Kong's political reforms before and after 1997. This chapter also argues that the Basic Law represents the interests of the business and professional communities rather than those of the radical liberals.

Chapter 4 compares the operation of autonomous regions worldwide—examined by Hurst Hannum and Richard B. Lillich[2]—with the autonomous arrangement for the SAR as defined by the Basic Law. Hannum and Lillich's study is the only comprehensive research on the topic of nonsovereign regional autonomy, and offers a general examination of what characterizes a high degree of autonomy. The purpose of the comparison is to determine whether the SAR will have a high degree of autonomy.

Chapter 5 examines how the Beijing authorities' interpretation of sovereignty affected the drafting of the Basic Law. The section also examines how differences in the interpretation of sovereignty by Chinese Basic Law drafters and some Hong Kong citizens—state sovereignty vs. sovereign people—are a major source of dispute about the SAR's autonomy. It is expected that this disagreement between Beijing and Hong Kong will continue in the future.

Chapters 6 and 7 examine political and economic factors in China that will affect China's policy toward Hong Kong. Because the Chinese policy toward Hong Kong will not be implemented until 1997, how can one know that this policy will be workable? The best way to answer this question is to examine the current situations of both China and Hong Kong: how is China preparing for the reunification with Hong Kong after 1997; and how did Hong Kong respond to China's one country, two systems policy after the 1984 Sino-British agreement (Chapter 6)? Also, what has been the Chinese policy toward Hong Kong during the transition period before 1997 (Chapter 7)?

Chapter 6 shows how Deng Xiaoping's[3] reforms since 1978 paved the way for reunification. Deng's achievements include liberalization of the countryside, introduction of the concept of the free market, reform of the centrally planned economic system, and the "open door policy." With the open door policy, China established five Special Economic Zones (SEZs) and opened up coastal cities and regions to attract foreign investment and bridge the Chinese economy with the world economy. Hong Kong businessmen responded by investing heavily in the SEZs, the southern China regions, and other major coastal and industrial cities. As a result of Deng's economic reform and open door policy, China and Hong Kong have become economically interdependent. Moreover, Deng's market-oriented economic reform stimulated great changes in the Chinese economic system. The private and collective sectors became the engine for China's fast economic growth while the state-owned sector diminished, and in 1992 the Chinese government officially adopted the policy of a "socialist market economy." Deng's economic revolution in the last sixteen years has reshaped Chinese society, creating conditions that are impossible to reverse. Obviously, China's reform toward market economy has further assured Hong Kong's capitalism after 1997.

Chapter 7 examines Chinese policy toward Hong Kong in the transition period. In this period, China's policy included (1) trying to assure a stable transition by winning the cooperation of British authorities in both London and Hong Kong, (2) attempting to win support from the people of Hong Kong, and (3) using the Basic Law to influence Hong Kong's political reform.

Sino-British cooperation was effective in Hong Kong's political reform as well as in nonpolitical issues from 1984 to 1991. Although the two governments had differences on issues, such as the British package of Hong Kong citizens' "right of abode in Britain" and the Bill of Rights introduced by the colonial government, they settled important issues on transfer of sovereignty, such as of Hong Hong's new airport and of the Court of Final Appeal. But after 1991, with the collapse of the communist regimes of Eastern Europe and the former Soviet Union, London changed its Hong Kong policy. Britain's new policy was to abandon its previous commitment to cooperate with China on Hong Kong's political reform. The Beijing regime wanted to maintain Hong Kong's current system and insisted that Britain should keep its promise that Hong Kong's political reform before 1997 would accord with the Basic Law. But Britain was determined to place a more democratic system in Hong Kong by dramatically changing the current system before 1997. As a result, Sino-British cooperation on Hong Kong's political reforms ended. Beijing pledged that Hong Kong's governmental establishments would be dismantled in 1997 and that Hong Kong's first government and legislature would be based on the Basic Law.

The final chapter, Chapter 8, summarizes discussions and conclusions in this book. This chapter also examines the challenges to the one country, two systems policy and to the Basic Law since 1990, and the likelihood of implementation of the Chinese policy in 1997.

In this introduction, it is also necessary to discuss the origin of the Hong Kong question, the content of the 1984 Sino-British Declaration, and the making of the Basic Law of the Hong Kong Special Administrative Region. The paragraphs below introduce and provide basic background information on these three important events in modern Hong Kong history, and outline a context for the argument being made.

The Origin of the Hong Kong Question

Hong Kong includes three distinct parcels of land: the island of Hong Kong, the Kowloon Peninsula, and the New Territories as well as surrounding islands. Hong Kong was an integral part of China prior to 1840. Great Britain acquired these territories during the nineteenth century, a period when Imperial China, ruled by the Qing Dynasty, was a moribund empire, while Great Britain, which had completed its industrial revolution, was the most powerful nation in the world.

Britain first occupied Hong Kong, which is about 29.2 square miles, after the British defeated China in the First Opium War (1839–1842). According to the 1842 Treaty of Nanjing, the island of Hong Kong was ceded by China to Britain "in perpetuity." The British then forced China to cede the Kowloon Peninsula and nearby Stonecutters Island in perpetuity in the 1860 Treaty of Beijing. This agreement was reached after Britain won the Second Opium War (1858–1860), during which British and French forces sacked Beijing, the capital of the Qing Dynasty, and destroyed China's biggest royal gardens, Yuanmingyuan. The Kowloon Peninsula is only 4.2 square miles, but it is located strategically at the entrance to Hong Kong's harbor and provided a first step for the British entering China.

About forty years later, the British finally acquired the third and final parcel of land, the New Territories. This time Britain's acquisition did not result from a war with China but from diplomacy. The two Opium Wars had greatly weakened the Chinese Empire, and by the end of the nineteenth century much of coastal China had been divided by Western powers into several "spheres of influence."[4] China's defeat in the Sino-Japanese War (1894–1895) was followed by further incursions: Germany seized Jiaozhou Bay, a coastal area in Shandong Province, and secured a ninety-nine-year "lease" on it from the Chinese government. Russia acquired a twenty-five-year lease on Jinzhou Bay and Dalian Bay on the Liaodong peninsula. France leased Guangzhou [Canton] Bay for ninety-nine years. Great Britain, the biggest winner in the Western powers' partition of China, took the opportunity to lease two important parcels of land. Weihaiwei was rented for twenty-five years, countering expansion of Russian and German spheres of influence in Northern China, and in Southern China, an area already within the British sphere of influence, Britain obtained a ninety-nine-year leasehold. According to the 1898 Convention of Beijing:[5]

> it has now been agreed between the Governments of Great Britain and China that the limits of British territory shall be enlarged under lease to the extent indicated generally on the annexed map. The exact boundaries shall be hereafter fixed when proper surveys have been made by officials appointed by the two Governments. The term of this lease shall be ninety-nine years.[6]

The leased area, later called the New Territories, was located just north of the Kowloon Peninsula and comprised 370.4 square miles, including 235 islands and two bays. The British presence in today's Hong Kong region resulted from these three treaties. The Chinese insisted, as Chapter 1 will show, that the three international agreements were coerced. China's struggle for abrogation of the three agreements, as well as other "unequal treaties"[7] with Western powers, became important chapters in modern Chinese history.

Though the three parcels of land—Hong Kong island, Kowloon, and the New Territories—that make up today's British colony of Hong Kong were either ceded in perpetuity or leased for ninety-nine years, since 1898 the British have for administrative purposes considered them as a single unit. In retrospect, the historical development of Hong Kong demonstrates that the lease of the New Territories was the most important gain of the British colonial expansion in China. The New Territories is ten times larger in area than Hong Kong and Kowloon together and constitutes 90 percent of the land mass of the colony. Moreover, the New Territories provides much of the colony's water and power supply and space for manufacturing. Without this land, it would be impossible for Hong Kong to carry out normal economic operations and to maintain its prosperity.

Several books have been written about Hong Kong's history,[8] and it is not necessary to reiterate it here. However, it should be mentioned that since the nineteenth century Great Britain and China had approached the Hong Kong issue with diametrically opposed perspectives. In the British view, the purpose of initiating the Opium Wars with the Chinese was to gain free trade in China. The Chinese government restricted purchases of goods produced by "barbarian" countries like Britain, and, as a result, Britain's purchase of Chinese silk, porcelain, tea, and spices drained gold and silver specie out of the British treasury. Furthermore, the British regarded the nineteenth-century treaty settlements as perfectly legal documents sanctioned by international law and the territories so acquired as justified spoils of war or fruits of diplomatic negotiations. Therefore they were concerned with the ways in which their interests and privileges under those treaties could be protected. As will be shown in Chapter 1, however, for the Chinese the Opium Wars and the treaties were both a symbol and the origin of national humiliation. For generations the Chinese tried to abolish those "unequal treaties"—endeavors that finally led to the 1984 Sino-British agreement.

The 1984 Hong Kong Agreement

In 1984, the British and the Chinese governments issued a joint declaration. The British government declared that Hong Kong (including Hong Kong island, Kowloon, and the New Territories) would be returned to China in 1997, and the Chinese government announced that it would resume sovereignty over Hong Kong the same year. The Chinese government also announced its intended policy toward Hong Kong after the region was returned to China.

Though the transfer of sovereignty over Hong Kong was the primary content of the declaration, the long and detailed statement of Chinese policy toward Hong Kong was an important part of the document. According to the declaration, Hong Kong was to become a Special Administrative Region (SAR) of the People's Republic of China (PRC) and as such would enjoy a high degree of autonomy. The Hong Kong SAR's autonomy would include executive, legislative, and independent judicial power, including that of final adjudication. (The SAR would have its own Court of Final Appeal within the region.) The people of Hong Kong, not the officials from Beijing, were to run the SAR. Most importantly, the current economic system in Hong Kong was to remain unchanged, and so was the way of life.[9] The SAR was to maintain the economic and trade systems that previously existed in Hong Kong, and its status as a free port, a separate customs territory, and an international financial center would be maintained.[10]

Thus, in most respects, Hong Kong's status quo will be maintained. The major exception is the matter of sovereignty. The Chinese policy toward Hong Kong is founded on the principle of one country, two systems, which means that Hong Kong's capitalism will remain unchanged after sovereignty is transferred while the remainder of China will continue to practice socialism. The Chinese government also stated that all Chinese policies toward Hong Kong contained in the declaration would be stipulated, in the form of the Basic Law of the Hong Kong SAR, by the National People's Congress (NPC), China's legislature. The Beijing regime pledged that those policies would remain unchanged for fifty years after 1997.

The Basic Law

Immediately after the signing of the Sino-British Joint Declaration in December 1984, a Basic Law Drafting Committee (BLDC) was established by the NPC. The BLDC was a working group for the drafting of the "miniconstitution," as some Hong Kong citizens called it,[11] of the SAR. BLDC committee members were appointed by the NPC from both China and Hong Kong; of the fifty-nine members, thirty-six were from the PRC and twenty-three were from Hong Kong. Because the final draft was decided by a two-thirds majority of votes within the BLDC, the number of Hong Kong members was important in preventing China's domination over the drafting work. During the drafting process, three members from the mainland and one member from Hong Kong died. Two members from Hong Kong resigned from the BLDC and another two members were dismissed by the NPC Standing Committee for "their activities that did not accord with their status as a member of the BLDC." These two dismissed members supported the 1989 Beijing student demonstrations and actively participated in anti-Beijing demonstrations in Hong Kong after the Tiananmen Square incident that year.[12]

The BLDC was a working body under the NPC Standing Committee, which is responsible for the routine work of the NPC when it is not in session. The chair of the BLDC was Ji Pengfei, director of the Hong Kong and Macao Affairs Office under the State Council. Of the eight vice-chairs, four were from the mainland and four were from Hong Kong. The four mainland vice-chairs were Xu Jiatun, Wang Hanbin, Hu Sheng, and Fei Xiaotong. Xu Jiatun was director of the Hong Kong branch of Xinhua News Agency, and was actually the equivalent of China's ambassador to Hong Kong. Wang Habin was secretary general (later vice-chair) of the NPC Standing Committee and director of the NPC Working Committee on the legal system as well as director of the Legal Committee of the NPC. Hu Sheng had several titles: president of the China Academy of Social Sciences; director of the Party History Research Center of the Chinese Communist Party Central Committee; member of the Constitution Amendment Committee; and, since 1988, vice-president of the Chinese People's Political Consultative Conference (CPPCC). The CPPCC is a united front organization including communist and noncommunist personalities as well as political groups that support the leadership of the Communist Party. Fei Xiaotong was an internationally known sociologist, vice-chair of the CPPCC, and later vice-chair of the NPC Standing Committee.

Of the remaining mainland members, some were experts on Chinese law or drafters of China's constitution, like Zhang Youyu, Xiao Weiyun, and Wang Shuwen. Some were Chinese diplomats who participated in the Sino-British negotiations, like Zhou Nan and Lu Ping. The other members were well-known personalities in China and generally not Communist Party members.

Although all the participants of the BLDC were selected by the NPC, the majority of Hong Kong's BLDC members were from big business. The four Hong Kong vice-chairs in the BLDC were Sir Pao Yue-kong, the famous "king of the shipping industry" who died in 1991; Ann Tse-kai, a successful industrialist, a member of the CPPCC Standing Committee,[13] and a former member of the Executive and Legislative Councils of Hong Kong's government; David Li, the chief manager of the Bank of East Asia and a jurist and an elected member of the Legislative Council; and Fei Yimin, a former director of *Ta Kung Pao*, a pro-Beijing newspaper, and a member of the NPC Standing Committee who died in 1988. Other business tycoons included Henry Fok Yin-tung, chair of the Hong Kong Chinese General Chamber of Commerce, a member of the CPPCC Standing Committee, and an NPC delegate since 1988; and Li Ka-shing, a property and business magnate and the wealthiest person in Hong Kong. Of the twenty-three Hong Kong BLDC members, nine were or had been members of the Executive and Legislative Councils of the Hong Kong government. A number of professionals were also included. Among them were Ma Lin, former vice chancellor of the Chinese University; Szeto Wah, a member of the Hong Kong Legislative Council and president of the Hong Kong Professional Teachers' Union, a powerful organization with 30,000 members; and, as the representative of lawyers, Martin Lee, a jurist and an elected member of the Legislative Council. Lee and Szeto strongly advocated a Western-style political system and appealed to the colonial government to introduce democracy to Hong Kong. Lee and Szeto were the two members dismissed by the NPC Standing Committee after the Tiananmen incident of 1989 because they supported the students.[14] Generally, the BLDC had an overwhelming majority of conservatives.

A Basic Law Consultative Committee (BLCC), headed by Ann Tse-kai, was established by the NPC Standing Committee in 1985. The BLCC consisted of 180 Hong Kong residents; its mission was to solicit opinions of the people of

Hong Kong on the draft of the Basic Law for the BLDC. Copies of the Basic Law draft were sent to each section of Hong Kong, and citizens sent their opinions to the BLCC members in their section or for their social group. The BLCC collected five volumes of opinions,[15] which were helpful in revising the Basic Law draft.

Three revisions based on the solicited opinions were made before the Basic Law draft was sent to the NPC for final approval. The Basic Law passed the NPC on April 4, 1990, and became, as the law itself states, the highest law of the Hong Kong SAR.[16] But the Basic Law is only one of the internal laws of China, and is not a part of the Chinese Constitution.[17] The Basic Law will take effect on July 1, 1997.

The 1984 Joint Declaration did not mention when the Basic Law should be completed. Why was it completed seven years before it would take force? The Beijing authorities believed that the one country, two systems policy was generally acceptable to the people of Hong Kong and that an early enactment of the Basic Law, which is in fact the constitution of the Hong Kong SAR, and legalization of the Chinese policy in that law would help maintain Hong Kong's stability in the transition period. Moreover, China and Britain agreed that Hong Kong's political reform before 1997 should converge with the system of the SAR provided by the Basic Law. For these reasons, the Basic Law became the Beijing regime's blueprint for Hong Kong's political reforms before and after 1997.

Notes

1. See *Jibenfa de Dansheng* [The Birth of Basic Law] (Hong Kong: Hong Kong Wen Wei Publishing Company, 1990); Peter Wesley-Smith and Albert H. K. Chen, eds., *The Basic Law and Hong Kong's Future* (Hong Kong: Butterworths, 1988); William McGurn, ed., *Basic Law, Basic Questions* (Hong Kong: Review Publishing Company, 1988); and Kevin P. Lane, *Sovereignty and the Status Quo: The Historical Roots of China's Hong Kong Policy* (Boulder: Westview Press, 1990).

2. Regarding this study, see Chapter 4.

3. Because Chinese names and terms have been romanized with both the Wade-Giles system and pinyin, it is difficult to transcribe all names and terms with a single system. This book uses both pinyin and Wade-Giles systems. Generally, the names and terms from the mainland and historical personalities use pinyin. Examples are Mao Zedong [Mao Tse-tung], Zhou Enlai [Chou En-lai], Beijing [Peking], Guangzhou [Canton], and Qing [Ch'ing] Dynasty. If the names have not been romanized or have been romanized in more than one system, pinyin is favored. Names that were used by the Nationalists and names used in Taiwan's traditional transliteration, Wade-Giles, continue to be rendered in that manner. Examples are Chiang Kai-shek, Lee Teng-hui, and Chiang Ching-kuo. Names of Hong Kong personalities are used as transliterated currently in Hong Kong's English newspaper and literature, if such transliterations are available. Examples are Ann Tse-kai, David Lee, Martin Lee, Henry Fok Ying-tung, and Li Ka-sheng. If Hong Kong personalities' English names are not available, pinyin is employed.

4. Between the end of the nineteenth century and the 1940s, China was gradually partitioned by the major world powers into their spheres of influence. These were Chi-

nese regions where a Western power maintained special control of local political and economic affairs and enjoyed special privileges. For example, the provinces in the lower and middle Changjiang [Yangtze] valley were specified as the sphere of influence for Great Britain; Shandong Province for Germany; the provinces of Guangdong, Guangxi, and Yunnan for France; the southern part of today's three northeast provinces—Heilongjiang, Jilin, and Liaoning, as well as Fujian Province—for Japan; and the northern part of the three northeast provinces for Russia. The powers' influence in China began after the two Opium Wars and did not end until the 1940s. Concerning the powers' spheres of influence, also see Harold R. Isaacs, *The Tragedy of the Chinese Revolution*, 2nd ed. (Stanford, Calif.: Stanford University Press, 1961).

5. Concerning the Western powers' division of China's territories in the nineteenth century, see Henry Kittredge North, *China and the Powers* (New York: John Day, 1927), 22–51. North offered a Western view on the issue. Hu Sheng, *Imperialism and Chinese Politics* (Beijing: Foreign Language Press, 1955; reprint, Westport, Conn.: Hyperion Press, 1973); and Zhang Haiping, "The Revolution and Sun Yat-sen," *Beijing Review* 34, no. 41 (14 October 1991): 25–26, represent the Chinese view.

6. Peter Wesley-Smith in "The Convention of Peking, 1898," *Unequal Treaty 1898–1997: China, Great Britain and Hong Kong's New Territories* (Hong Kong: Oxford University Press, 1980).

7. The concept "unequal treaty" is controversial. For example, Lung-Fong Chen defined an unequal treaty as "a treaty of unequal and nonreciprocal nature contrary to the principles of equality of states and of reciprocity in the making, obligations, rights and performance of the treaty." Lung-Fong Chen, *State Succession Relating to Unequal Treaties* (Hamden, Conn.: Archon, 1974), 34. Ian Brownlie, professor of public international law at Oxford University, defined unequal treaties as follows: "The doctrine of international law in Communist states, invoked by their representatives in organs of the United Nations, holds treaties not concluded on the basis of the sovereign equality of parties to be invalid. . . . While 'Western' jurists oppose the doctrine on the ground that it is too vague, the principle is regarded as entirely just by newly independent states, and it is no longer confined to the thinking of jurists from Communist states." Ian Brownlie, *Principles of Public International Law* (New York: Oxford University Press, 1990), 615–616. However, Fariborz Nozari argued: "An unequal peace treaty imposed by a victorious aggressor lacks legal validity. The *de facto* enforcement of such a treaty does not change its *de jure* invalidity. As soon as the means of force disappear, the situation must be brought back to the state which existed before the time the treaty was put into operation." Fariborz Nozari, *Unequal Treaties in International Law* (Stockholm: S-Byran Sundt, 1971), 286. In addition, concerning the history of conclusions and terminations of the unequal treaties between China and the powers, see William L. Tung, *China and the Foreign Powers: The Impact of and Reaction to Unequal Treaties* (Dobbs Ferry, N.Y.: Oceana, 1970).

8. See G. B. Endacott, *A History of Hong Kong*, 2nd ed. (Hong Kong: Oxford University Press, 1978); Wesley-Smith, *Unequal Treaty, 1898–1997*; and Lane, *Sovereignty and the Status Quo*.

9. The term "way of life" is clarified by the 1984 Sino-British Declaration thus: "The current social and economic systems in Hong Kong will remain unchanged, and so will the life-style. Rights and freedoms, including those of the person, of speech, of the press, of assembly, of association, of travel, of movement, of correspondence, of strike, of choice of occupation, of academic research and religious belief will be ensured by law in the Hong Kong Special Administrative Region. Private property, ownership of enterprises, legitimate right of inheritance and foreign investment will be protected" (Article 3, Section 5).

10. Chapter 4 will discuss the SAR's high degree of autonomy, which is stipulated by the 1984 Joint Declaration and the Basic Law of the Hong Kong SAR.

11. Emily Lau, "The Early History of the Drafting Process," in Wesley-Smith and Chen, eds., *The Basic Law and Hong Kong's Future*, 90.

12. *Jibenfa de Dansheng* (Hong Kong Wen Wei Publishing), 212–213.

13. The Chinese government also appoints Hong Kong and Macao elites to be delegates to the NPC or the CPPCC, because the People's Republic insists that Hong Kong and Macao are Chinese territories and that their citizens are Chinese patriots.

14. Concerning the Basic Law Drafting Committee, see Lau, "The Early History of the Drafting Process," in Wesley-Smith and Chen, eds., *The Basic Law and Hong Kong's Future*, 90–104; and *Jibenfa de Dansheng* (Hong Kong Wen Wei Publishing), 212–230.

15. Zhonghua Renmin Gongheguo Xianggang Tebie Xingzhengqu Jibenfa Zixun Weiyuanhui (hereafter Jibenfa Zixun Weiyuanhui) [The Consultative Committee of the Basic Law of the Hong Kong Special Administrative Region of the People's Republic of China], *Zixun Baogao* [Consultative Reports], vols. 1–5 (Hong Kong: Zhonghua Shangwu Caise Yinshua Youxian Gongsi, 1988 and 1989).

16. The Basic Law states: "In accordance with Article 31 of the Constitution of the People's Republic of China, the systems and policies practised in the Hong Kong Special Administrative Region, including the social and economic systems, the system for safeguarding the fundamental rights and freedoms of its residents, the executive, legislative and judicial systems, and the relevant policies, shall be based on the provisions of this Law. No law enacted by the legislature of the Hong Kong Special Administrative Region shall contravene this Law" (Basic Law [hereafter BL], Article 11).

17. Norman Miners's suggestion may be inaccurate. He thought that the Basic Law would "form part of the Constitution of the People's Republic of China." See Norman Miners, *The Government and Politics of Hong Kong*, 4th ed. (Hong Kong: Oxford University Press, 1986), 67. The Basic Law is not included in the Chinese Constitution.

1

Chinese Policy Toward Hong Kong: A Limited Choice

Since the announcement of the 1984 Sino-British Declaration, the Hong Kong question has become a controversial issue and aroused worldwide attention. This chapter will show that the outcome of the 1984 Hong Kong agreement—the transfer of sovereignty in 1997 and the adoption of the one country, two systems policy after sovereignty is transferred—was determined by several factors. In fact, the policymakers in Beijing had limited options on the issue of sovereignty, and the Hong Kong question posed a great challenge. The Chinese government's choice of a flexible policy toward Hong Kong was a pragmatic solution. What were the factors determining the 1984 Hong Kong settlement? Why did the Beijing regime choose the one country, two systems policy toward Hong Kong?

Sovereignty

The meaning of the concept of sovereignty is central to the Hong Kong question. First, differences between Great Britain and the People's Republic in the interpretation of the term led to conflict before the 1984 agreement. Then, after the agreement was made, differences between Beijing and Hong Kong over the interpretation of sovereignty affected the drafting of those portions of the Basic Law that concerned the relationship between a sovereign China and an autonomous Hong Kong. The Chinese government and mainland scholars stressed state sovereignty while officials and scholars from Hong Kong, particularly the prodemocracy liberals, favored the theory of a sovereign people. Moreover, as Chapter 2 will show, the concept of sovereignty linked China's internal politics with international issues in the Hong Kong, Macao, and Taiwan questions, all of which involved reunification with regions in which different political systems had evolved. The Chinese authorities maintained that the three questions must be settled according to the single formula of one country, two systems. At

13

the same time, Beijing insisted that China would resume sovereignty over Hong Kong and Macao, that the issue of Taiwan was internal to China, and that Beijing must be sovereign over Taipei after the mainland's reunification with that island. In addition, conflicts developed between China and Britain and between Beijing and Hong Kong concerning the interpretation of Chinese sovereignty over Hong Kong, as written in the Basic Law, during the transition period. Deng Xiaoping was convinced that the settlement of the Hong Kong, Macao, and Taiwan questions would serve China's modernization drive. Therefore, the issue of sovereignty took on a symbolic appeal in relation to China's nationalism, reunification, and industrialization.

The term "sovereignty" is defined by the *International Encyclopedia of the Social Sciences* as:

> a theory of politics which claims that in every system of government there must be some absolute power of final decision exercised by some person or body recognized both as competent to decide and as able to enforce the decision. This person or body is called the sovereign. The simplest form of the theory is the common assertion that "the state is sovereign," which is usually a tautology, just as the expression "sovereign state" can be a pleonasm.[1]

According to this definition, the concept of sovereignty has two interpretations. First, sovereignty is a power of highest authority and that power is supreme, absolute, and independent. Second, sovereignty is a special attribute of the independent state.

An early theory of sovereignty can be found in Aristotle's *Politics* and in the classical works of Roman law. Aristotle argued that "citizen body is the sovereign power in states. Sovereignty must reside either in one man, or in a few, or in a bulk of the citizens," and he distinguished these three different institutions as "Kingship," "Aristocracy," and "Polity." Obviously, Aristotle believed that sovereignty existed in all three forms of government.[2] The Romans also clearly expressed the idea of sovereignty in their well-known saying that "the will of the Prince has the force of law, since the people have transferred to him all their right of power."[3]

It was the modern French thinker Jean Bodin who first systematically discussed the theory of sovereignty. In his *Six Books of the Commonwealth*, the cornerstone of modern thinking on political science, Bodin defined sovereignty as "the absolute and perpetual power of a commonwealth."[4] For Bodin, the supreme power is absolute and is totally free and independent from any restraint of law above. Bodin asserted that the sovereign has "the power to make law binding on all his subjects in general," and that other rights of sovereignty include making peace and war, hearing appeals from the sentences of all courts, appointing and dismissing state officials, taxing, granting privileges of exemption to all subjects, determining coinage, and receiving oaths of fidelity from subjects.[5]

It should be noted that Bodin's theory of sovereignty was accompanied by the emergence of the modern nation-state in Europe. In a sense, Bodin's theory of sovereignty was a product of his era. In the Middle Ages, the monarchies of Europe were hierarchical systems of allegiances, based on mutual rights and obligations, in which the king was subordinate to the emperor and the duke to the king, and so on. The Reformation from the fifteenth to seventeenth centuries disturbed the order of the existing religious and political systems. Protestant kings challenged the authority of Roman Catholic emperors and Protestant dukes fought Roman Catholic kings. The modern concept of sovereignty and the state system were expressed in the Treaty of Westphalia of 1648, and the concept of sovereignty is the key to understanding the state system that emerged thereafter. In order to gain sovereignty, a regime must first have its territory, its population, the ability to maintain order within the state, and recognition by other existing sovereign states. Obviously, the modern concept of sovereignty is different from Aristotle's, in which sovereignty was regarded as the highest authority but not related to the nation-state. In Bodin's era, sovereignty became a special attribute of the nation-state. In other words, only nation-states could enjoy sovereignty; state and sovereignty were inseparable.

Philosophers such as Thomas Hobbes, John Locke, Jean-Jacques Rousseau, and Karl Marx further developed the theory of sovereignty. After Bodin, Hobbes was the first thinker to make great contributions in the development of the theory of sovereignty. In his *The Leviathan*, published in 1651, Hobbes argued that sovereign power is necessary for men to "defend them from invasion of foreigners, and the injuries of one another." For defense against foreign invaders and for preventing individuals from destroying each other, Hobbes suggested that all men should make a contract, or covenant, in which they agree to give up their rights of governing themselves to "some man, or assembly of men. . . . This done, the multitude so united in one person, is called a Commonwealth," a "Leviathan." In this institution of the commonwealth, the man or the assembly of men will have, for the interests of commonwealth, a sovereign power that will not be limited.[6]

Bodin's and Hobbes's theories of sovereignty were challenged by Locke and Rousseau. Locke did not directly reject Hobbes, but reinterpreted natural law as encompassing innate and inalienable rights inherent in each individual. Society and the state exist to protect these individual rights, including the right of property. Locke moderated Hobbes's view that state sovereignty is coercive and supreme, and he argued that the government should rule with the consent of the governed.[7]

In his *The Social Contract*, published in 1756, Rousseau agreed with Hobbes that state sovereignty is absolute, indivisible, inalienable, and infallible; it is the result of a contract in which individuals surrender their will. However, unlike Hobbes, Rousseau considered the state a "body politic" in which the government has not even a delegated power. It is the people who are the bearer of sovereignty.[8]

Marx argued that previous approaches to the theory of state sovereignty were actually philosophical formulations rather than political reality. The state only represented the interests and will of the ruling class, not the general interests of society. He did not believe such a general interest existed in a capitalist society. It was only under socialism that the government of the working class would represent the interests of the working people.[9]

Though these modern thinkers, from Bodin to Marx, differed about who is sovereign and how sovereignty functions within a state, they did not deny that sovereignty—a supreme and absolute power—exists. Under the concept of sovereignty, unchallenged authorities are created to settle legal disputes and to maintain social order within the nation-state. In addition, sovereignty has become a fundamental concept in international relations.

However, there is an essential difference between the practice of sovereignty in domestic politics and in international politics. In domestic politics, sovereignty is generally a source of order. National authorities in such forms as governmental, legal, and judicial agencies, military forces, and the police maintain the normal operation of national affairs. In most cases, these authorities have the ability to enforce the law, settle conflicts or disputes, and maintain social order. For instance, if two parties dispute over a piece of land, they can bring the case to the court for a ruling. The court has the authority of a sovereign government to settle disputes, and the two disputing parties have to respect the court's ruling. The defeated party may appeal the case to a higher court, even to the supreme court of the state, but ultimately the court's ruling binds the two disputing parties, even if one party still disagrees with the decision. This description demonstrates how the concept of sovereignty authorizes the maintenance of social order within a state.

In international politics, however, the application of sovereignty has opposite consequences as regards the authority of the state. Because each state is sovereign, there is no authority that is superior to any one state. Therefore, each state has the authority to interpret international laws and defend its own interests. If one state claims a piece of territory over which another exercises sovereignty, there is no authority above the state, such as a world government, to settle that dispute. However, because the possession of territory is essential to the existence of a nation-state, no state is willing to share sovereignty over its own territory with another state if the former is powerful enough to resist occupation and defend itself. It is less likely for states to agree to compromise over territorial disputes than over other matters.[10] In most cases, in a dispute over territorial matters the stronger power or powers (military, economic, political, or technological)[11] are likely to gain no matter how the two parties interpret international law and defend their positions theoretically. This situation explains most changes on the political map of the world in the centuries after a modern interstate system was established under the concept of sovereignty.

This argument also explains the change in sovereignty over Hong Kong in 1842 as well as the expected change in 1997. First, the above review of the concept of sovereignty shows that it was itself a factor in the conclusion of the 1984 agreement. As will be discussed in detail later in this chapter, both Britain and China claimed sovereignty over Hong Kong during the negotiations in the early 1980s. Britain proposed a policy of "divided sovereignty" over Hong Kong after 1997, according to which China would resume sovereignty over Hong Kong but the British would continue their administrative rule over the region. However, China insisted that sovereignty was nonnegotiable and could not be divided or commuted. The Chinese also believed that China would be able to take Hong Kong back with fewer losses under the one country, two systems formula. Second, because the Hong Kong question involved the sensitive issue of territorial sovereignty, there was less likelihood that the two parties could compromise. Pragmatically, there were two possible outcomes for the settlement in the 1980s: First, Great Britain would continue to rule Hong Kong under the theory of divided sovereignty. This would be the likely outcome if Britain continued to maintain its dominant position over China and could defeat China militarily in the 1980s, as it had in the 1840s and 1850s. For the Chinese, the application of divided sovereignty would be another form of British colonial rule over Hong Kong. Second, China would resume its sovereignty over Hong Kong.

Chinese Nationalism
and the Hong Kong Question

The Pre-1949 Period

The foreign occupation of Chinese soil through various treaties and conventions on the one hand, and strong anti-imperialist and anticolonialist movements on the other, form the main content of modern Chinese history. Even during the last years of the Qing Dynasty—which submitted to Great Britain in signing the three treaties about Hong Kong (the Treaty of Nanjing of 1842, the Treaty of Beijing of 1860, and the Convention of Beijing of 1898) as well as other unequal treaties—Chinese intellectuals called on the Western powers to return Chinese territories. The intellectuals argued that the circumstances under which the treaties were conducted had changed.[12] In the 1890s, Kang Youwei, a well-known leader of 1898 Hundred Day Reform, criticized the imperialist countries' treatment of China. Kang said that although China was nominally still an independent country, Chinese territory and major economic systems such as railways, shipping, trade, and banks were under the control of powers who "can grab whatever they like." Kang argued that China "is really no longer independent although outwardly it remains so."[13] Kang also pointed out that the unequal treaties imposed on China were "an extreme national shame."[14]

   Dr. Sun Yat-sen, the first President of the Republic of China after the Chinese Revolution of 1911, also criticized as unequal treaties the agreements concluded by the Qing Dynasty and the Western powers. Sun argued that the Western powers' political and economic oppression made China a "hypo-colony." He wrote:

> The result is that China is everywhere becoming a colony of the Powers. The people of the nation still think we are only a "semi-colony" and comfort themselves with this term, but in reality we are being crushed by economic strength of the powers to a greater degree than if we were a full colony. China is not the colony of one nation but of all, and we are not the slaves of one country but of all. I think we ought to be called a "hypo-colony."[15]

In his short will, Sun urged his followers again that "the abolition of unequal treaties should be carried into effect with the least possible delay."[16]

The overthrow of the Qing Dynasty in the Revolution of 1911 did not end foreign partition of Chinese territory. The Western powers and Japan, a power that had newly emerged in Asia, continued to preserve and even increase their privileges in China. The powers continued to ask China to cede or lease Chinese territories, established their extraterritorial concessions,[17] enjoyed extraterritorial rights, and directed the Chinese Customs to permit the entry of powers' goods into the Chinese market under low tariffs.[18]

At the 1919 Paris Peace Conference, China, as one of the victor states of the First World War, expected to recover its Shandong Province, which had been occupied by the defeated Germany. However, the powers decided to grant that territory to Japan. China's diplomatic failure and the powers' decision shocked Chinese students and intellectuals. On May 4, 1919, the students of Beijing University took to the streets to protest *qiangquan* [the powers] and *guozei* [traitors]. The protest aroused an anti-imperialist and antifeudal movement that spread throughout the country. The May Fourth Movement became a history-making event in modern Chinese history, and awakened the Chinese people to the struggle for independence and the struggle to end feudalism, which had lasted for 2,000 years.

Anti-imperialism and national independence were the mission of the Kuomintang (KMT), or the Nationalists, the first major political party of China. Under the leadership of Dr. Sun Yat-sen, the KMT held its first National Congress in January 1924. Leading Chinese Communists also joined the KMT and participated in the KMT's Congress. In its manifesto, the KMT declared its anti-imperialist foreign policy and the party's position on the unequal treaties:

> (1) All unequal treaties such as those providing for leased territories, extraterritorial privileges, foreign control of the customs tariff, and exercise of political authority on Chinese territories which impair the sovereignty of the Chinese nation, should be abolished, and new treaties should be concluded on the basis of absolute equality and mutual respect of sovereign rights.
>
> (2) All countries that are willing to abandon their special privileges in China and to abolish their treaties which impair Chinese sovereignty should be accorded most-favored-nation treatment.
>
> (3) All other treaties between China and the foreign powers which are in any way prejudicial to the interests of China should be revised according to the principle of non-infringement of each other's sovereignty.[19]

After the death of Sun Yat-sen in 1925, the Nationalists continued their cooperation with the Communists in the Northern Expedition of 1926–1927.[20]

However, in April 1927 the Nationalists, under the leadership of Chiang Kai-shek, broke off their cooperation and established their government in Nanjing. In the following years, the Nationalists successfully defeated the remaining warlords and unified China. In 1928, the government in Nanjing pronounced that it would recover all Chinese territories occupied by the powers, and in June 1928 of that year declared:

> For 80 years China has been under the shackles of unequal treaties. These restrictions are a contravention of the principle in international law, of mutual respect and sovereignty and are not allowed by any sovereign state. . . . Now that the unification of China is being consummated we think the time is ripe for taking further steps and begin at once to negotiate—in accordance with diplomatic procedure—new treaties on a basis of complete equality and mutual respect for each other's sovereignty.[21]

In addition, Chiang Kai-shek asserted that China's weakness was mainly a result of Western powers' exploitation under unequal treaties. He continued, "The implementation of unequal treaties constitutes a complete record of China's national humiliation."[22] At the 1931 National People's Convention, Chiang's Nationalist government proclaimed the "Manifesto Concerning the Abrogation of Unequal Treaties" and concluded:

> 1) The Chinese people will not recognize all the past unequal treaties imposed by the Powers on China.
> 2) The National Government shall, in conformity with Dr. Sun Yat-sen's testamentary injunction, achieve with least possible delay China's equality and independence in the Family of Nations.[23]

As a result of Chinese pressure and a stronger Chinese government under Chiang, the powers considered giving up part of their privileges in China, among them extraterritoriality. By the end of 1928, the Nationalist government successfully terminated or modified some of the powers' privileges and recovered China's tariff autonomy.[24] Great Britain also was pressured to renounce its concessions at Hankou and Jinjiang in 1928 and to return the leased territory of Weihaiwei in 1930. But the British did not return Hong Kong, including the New Territories, to China. By the 1920s Hong Kong was important to the British for Far Eastern trade, as will be discussed later, and it remained in Britain's interest to continue to rule Hong Kong while relinquishing some extraterritorial privileges in China.[25] Britain and other powers could not accept the Chinese government's request that all extraterritorial privileges be terminated by January 1, 1930, even though the powers agreed to the principle of a gradual withdrawal after that date. For the Nationalist government, the existence of foreign extraterritoriality, which was established in major Chinese cities and was a symbol of Chinese humiliation, was more intolerable than the British presence in Hong Kong, located far from China's political and economic centers. Also,

Chiang's government was not powerful enough to gain abrogation of all the treaties in one move. Another reason that Chiang's government could not abolish all the treaties was the Japanese threat to China. In 1931, Japan occupied Manchuria, and the next year attacked Shanghai. In 1933, the Japanese established a puppet government that ruled the Rehe, Chahaer, and Inner Mongolian regions. Japan's rapid encroachment upon large Chinese territories threatened China's survival, and response to Japan was more urgent than abolition of the unequal treaties.

The Nationalists' diplomatic efforts to terminate foreign privileges in China were suspended after the Japanese occupation of Manchuria in 1931. Japan's invasion of China in 1937 and its occupation of major ports also weakened the Western extraterritoriality system. After the Japanese attack on Pearl Harbor and Hong Kong in 1941, China became an ally of the United States and Great Britain against the Japanese; and Chiang's government took the opportunity to ask Britain to give up colonial rule in Hong Kong. In 1942, the 100th anniversary of the signing the Treaty of Nanjing, the Nationalist government made a public appeal to abolish all the unequal treaties. China's position was supported by the United States, where anticolonialism was strong. United States President Franklin D. Roosevelt clearly stated several times from 1943 to 1945 that Britain should return Hong Kong to China, because Clause Three of the Atlantic Charter of 1943 called for the liberation of all peoples and applied to the people overrun by the Germans and Japanese as well as to the people under British colonial rule.[26] However, the British rejected the Chinese proposal and refused to relinquish Hong Kong. They did promise to reconsider the Hong Kong question when the war was over.[27]

The Japanese defeat in 1945 aroused tensions between China and Britain over which country should accept Japan's surrender at Hong Kong. When the British got support from United States President Harry S. Truman, Chiang's government had to allow Britain to accept Japanese surrender and to continue colonial rule. To comfort the Chinese people concerning the future of Hong Kong, Chiang promised that his government would continue to negotiate with the British for the settlement of the Hong Kong question through diplomatic channels.[28] Chiang's decision demonstrated that he could do nothing but accept the status quo on the Hong Kong issue. In 1949, Chiang's government was overthrown by the Chinese Communists, ending his opportunities to settle the Hong Kong issue.

This review of Chinese history has disclosed a simple fact: the unequal treaties concluded between the Qing Dynasty and the Western powers were a national humiliation for generations of Chinese. Chinese elites and political leaders, such as Kang Youwei, Sun Yat-sen, and Chiang Kai-shek, all strongly condemned the unequal treaties, including the three treaties involving Hong Kong. The Chinese thought that Britain's rule in Hong Kong challenged Chinese national dignity.

The Post-1949 Period

From the time of its establishment on July 23, 1921, the Chinese Communist Party (CCP) was a strong anti-imperialist and anticolonialist organization adhering to Marxist-Leninist doctrine. The Manifesto of the Second Congress of the Party, published in 1922, pointed out that China was under "the domination of international imperialism" and had been "trampled underfoot by Britain, the United States, France and Japan." The manifesto further stated that the imperialist oppression of China and competition among imperialist powers for economic interests in China "accounts for China's present special status in the field of international relations." The imperialist aggression, the manifesto continued,

> is bound to deprive the Chinese people completely of their economic independence and reduce the four hundred million oppressed people of China to slaves of the international trusts, these new masters of a new type. The time has come when we cannot but rise to give battle, for the Chinese people face a life-and-death struggle.[29]

Mao Zedong, one of the founders of the CCP, offered his view on modern Chinese foreign relations. He argued that since the First Opium War of 1840, the Western powers had invaded China and opened China's "door," which had been closed to international intercourse. The Chinese suddenly found that their country was much more backward than the Western countries. Thereafter, members of the progressive Chinese elite, including Dr. Sun Yat-sen, traveled abroad, mainly to the West and Japan, to gain information for the benefit of their nation and their people. Mao continued by stating that these elite could not understand why their "teachers" (Western powers, from which the Chinese were learning) always invaded "students" (China). In his 1939 essay, "The Chinese Revolution and the Chinese Communist Party," Mao argued that the purpose of the "imperialist powers" in invading China was not to transform feudal China into a capitalist China, but "to transform China into their semi-colony or colony." Mao further listed a number of undertakings by which the imperialist powers were able to realize their purpose, among them that the powers started war against China, including the two Opium Wars, and that the powers seized and "leased" Chinese territories. Mao particularly mentioned the British seizure of Hong Kong. Then the powers "forced China to conclude numerous unequal treaties"; the imperialists gained control of all the important trading ports in China by unequal treaties; and the powers monopolized industries and banks in China and hampered the development of China's own industry and banking system. Mao also pointed out: "Imperialism controls not only China's vital financial and economic arteries but also her political and military powers." For instance, in the Japanese-occupied areas, "everything is monopolized by Japanese imperialism." Mao concluded that "the contradiction between imperialism and the Chinese nation . . . is the principal one among the various contradictions." He continued that the primary task of the Chinese revolution was "the national revolution for the overthrow of imperialism."[30]

In April 1949, when the Chinese Communists' military forces, the People's Liberation Army (PLA), skirmished with the *Amethyst* and three other British warships in China's Yangtse River, Mao stated:

> The Yangtse is an inland waterway of China. What right have you British to send in your warships? You have no such right. The Chinese people will defend their territory and sovereignty and absolutely will not permit encroachment by foreign governments.[31]

On the eve of the founding of the PRC on October 1, 1949, the First Session of the Chinese People's Political Consultative Conference (CPPCC) was held on September 21–30, 1949. The CPPCC represented delegations from all procommunist political parties, groups, and organizations. As a constituent body of the PRC, the CPPCC adopted a Common Program as the fundamental law of the New China prior to the enactment of a constitution in 1954. The Common Program declared the PRC's opposition to imperialist aggression; cooperation with all peace-loving countries, especially with the Soviet Union; and "protection of independence, freedom, integrity of territory and sovereignty of the country." As regarded treaties concluded between previous Chinese governments and foreign powers, the Common Program stated that the PRC would "recognize, abrogate, revise, or re-negotiate them according to their respective contents."[32] Later the PRC adopted "five principles" for conducting foreign relations, the first of which was mutual respect for other nations' territorial integrity and sovereignty.[33] Obviously, the British occupation of Hong Kong under unequal treaties was a great challenge to the principles of the PRC's foreign policy. The incompatibility of the unequal treaties with China's "five peaceful principles" indicated that someday China would no longer tolerate British rule of Hong Kong.

The Communists also thought their course was to continue the national liberation movement of fighting colonialism and imperialism, dating from the Opium War of 1840.[34] In his opening speech at the First Plenary Session of the CPPCC on September 21, 1949, Mao said:

> For over a century our forebears have never stopped waging tenacious struggle against domestic and foreign oppressors, including the Revolution of 1911 led by Mr. Sun Yat-sen, the great forerunner of the Chinese revolution. Our forebears have instructed us to fulfill their behest, and we have now done so accordingly.[35]

In his draft for the inscription on the Monument to the People's Heroes established in Tiananmen Square in Beijing, Mao wrote that the Communists' course was to continue the struggle begun in 1840 to "resist the enemy, domestic and foreign, to strive for the independence of the nation and the freedom of the people."[36]

Even after Deng Xiaoping reemerged to power in 1978 and the new Chinese government announced that the country would be open to the outside world, the Chinese nationalistic theme continued among the reform leaders in terms of their attitude toward foreign nations. In his report to the Twelfth Party Congress held in September 1982, Hu Yaobang, general secretary of the party, declared, "Being patriots, we do not tolerate any encroachment on China's national dignity or interests." Hu continued, "Having suffered aggression and oppression for over a century, the Chinese people will never again allow themselves to be humiliated as they were before."[37] Deng Xiaoping's speech at the same congress was also full of nationalistic language:

> Independence and self-reliance have always been and will forever be our basic stand. We Chinese people value our friendship and cooperation with other countries and peoples. We value even more our hard-won independence and sovereign rights. No foreign country can expect China to be its vassal or expect it to swallow any bitter fruit detrimental to its own interests.[38]

Hu's and Deng's speeches were made a few days before British Prime Minister Margaret Thatcher's historic visit to Beijing for the settlement of the Hong Kong question in September 1982. The Chinese leaders' remarks indicated that it was not likely that they would make concessions on the question of sovereignty of Hong Kong.

When Prime Minister Thatcher formally talked with Deng Xiaoping on the question of Hong Kong, Deng expressed that the three Sino-British treaties on Hong Kong were unequal treaties and that they were invalid. Thatcher argued that those treaties might not have been equal but that they were valid under international law. Deng was angered by Thatcher's position on the unequal treaties and emotionally informed the British Prime Minister that China would recover all territories of Hong Kong under British rule by 1997. Deng said:

> On the question of sovereignty, China has no room for maneuver. To be frank, the question is not open to discussion.
> . . . If China failed to take Hong Kong back in 1997, when the People's Republic will have been established for 48 years, no Chinese leaders or government would be able to justify themselves for that failure before the Chinese people or before the people of the world.
> It would mean that the present Chinese government was just like the government of the late Qing Dynasty and that the present Chinese leaders were just like Li Hongzhang!
> . . . If we failed to take Hong Kong back in 15 years, the people would no longer have any reason to trust us, and any Chinese government would have no alternative but to step down and voluntarily leave the political arena.[39]

Zhao Ziyang, the Chinese premier, also stated that China would regain sovereignty over Hong Kong.[40] Both Deng and Zhao made it clear that sovereignty was not negotiable. The Chinese expressed their intolerance of Thatcher's position on the Hong Kong question and the unequal treaties:

These treaties, which were forced upon the Chinese people, provide an iron-clad proof of British imperialism's plunder of Chinese territory. The Chinese people have always held that these treaties are illegal and therefore null and void. Even when they were still in a powerless status, the Chinese people waged a protracted, unremitting and heroic struggle against imperialist humiliation and oppression and against the series of unequal treaties forced upon them by imperialism. It was not until the founding of the People's Republic of China in 1949 that the Chinese people finally won independence and emancipation. Now that Chinese people have stood up, it is only natural that they find these treaties . . . unacceptable.[41]

In conclusion, though the Communists and the Nationalists differed fundamentally in ideology, their strong nationalism was almost identical. Chinese nationalism was an important reason for China's decision to recover Hong Kong in the 1984 agreement. In modern Chinese history, all those who fought against the colonialists and imperialists were praised. Lin Zexu, Feng Zicai, Deng Shichang, and Zhang Zizhong[42] were national heroes to the Nationalists and the Communists alike. On the other hand, those who compromised or surrendered to the imperialist powers were considered national traitors. Qi Ying, Li Hongzhang, and Wang Jingwei[43] were all condemned by generations of Chinese. It was unthinkable that during the Sino-British negotiations in the early 1980s the policymakers in Beijing would agree to a continuation of Hong Kong's British rule, because no Chinese leader wanted to be viewed as a national traitor in history or to be condemned by his people. Deng Xiaoping may have summed up the real feelings of the policymakers in Beijing when he said that he would not be a second Li Hongzhang. Strong Chinese nationalism, reinforced by the PRC's military power, explains why Beijing was determined to recover Hong Kong in 1997. The tradition of nationalism was the real crux of Chinese efforts leading to the 1984 Hong Kong settlement, and the outcome of the settlement cannot be correctly explained without an understanding of that tradition.

Beijing's Official Position
on the Hong Kong Question, 1949–1970s

Though the Communists had strong nationalistic feelings on the issue of the unequal treaties, the government in Beijing was cautious on the Hong Kong question. From the 1950s to the 1980s, China never initiated any negotiations with Great Britain over Hong Kong. In principle, Mao's government repeated the Nationalist position that all the unequal treaties on Hong Kong were invalid, and that China would settle the Hong Kong question "in an appropriate way when conditions are ripe."[44] In practice, the People's Republic tolerated British rule of Hong Kong for diplomatic and economic reasons. In 1949, the PLA swept all of China and approached the China–Hong Kong border. However, it did not cross that border. The British promised to recognize the newly established government in Beijing, and in return the People's Republic was to tolerate British presence in Hong Kong. At that time, though Chiang's Nationalist government was defeated and had moved to Taipei, Taiwan, his regime was still recognized by the major powers, including the United States and Great Britain. Because Chiang's Nationalists pledged they would return to the mainland at any moment, Beijing's first priority was to wipe out Chiang's remaining forces in Taiwan. Therefore, Hong Kong remained a less consequential question. However, the British decision to recognize Beijing was an important diplomatic victory for the PRC. In January 1950, London kept its word by establishing formal relations with the government in Beijing while cutting off diplomatic relations with Taipei. Great Britain was the first major Western power to extend its recognition to the People's Republic. France's diplomatic relations with the PRC were established only in 1965, and the United States' in 1979.

After the Korean War, because of the American-led United Nations trade embargo against the PRC, Hong Kong became the only channel by which China could maintain a limited economic tie with the West. In the 1950s, China exported through Hong Kong to the rest of the world. In the next decade, after the Soviet Union initiated an economic blockade against China, China imported, also through Hong Kong, complete industrial plants from European countries and Japan.[45] Moreover, Hong Kong became an increasingly important source of foreign exchange for China.[46] The foreign exchange acquired from China–Hong Kong trade was over 50 percent of China's total foreign exchange earnings from 1952 to the 1970s, and about 30 to 40 percent in the 1980s.[47] Since the 1960s, Beijing and the British Hong Kong government have maintained friendly relations. China became a permanent and reliable supplier of water and food for Hong Kong. The British Hong Kong authorities understood that Beijing was sensitive about the issue of sovereignty, and carefully formulated public policies, both internal and external, to avoid any unnecessary provocations offensive to the colony's powerful neighbor. The colonial government banned any activities that used Hong Kong as a base from which to conduct political activities against China. Both the London and Hong Kong governments understood Beijing's stand on the Taiwan issue and the colonial government prohibited Taiwan from conducting any anti-Beijing activities in Hong Kong.[48]

However, the PRC was careful in all its actions and statements never to do anything that could possibly be construed as even tacit recognition of the legitimacy of British colonial rule over Hong Kong. On March 10, 1973, Huang Hua, China's ambassador to the United Nations, wrote a letter to the chair of the United Nations Special Committee on Colonialism, which had included Hong Kong and Macao in the list of remaining colonial territories. Huang asked the chair to remove Hong Kong and Macao from the committee's list. The letter stated:

As is known to all, the questions of Hong Kong and Macao belong to the category of questions resulting from the series of unequal treaties left over by history, treaties which the imperialists imposed on China.

> Hong Kong and Macao are part of Chinese territory occupied by the British and Portuguese authorities. The settlement of the questions of Hong Kong and Macao is entirely within China's sovereign right and does not at all fall under the ordinary category of colonial territories. . . .
>
> With regard to the questions of Hong Kong and Macao, the Chinese Government has consistently held that they should be settled in an appropriate way when conditions are ripe. The United Nations has no right to discuss these questions.[49]

China did successfully remove Hong Kong and Macao from the list of the colonial territories in the United Nations document.

China's tolerance of British rule over Hong Kong seemed contrary to the otherwise radical Chinese domestic and foreign policies from 1949 to the 1970s. Chinese policy toward Hong Kong also seemed contrary to Beijing's pledge to lead the world's revolution against imperialism and new colonialism. Some of China's supporters even criticized Beijing's position on the Hong Kong question. For example, in 1963 the Communist Party of the United States criticized China for its tolerance of the continuation of British rule over Hong Kong.[50]

In conclusion, China's position on Hong Kong was clear: Hong Kong and Macao were problems left over from history. China did not recognize the legitimacy of the British colonial rule, and at the appropriate time those issues would be settled peacefully through negotiations. Beijing's traditional position on the Hong Kong question actually made it impossible for the Chinese leaders in the 1980s to allow any concessions on the issue of sovereignty. If they had renewed the unequal treaties, they would have contradicted the traditional Chinese stand on the Hong Kong question.

Decolonization of the British Empire

From a historical point of view, the return of Hong Kong to China was the continuation of the decolonization of the British Empire in the twentieth century, especially in the post–World War II period. One of the major features of world history from the sixteenth to the twentieth centuries was the expansion of the European powers in Asia, Africa, and America. The conquering of the world by the European states was accomplished with a variety of policies: the establishment of settlement colonies; the carving out of dependencies where a local population was ruled by a few European officials; and the development of semicolonies, or "informal empire," where the conquered states remained nominally independent but had little economic and political freedom.[51] By the end of the nineteenth century, the United States and Japan, two newly emerged powers, had joined the European expansion movement, and by 1920 a large number of countries had been conquered as colonies, semicolonies, or spheres of influence of these powers. In Asia, most countries became colonies or semicolonies.

Great Britain, the most powerful nation in the world during this period, recorded more notable achievements in its colonialist expansion than the other powers and established a huge British empire. By 1920, the British Empire had conquered most regions in the world, including New Zealand, Australia, one-fourth of Borneo, Burma, India, Ceylon, and Malaya in Oceania and Asia; Iraq, Aden, Palestine, Transjordan, and Cyprus in the Middle East; Egypt, Sudan, Uganda, British Somaliland, Kenya, Tanganika, Rhodesia, Bechuanaland, South West Africa, the Union of South Africa, Cameroon, Nigeria, the Gold Coast, Sierra Leone, and Gambia in Africa; and Canada, Newfoundland, and British Guiana in America.[52] In addition, Britain occupied several Chinese territories and took central China as its sphere of influence.

However, the British Empire collapsed after World War II and British colonies in Asia, the Middle East, and Africa as well as in other regions were granted their independence one after another. By 1967, only a few British colonies remained.[53] The transfer of sovereignty over Hong Kong should be perceived as the continuation of Britain's decolonization. Hong Kong was one of the few British colonies remaining. The fact that Britain no longer had a strategic interest in that colony accounts for its willingness to withdraw in the 1984 agreement. During the nineteenth century, Great Britain monopolized China's trade, and in the 1920s, though the British suffered from American and Japanese competition, Britain and Hong Kong still controlled one third of China's foreign trade.[54] Britain's economic influence in the Far East was further strengthened by British naval bases at Hong Kong and Singapore and by privileged use of the Chinese city of Shanghai, where Britain had a dominant position.[55]

However, as the British Empire collapsed, Britain's political influence in the Asian region dramatically diminished. India, Malaysia, and China—colonies or semicolonies of British Empire—got their independence from Britain and from other powers after World War II. As the power relationships between Britain and its former colonies changed, Hong Kong lost its strategic importance for Great Britain. In 1952, the British government abandoned its plan to defend Hong Kong against a full-scale attack from China and decided to reduce its forces at Hong Kong to a level just capable of maintaining the internal security of the colony.[56] The British garrison at Hong Kong was cut from 30,000 in the early 1950s to 8,000 in the 1970s and thereafter. In the 1950s, ships of the British Royal Naval Forces harbored at Hong Kong moved to Singapore, and in 1958 the British permanently closed their naval dockyard at Hong Kong. However, it was still costly for the government in London to maintain the garrison of the colony. In 1971–1972, the garrison cost London £28 million, and the amount had risen to about £50 million by 1975–1976. To reduce the burden on the British government, in 1975 London asked the Hong Kong colonial authorities to pay 50 percent of the cost of the British garrison in 1976–1977, 62.5 percent in 1977–1978, and 75 percent thereafter. In 1985–1986, the garrison cost about £200 million, of which Hong Kong paid £150 million to London.[57]

Meanwhile, mainly because of economic pressure and devaluation of the pound sterling in 1967, the British government tried to reduce the toll of overseas spending. London finally decided to abandon its "East of Suez" policy and to withdraw all bases from those regions by 1971. The final withdrawal was completed in 1976. From then on, Britain's strategic defense was concentrated in Europe and the North Atlantic.

Britain's lack of strategic interest could also be seen in the parliamentary debate over the 1984 Sino-British draft agreement on December 5, 1984. Discussion of the agreement in the House of Commons was delayed for two hours as members of the Parliament (MPs) argued the issue of students' grants in Britain. When the debate over Hong Kong began, only 8 percent of the MPs showed up.[58]

In conclusion, the end of British colonial rule in Hong Kong was a continuation of Britain's dramatic decolonization after World War II. The diminished British strategic interest in maintaining Hong Kong as a colony and the declining economic importance of Hong Kong to Great Britain, which accompanied the fall of the British Empire, were the main factors that impacted the 1984 Hong Kong agreement.

The Emergence of the People's Republic as a Military Power

As the power of the British Empire diminished, China was getting stronger. In 1950, one year after the establishment of the PRC, China joined the Korean War and fought against the United Nations forces, which included the military forces of the United States, the most powerful country in the world. China's military capability, as demonstrated in the Korean War, proved that the People's Republic had become a military power. It is not clear how the Korean War affected British foreign policy toward Asia and in particular toward Hong Kong. However, in 1952 Great Britain did change its position on Hong Kong and abandoned its plan to defend Hong Kong if it came under a large-scale Chinese military attack. A British Cabinet memorandum (which was not released at that time to the public) stated: "We do not consider that our strategy in Hong Kong should be changed by a French withdrawal from Indo-China, although it may be necessary to maintain a larger garrison to ensure internal security and, if attacked, to cover an orderly evacuation."[59] This secret document revealed that in the early 1950s, Hong Kong's status became uncertain and the British were prepared to withdraw from their colony if the Beijing authorities determined to recover Hong Kong militarily.

After the Korean War, the PRC was more confident of its military capability and demonstrated that it was willing to use force to take disputed border territories. In 1962, China defeated its neighbor, India, in a war over a disputed border territory, and in 1969 fought with the Soviet Union for possession of Zhenbao Island, located on the Ussuri River border. In the 1970s and 1980s, the Chinese initiated several military attacks against the Vietnamese in the Spratly and Paracel Islands in the South China Sea, which both China and Vietnam claimed. Chinese military power could also be seen in its possession of an atomic bomb in 1964 and its production of a hydrogen bomb in 1967, and in its launching of a satellite in 1970. China's military capability may be one of the reasons that the Chinese were stubborn about sovereignty over Hong Kong in the 1980s. The Qing Dynasty lost Hong Kong when the Chinese were defeated in the Opium Wars 140 years ago. But in the 1980s, although Great Britain was still one of the military powers in the world, it had lost its dominant position in relation to China.

This review of China's military position does not assert that China wanted to settle the Hong Kong question via military means. On the contrary, China made it clear that the Hong Kong question could be settled peacefully through diplomatic negotiations. A Hong Kong destroyed by war was not in the interests of China. However, the Chinese military position may have strengthened China's negotiating resources.

The Hong Kong Question: A Challenge to Beijing

Though China was willing to resume sovereignty over Hong Kong, accomplishing the transfer presented great challenges to the Beijing authorities. The first challenge came from Great Britain. In the early 1980s, Hong Kong businessmen faced a serious problem: repayment periods for mortgages in the New Territories would extend beyond 1997, when the British lease of the New Territories would expire, but the Hong Kong government had no legal basis for leasing land in the New Territories during the period after 1997. To protect their interests, Hong Kong businessmen pressed the British government to negotiate the Hong Kong question with China.[60] In September 1982, British Prime Minister Margaret Thatcher made her historic trip to Beijing.

The British prime minister ignored the Chinese stand and took a hard line on the Hong Kong question. Thatcher disagreed with China's position that the unequal treaties were illegal and stated that all three treaties concerning Hong Kong were legal and valid under international law. Thatcher's strong position angered the Chinese leaders. Deng Xiaoping told the prime minister that he, on behalf of the government of the People's Republic, officially informed her government that China would recover all territories of Hong Kong by 1997. As a result of Thatcher's visit, neither China nor Great Britain was willing to make a concession on sovereignty, although they did agree to negotiate on the disputed territory and to maintain stability and prosperity in Hong Kong.

After leaving Beijing, Thatcher went to Hong Kong, where she held a news conference in which she repeated her position:

> Britain has three treaties. Two of those refer to sovereignty in perpetuity, one of them refers to a lease which ends in 1997. . . . I believe they are valid as international law, and if countries try to abrogate treaties like that, then it is very serious indeed, because if a country will not stand by one treaty it will not stand by another treaty, and that's why you enter into talks.[61]

Thatcher also insisted that Britain had moral obligations to the Hong Kong people, a statement that was seriously criticized by the Chinese. Thatcher's position was based on the concept of *pacta sunt servanda*, a principle of international law according to which "a treaty in force is binding upon the parties and must be performed by them in good faith."[62]

Sino-British negotiations started immediately after Thatcher's trip. The British proposed their plan for the settlement of the Hong Kong issue: Chinese sovereignty and British administration, or "divided sovereignty." This meant that China would resume sovereignty over Hong Kong but the British would continue to administer the region.

Why did the British favor a settlement based on the theory of divided sovereignty? In his interview with *Hu Bao*, a Hong Kong newspaper, on September 14, 1983, Colin Moynihan, secretary of the Foreign Affairs Committee of the British Conservative Party, said that "the British role in Hong Kong is the key to its economic stability," and that in order to "maintain Hong Kong's stability," Britain "cannot give up its right of administration over Hong Kong."[63] Some British scholars also believed that a continued British administration in Hong Kong would guarantee the prosperity of the region. An article published in *The Economist* asserted that there were only two alternatives for the Chinese leaders: they could either resume sovereignty and suffer a depression in Hong Kong, or ask the British to stay to assure the prosperity of Hong Kong.[64] Robert Skidelski and Felix Patrikeef, two British political scientists, suggested in September 1982 that Britain should take a tougher line on the Hong Kong issue. They argued that Hong Kong's prosperity, which China wanted to assure, was dependent on an economic "spine" that consisted of 20,000 people who would withdraw their investments in the colony if the status quo were not maintained. In addition, the two authors suggested that "the object of British diplomacy should be to secure a new lease of some 15 to 30 years for the territory after 1997." In thirty years, Hong Kong's economy would gradually and naturally merge with China's Special Economic Zones across the border.[65]

Anthony Dicks, a British scholar, defended Britain's position from a legal perspective. He asserted that the concept of divided sovereignty was the latest development of international law in the West. Dicks explained:

> Sovereignty is said to be divided where the sum total of powers accorded by international law to a fully sovereign state are exercised in respect of a territory by two or more states. The manner in which the powers are distributed varies. One state may exercise most or all of the plenary powers, and may be said to have "effective" sovereignty, while the other may have merely "titular" or "residual" sovereignty, as has been the case with most leased territories. Again, one state by reason of its small size or lack of defensive capacity may entrust its external relations and defence to a more powerful state, while retaining full control of its own internal affairs. Still more complex examples of divided sovereignty are provided by the United Nations Trust Territories.[66]

The essence of divided sovereignty, which was the solution to the Hong Kong question favored by the British government, is that sovereignty can be separated and shared *between* states. This is indeed an entirely new concept for the interstate system, since the modern concept of sovereignty means supreme and absolute power *within* a state. However, as Dicks suggested, a state that lacks the military capability to defend its sovereignty might accept the arrangement of divided sovereignty. But China in the 1980s had the military power to defend and to take the territories it claimed, and therefore was less likely to accept the British proposal.

The second and greater challenge came from a situation that was difficult for the Beijing authorities: Hong Kong differed greatly from China in political, economic, and legal systems as well as in way of life. As will be discussed below, it was possible that the integration of Hong Kong with China might result in political unrest and/or economic collapse in Hong Kong. The situation was further complicated by the fact that the settlement of the Hong Kong question was proposed at the same time that Deng Xiaoping had initiated an ambitious modernization drive, in which it was expected that Hong Kong would play an important role.[67] The death of Mao Zedong in 1976 and the subsequent downfall of the "Gang of Four," a left-wing faction of the Chinese Communist Party and the major force supporting the Cultural Revolution, had greatly changed China's politics. After Deng Xiaoping reemerged as China's de facto leader, he announced that in the next decades China would concentrate on its program of "four modernizations" (industry, agriculture, science and technology, and national defense). Modernization became the priority of Chinese policymakers.[68]

Before the 1970s, China had had limited foreign relations with the capitalist world. The PRC and the United States had no formal contact until 1972, when President Richard M. Nixon visited China. The two countries finally established formal relations in 1979. China's economic exchanges with other major Western industrial states, such as Britain, France, and Japan, were also conducted on a small scale, because the West had been maintaining economic sanctions against the People's Republic after the Korean War. Hong Kong, newly emerged as one of the world's financial and trade centers after the 1960s,[69] was in a unique position to help China in Deng's modernization drive.

Of China's two goals in settling the Hong Kong question—regaining sovereignty and maintaining Hong Kong's stability and prosperity—the second goal was the more difficult to achieve. There were tremendous political, economic, and social differences between China and Hong Kong. Hong Kong had been ruled by the British for 140 years. Except for the strong flavor of colonialism in Hong Kong's political system,[70] the people of Hong Kong enjoyed Western-style freedoms under the rule of common law. China, however, was a socialist country and its political system, characterized by the "four cardinal principles" (the leadership of the Communist Party, the dictatorship of the proletariat, the socialist road, and Marxism-Leninism and Mao Zedong Thought) was quite incompatible with Hong Kong's political tradition. A large number of the then 5.5 million Hong Kong inhabitants were refugees who had fled China as a result of the Communist takeover in 1949. According to a Hong Kong opinion poll released on August 12, 1982, 67 percent of people questioned said that "return to China" was "not acceptable," while only 26 percent said it was "acceptable." Ninety-five percent expressed the view that maintaining the status quo was an acceptable solution. Sixty-four percent believed the most acceptable solution would be for Hong Kong to come under Chinese sovereignty but remain under British administration—an alternative later proposed by the British government. Only 17 percent thought that such an outcome was not acceptable.[71] Obviously, Hong Kong residents were not ready to come under Beijing's sovereignty. The Chinese leaders had to face the problem of persuading those Hong Kong residents who were dissatisfied with China's socialist system to accept China's rule.

Economically, China had a planned state economy with public ownership, though that economic system had been changing as a result of the reforms begun by Deng Xiaoping in 1978.[72] In contrast, Hong Kong's economy was based on private ownership and the free market. Hong Kong was also a free port; and the Hong Kong dollar was convertible, as compared with the inconvertible Chinese currency, the renminbi.

Meanwhile, as the Beijing authorities had expected, Hong Kong had been playing an important role in financing China's modernization. Three of China's four newly established Special Economic Zones (SEZs) had been located adjacent to Hong Kong and Macao for the purpose of absorbing investment from those regions.[73] Of all the foreign investment in the Shenzhen SEZ, for example, 91 percent was from Hong Kong investors alone. By August 1981, the Shenzhen SEZ had signed 814 contracts with foreign investors, with total pledged investments of HK$2,760 million (US$465 million). According to a report in the *Asian Wall Street Journal Weekly*, in January 1982 foreign investment in Shenzhen was US$1,570.5 million, and most of this capital was from Hong Kong Chinese businesspeople.[74]

The Hong Kong market was also important to China as a source of badly needed hard currency. China's trade surplus with Hong Kong provided significant gains, increasing rapidly from HK$7,637 million in 1976 to HK$18,542 million in 1981.[75]

In conclusion, although Hong Kong and China have essentially two quite different systems in political and economic terms, as well as ways of life, Hong Kong played a key role in the Chinese modernization drive. Given this dynamic, what was the best course for policymakers in Beijing to take in order to resume sovereignty while maintaining Hong Kong's prosperity?

Beijing's Decisions on the Hong Kong Question in 1984

Beijing actually had limited choice on the issue of sovereignty over Hong Kong. The concept of sovereignty, strong Chinese nationalism, Beijing's traditional position on Hong Kong, decolonization of the British Empire, and the PRC's military power all played essential roles in determining China's decision. It was impossible for Deng Xiaoping and other leaders to renew the lease of the New Territories or to allow the British to remain in Hong Kong island and Kowloon, because for over a hundred years the Chinese had insisted that the British presence in Hong Kong was illegal. Also, in the 1980s China had enough military and political power to recover the territories under British colonial rule, and if Deng had allowed the British to continue their rule in Hong Kong, his authority would have been greatly weakened.

China's theoretical defense of its decision to recover sovereignty was stated by Jin Fu, a Chinese expert on international law. He responded to the British position on the unequal treaties by arguing that "it is true that 'pacta sunt sevanda' is an established principle of international law, but international law does not recognize the validity of all treaties, irrespective of their nature and the circumstances in which they are concluded." Jin asserted that the three treaties on Hong Kong are "null and void according to basic principles of international law concerning treaties." Jin explained:

> 1. According to a basic principle of international law, wars of aggression are unjust and unlawful, 'ex injuria jus non oritur.' Therefore, treaties concluded in connection with the spoils of such wars are invalid. . . . 2. According to a principle of the law of treaties, a treaty is null and void if it is imposed by a contracting party by the threat or use of force against another. . . . 3. According to the relevant provisions of the Law of Treaties, any treaty that violates the peremptory norms of international law is null and void. This is a generally acknowledged principle.[76]

Jin also criticized the British proposal of "divided sovereignty":

> Sovereignty as a legal concept is indivisible in itself. What is sovereignty? It is the inherent right of a state, which manifests itself internally as supreme authority, namely, the exclusive jurisdiction of a state over its territory and, externally, as the right of independence, namely, the complete independent exercise of right by a state in international relations free from any outside interference. What is administration? It means administrative power, the power of a state to rule in its territory. It is a concrete expression of sovereignty. The concept of sovereignty naturally embraces administration. Since the two are indivisible, there can be no question of exchanging one for the other.[77]

This argument was repeated by *New China News Agency (NCNA)*, which published the statement that: "if administrative powers remain in the British hands, how can China be said to have recovered sovereignty? In what sovereign state in the world is administrative power in the hands of foreigners?"[78]

The Chinese could not make any concessions on sovereignty, but they did have choices about the ways that sovereignty would be transferred and about policy toward Hong Kong after 1997. However, Chinese governmental options were limited by the great differences between the mainland and Hong Kong.

The most important decision made by the Chinese government in the early 1980s was to establish its policy toward Hong Kong under the principle of one country, two systems. The Beijing authorities understood that the stability and prosperity of Hong Kong could not be maintained without British cooperation in the transfer of sovereignty, so China made concessions to Great Britain in the 1984 agreement. Thus, the 1984 Sino-British Joint Declaration states: "The Hong Kong Special Administrative Region may establish mutually beneficial economic relations with the United Kingdom and other countries, whose economic interests in Hong Kong will be given due regard" (art. 3, sec. 9). The declaration also provided that Chinese and foreign nationals previously working in the public and police services in the British colonial government could remain in employment. "British and other foreign nationals may also be employed to serve as advisers or hold certain public posts in government departments of the Hong Kong Special Administrative Region" (art. 3, sec. 4). These Chinese concessions were helpful in concluding the 1984 agreement. They assured the British that their economic interests in Hong Kong would be maintained after 1997 and that British citizens residing in Hong Kong could continue working there.

This discussion has disclosed the complex historical conditions that made the transfer of sovereignty the most probable outcome of the Hong Kong question, and explained why the Chinese policy toward Hong Kong—one country, two systems—might not have been ideal but was pragmatic and reasonable. That policy has served the interests of Beijing, London, and Hong Kong.[79] Any arguments about Chinese policy toward Hong Kong that are not based on an analysis of the complicated conditions under which that policy was made are meaningless.

Notes

1. *International Encyclopedia of the Social Sciences*, 1968 edition, s.v. "sovereignty."

2. Aristotle, *The Politics*, Book III (Baltimore, Md.: Penguin Books, 1966), 115–116.

3. C. E. Merriam, Jr., *History of the Theory of Sovereignty Since Rousseau* (New York: Arms Press, 1968), 11. Also see F. H. Hinsley, *Sovereignty* (New York: Cambridge University Press, 1986), 36–44.

4. Jean Bodin, *Six Books of the Commonwealth*, published in 1576, M. J. Tooley, trans. and ed. (Oxford: Basil Blackwell, 1962), 43–44.

5. Ibid., 43–45.

6. Thomas Hobbes, *The Leviathan*, Michael Oakeshott, ed. (Oxford: Basil Blackwell, 1960), 107–120.

7. John Locke, *The Second Treatise of Government*, J. W. Gough, ed. (Oxford: Basil Blackwell, 1976).

8. Jean Jacques Rousseau, *The Social Contract*, Charles Frankel, ed. (New York: Hafner Publishing, 1966).

9. Karl Marx, "The Communist Manifesto," "The Class Struggle in France," and "The Civil War in France" in *Selected Writings*, David Mclellan, ed. (Oxford: Oxford University Press, 1977), 211–247, 286–297, 539–558. V. I. Lenin expressed Marx's idea on the function of state as, "According to Marx, the state is an organ of class *domination*, an organ of *oppression* of one class by another; its aim is the creation of 'order' which legalizes and perpetuates this oppression by moderating the collisions between the classes." V. I. Lenin, *State and Revolution* (New York: International Publishers, 1968), 9.

10. Donald M. Snow, *National Security: Enduring Problems of U.S. Defense Policy* (New York: St. Martin's Press, 1987), 9.

11. Hans J. Morgenthau, *Politics Among Nations: The Struggle for Power and Peace* (New York: Alfred A. Knopf, 1962), 101–147; and Robert Gilpin, *War and Change in World Politics* (New York: Cambridge University Press, 1986), 13–14.

12. Lane, *Sovereignty and the Status Quo*, 20.

13. See Hu, *Imperialism and Chinese Politics*, 123.

14. Cited in Tung-ming Lee, "The Sino-British Joint Declaration on the Question of Hong Kong: A Political and Legal Perspective" (Ph.D. diss., University of Oklahoma, 1985), 87.

15. Sun Yat-sen, *San Min Chu I: The Three Principles of the People*, Frank W. Price, trans., The Commission for the Compilation of the History of the Kuomintang (Taipei, Taiwan: China Publishing, n.d.), i, 10.

16. Ibid. Sun's appeals represented the voice of the Chinese people. In 1895 Kang Youwei made a similar argument. He wrote, "It is a well-known fact that in ancient times, countries were destroyed by the armed might of other countries. But today countries are ruined by foreign trade, a thing which is overlooked by everybody. When a country is conquered by the armed forces of another country, it perishes but its people remain; when a country is destroyed by trade, its people perish together with it. This is the danger now facing China." *Nanhai Xiansheng Si Shangshu Ji* [Notes on Kang Youwei's Four Memorials to the Emperor] (n.p., n.d.), 15, 21. Current Chinese Marxist historians have discussed, using dependency theory and Lenin's theory of imperialism, the relationship of the Western powers to the Chinese economy. See Hu, *Imperialism and Chinese Politics*. However, some Western scholars assert that Western imperialism played a positive role in the development of Chinese industry in the late nineteenth century and the twentieth century. Foreign industries in treaty ports provided capital equipment and stimulated growth of Chinese industries elsewhere on the mainland. Foreign capital supported the modernization of transportation and communication and the establishment of heavy industry, and foreigners brought the Chinese new technology. See Robert Dernberger, "The Role of the Foreigners in China's Economic Development, 1840–1949," in Dwight H. Perkins, ed., *China's Modern Economy in Historical Perspective* (Stanford University Press, 1980), 19–48. Concerning foreign investment in China in the early twentieth century and China's antiforeignism, see Kuang-sheng Liao, *Antiforeignism and Modernization in China, 1860–1980: Linkage between Domestic Politics and Foreign Policy* (New York: St. Martin's Press, 1984), 64–79.

17. An exterritorial concession was a tract of land in a Chinese port or city supposedly on lease to, but actually seized by, other powers. The concession became an enclave on Chinese soil, in which China had no jurisdiction. For instance, if a foreign national in China, who was a citizen of a country granted the exterritorial concession, was a defendant in a law suit, civil or criminal, he was not to be tried by Chinese court but by a court of his own country. For details about the extraterritorial system in China, see George Keeton, *The Development of Extraterritoriality in China* (New York: Howard Fertig, 1969); John Carter Vincent, *The Extraterritorial System in China: Final Phase* (Cam-

bridge, Mass.: Harvard University Press, 1970); and Wesley R. Fishel, *The End of Extraterritoriality in China* (New York: Octagon Books, 1974).

18. Concerning the benefits that the powers obtained through control of Chinese customs, see Sun, *San Min Chu I: The Three Principles of the People*, 103, 186, 209.

19. This is only part of the KMT's foreign policy as announced in the 1924 manifesto. Concerning the whole text see Liao, *Antiforeignism and Modernization in China*, 82–83.

20. This military campaign was mounted against the warlords who ruled the divided China after the collapse of Yuan Shikai's regime (1912–1916).

21. *Foreign Relations of the United States, 1928*, vol. 2 (Washington, D.C.: U.S. Government Printing Office), 413–414.

22. Chiang Kai-shek, *China's Destiny and Chinese Economic Theory* (New York: Roy Publishers, 1947), 44.

23. "Manifesto of the National People's Convention Concerning the Abrogation of Unequal Treaties," *The Chinese Social and Political Science Review*, vol. 15 supplement (1931–1932): 461–465.

24. Tung, *China and the Foreign Powers*, 249–257.

25. Lane, *Sovereignty and the Status Quo*, 44–45.

26. Endacott, *A History of Hong Kong*, 304.

27. Lane, *Sovereignty and the Status Quo*, 49.

28. Chinese Ministry of Information, *The Collected Wartime Messages of Generalissimo Chiang Kai-shek, 1937–1945* (New York: John Day, 1946), 718.

29. See Hu, *Imperialism and Chinese Politics*, 269–270.

30. Mao Zedong, "The Chinese Revolution and the Chinese Communist Party," *Selected Works of Mao Tse-tung*, vol. 3 (London: Lawrence & Wishart, 1954), 78–87.

31. Mao Zedong, "On the Outrages by British Warships—Statement by the Spokesman of the General Headquarters of the Chinese People's Liberation Army," *Selected Works* (New York: International Publishers, n.d.), 5:401.

32. Articles 11, 54, 55. The full text of the Common Program can be found in Albert P. Blaustein, ed., *Fundamental Legal Documents of Communist China* (South Hackensack, N.J., 1962), 96–103.

33. The Five Principles of Peaceful Coexistence were promulgated by Premier Zhou Enlai of China and Prime Minister Nehru of India in 1954, to guide relations between the two states. The Five Principles are: (1) mutual respect for each other's territorial integrity and sovereignty, (2) nonaggression, (3) noninterference in each other's internal affairs, (4) equality and mutual benefit, (5) peaceful coexistence. See Robert C. North, *The Foreign Relations of China* (North Scituate, Mass.: Duxbury Press, 1978), 132.

34. Ibid., 82.

35. Michael Y. M. Kau and Jogh K. Leung, eds., *The Writings of Mao Zedong 1949–1976*, vol. 1 (Armonk, N. Y.: M. E. Sharpe, 1986), 5.

36. Ibid., 9.

37. Hu Yaobang, "Create a New Situation in All Fields of Socialist Modernization—Report to the 12th National Congress of the Communist Party (1 September 1982)," *Beijing Review* 25, no. 37 (13 September 1982): 29–30.

38. "12th National Party Congress Opens," *Beijing Review* 25, no. 36 (6 September 1982): 5.

39. Deng Xiaoping, "Our Basic Position on the Hong Kong Question," *Beijing Review* 36, no. 41 (4 October 1993): 7–8. Li Hongzhang was a minister of the Qing Dynasty at the end of the nineteenth century, who signed, on behalf of the Qing Dynasty, several unequal treaties.

40. "AFP: PRC Confirms Intent to Regain Hong Kong," Foreign Broadcast Information Service (FBIS), *Daily Report: China*, 23 September 1982, G4. Since all citations

from FBIS in this book are in the China series, the title *Daily Report: China* after FBIS is exempted hereafter.

41. "China's Stand on Hong Kong Issue Is Solemn and Just," *NCNA*, 30 September 1982, in FBIS, 1 October 1982, E1.

42. Lin Zexu was a special commissioner sent to Guangzhou (Canton) by the Qing court in 1839 to put an end to the opium trade. He confiscated and burned more than one million kilograms of opium smuggled into Guangzhou by British and American merchants and announced strict rules prohibiting foreigners from bringing opium to Chinese ports. On the pretext of protecting trade, the British government sent military forces to China in 1840 and initiated the First Opium War. Lin organized Chinese forces to resist the British forces at the beginning of the war. Feng Zicai was a Chinese general whose troops defeated the French forces in the Sino-French War in the 1870s. Deng Shichang was a Chinese naval official who died a heroic death in the 1895 Sino-Japanese War, and Zhang Zizhong was a Kuomintang general who died in action during China's War of Resistance against Japan (1937–1945).

43. Qi Ying was a high-ranking official of Qing Dynasty, who insisted during the First Opium War that China should compromise with Britain and satisfy the needs of the British. As a result, the Qing court signed the 1842 Nanjing Treaty. Wang Jingwei was chair of the Chinese Nationalist Party, who surrendered to the Japanese during China's War of Resistance against Japan (1937–1945).

44. See Joseph Y. S. Cheng, *Hong Kong: In Search of a Future* (Hong Kong: Oxford University Press, 1984), 54.

45. Yun-wing Sung, *The China–Hong Kong Connection: The Key to China's Open-Door Policy* (New York: Cambridge University Press, 1991), 5.

46. China's trade surplus against Hong Kong from 1950 to 1959 amounted to US$772.83 million. From 1960 to 1969, China's trade surplus from China–Hong Kong trade increased to US$3,202.83 million, to US$13,319.95 million from 1970 to 1979, and to US$13,032.8 million from 1977 to 1981. China's total surplus in the China–Hong Kong trade in the period between 1950 and 1981 amounted to US$23,783.21 million. In other words, in the 1960s China's surplus against Hong Kong was 314 percent higher than in the 1950s, and 315 percent higher in the 1970s than in the 1960s. The trade surplus in the four years between 1977 and 1981 was three times higher than in the 1950s and 1960s and almost equal to the total of the 1970s. Y. C. Jao, "Hong Kong's Role in Financing China's Modernization," in A. J. Yongson, ed., *China and Hong Kong: The Economics Nexus* (Hong Kong: Oxford University Press, 1983), 17.

47. Lane, *Sovereignty and the Status Quo*, 80.

48. The People's Republic of China has long stated that Beijing is the only legal government of China and that Taiwan is part of China. See Norman Miners, *The Government and Politics of Hong Kong*, 4th ed. (Hong Kong: Oxford University Press, 1986), 235–237.

49. Quoted in J. A. Cohen and Hungdah Chiu, eds., *People's China and International Law, A Documentary Study*, 2 vols. (Princeton, N.J.: Princeton University Press, 1974), 1:384.

50. See Lane, *Sovereignty and the Status Quo*, 65.

51. John Darwin, *Britain and Decolonization: The Retreat from Empire in the Post-War World* (New York: St. Martin's Press, 1980), 1.

52. Ibid., see the map of "The British Empire in 1920," x.

53. Ibid., see the map of "Colonies and Bases 1967," xi.

54. Parker Thomas Moon, *Imperialism and World Politics* (New York: Macmillan, 1939), 359.

55. Stephen Lyon Endicott, *Diplomacy and Enterprise: British China Policy, 1933–1937* (Vancouver, University of British Columbia, 1975), 22. Also see Miners, *The Government and Politics of Hong Kong*, 4th ed., 15–16.

56. Ibid., 18–19, 235.

57. Ibid., 17, 20.

58. David Bonavia, *Hong Kong 1997: The Final Settlement* (Hong Kong: South Morning Post, 1985), 144.

59. Miners, *The Government and Politics of Hong Kong*, 4th ed., 233, 246.

60. Lane, *Sovereignty and the Status Quo*, 89.

61. "Prime Minister Thatcher Holds Press Conference," *Hong Kong Television Broadcast Limited*, 27 September 1982, in FBIS, 28 September 1982, W4, W6.

62. Ian Brownlie, *Principles of Public International Law*, 4th ed. (Oxford, Clarendon Press, 1990), 616.

63. "Britain's Argument Is Untenable," *Beijing Review* 26, no. 41 (10 October 1983): 10.

64. See "Hong Kong's Future: That Ring of Confidence is Fading," *The Economist*, 12 March 1983, 52–54.

65. Robert Skisdelski and Felix Patrikeeff, "Trumping the China Cards," *The Times*, 21 September 1983, 12.

66. Anthony Dicks, "Treaty, Grant, Usage or Suffrage? Some Legal Aspects of the Status of Hong Kong," *The China Quarterly*, no. 95 (September 1983): 437.

67. After Deng announced his modernization program in 1978, a Hong Kong and Macao Affairs Office under the State Council was established. This office was organizationally distinct from the Hong Kong and Macao Office under the Ministry of Foreign Affairs, which had the primary responsibility for making Hong Kong policy. In November, China's vice-minister of foreign affairs expressed the view that Hong Kong and Macao were important for China's modernization drive. In the following years, Li Qiang, Chinese foreign trade minister, and Wang Kuang, director of New China News Agency Hong Kong Branch, asked Hong Kong's assistance for China's four modernizations. When Sir Murray Maclehose, governor of Hong Kong, visited Beijing, Chinese officials further affirmed that Hong Kong was important to Chinese modernization and expressed the hope that Hong Kong businesspeople would increase investment in China. When a delegation of the Chinese Chamber of Commerce of Hong Kong, headed by Ngai Shiu-kit, visited Beijing, Gu Mu, China's vice-premier, told his guests that Hong Kong was a financial and commercial center in Asia and that it would help China in its economic reconstruction. See "PRC Vice Foreign Minister Stresses Importance of Hong Kong, Macao," in FBIS, 27 November 1978, A14; Dende Montalla, "Li Chiang [Li Qiang]: Hong Kong Can Assist in Modernization," *South China Morning Post*, 20 December 1978, 1, in FBIS, 20 December 1978, A27; "Governor's Banquet," *AFP*, 29 March 1979, in FBIS, 30 March 1979, E7; and "Delegation of Industrialists, Businessmen Asks About Hong Kong's Prospects; Gu Mu Says Its Prosperity Will Continue," *Wen Wei Pao*, 12 August 1982, 1–2, in FBIS, 12 August 1982, W1. The PRC's expectation of Hong Kong's major role in Chinese economic development can be traced to early 1960, when Premier Zhou Enlai announced that in order to help the region's economic development all Chinese provinces had a responsibility to provide supplies to Hong Kong. As a result, China became Hong Kong's reliable supplier of food and water and made it a goal to "provide" for the needs of Hong Kong. Joseph Y. S. Cheng, *Hong Kong: In Search of a Future* (Hong Kong: Oxford University Press, 1984), 45.

68. Concerning details of Deng's modernization drive, see Chapter 6.

69. At the end of the 1940s, when the British had ruled for over a century, Hong Kong was still a "relatively poor and obscure entrepôt." In 1947, Hong Kong's per capita gross domestic product (GDP) was about only HK$1,250 (US$243). It was in the early 1960s that Hong Kong's economy took off, and by the end of the 1970s Hong Kong had become a leading financial center in the Asian-Pacific region—an "East Asian New York." In 1981, Hong Kong's per capita GDP was HK$32,080 (US$5,638), an increase

of twenty-three times that of 1947. See Y. C. Jao, "Hong Kong's Economic Prospects After the Sino-British Agreement: A Preliminary Assessment," in Hungdah Chiu, Y. C. Jao, and Yuan-li Wu, eds., *The Future of Hong Kong: Toward 1997 and Beyond* (New York: Quorum Books, 1987), 57–58; and Ken Davies, *Hong Kong to 1994: A Question of Confidence* (New York: The Economist Intelligence Unit, 1990), 4–13.

70. Regarding characteristics of Hong Kong's current political system, see Chapter 3.

71. Mary Lee, "Hong Kong: The Point of No Return," *Far Eastern Economic Review (FEER)*, 20 August 1982, 14.

72. Concerning details of Deng's reforms, see Chapter 6.

73. Concerning China's Special Economic Zones, see Chapter 6.

74. See Y. C. Jao, "Hong Kong's Role in Financing China's Modernization," in A. J. Youngson, ed., *China and Hong Kong: The Economic Nexus* (Hong Kong: Oxford University Press, 1983), 51.

75. Ibid., Table 1.1, 15.

76. Jin Fu, "China's Recovery of Xianggang (Hongkong) Area Fully Accords with International Law," *Beijing Review* 26, no. 39 (26 September 1983): 15–16.

77. Ibid., 17.

78. *NCNA*, 21 September 1983, in FBIS, 16 September 1983, E1.

79. Between October 16 and November 2, 1984, Survey Research Hong Kong Ltd. (SRH), a market research company, conducted a poll of the Hong Kong community that indicated general acceptance of the 1984 agreement. The SRH's poll reported that 81 percent of those interviewed thought that the agreement was good for the people of Hong Kong, and 71 percent believed that the agreement was "quite good." Those who Lelieved that the agreement was bad comprised only 1 percent. In addition, 79 percent of those polled agreed that sovereignty over Hong Kong should be returned to China; 73 percent believed that the agreement provided a framework within which Hong Kong's prosperity and stability would be maintained; 73 percent indicated that the agreement was better than expected, and 77 percent considered that the arrangement was the best that could be expected under the circumstances. Opinion was divided, however, on the question of whether the one country, two systems policy would work, with 45 percent expressing positive and 30 percent negative views. See Joseph Y. S. Cheng, ed., *Hong Kong in Transition* (Hong Kong: Oxford University Press, 1986), 11–12.

2

China's "One Country, Two Systems" Policy Toward Hong Kong

During the Sino-British negotiations over Hong Kong between 1982 and 1984, the Chinese government made it clear that even if an agreement between the two countries could not be reached, China would announce its own policy toward Hong Kong. This raises the question of whether the Chinese policy toward Hong Kong announced in the 1984 Sino-British Joint Declaration was a temporary Chinese concession. Would China have announced a different policy if no agreement had been made?

This question is important, because if China's policy toward Hong Kong is only a temporary, tactical concession,[1] China could fundamentally change its orientation when British influence is removed. Moreover, since the joint declaration outlined the later-enacted Basic Law, if China changed its policy toward Hong Kong as stated in the declaration it would naturally change the Basic Law after 1997. In that case, the basic policy of one country, two systems—including the promised Hong Kong SAR's high degree of autonomy and the maintenance of current economic and legal systems as well as way of life—would be fundamentally altered. After 1997, there would be "one country, one system."

Another question to be examined in this chapter concerns the application of the Hong Kong model of peaceful settlement under the one country, two systems formula to Taiwan. As will be discussed, in the Beijing authorities' thinking about China's reunification the Hong Kong and Taiwan issues are closely related. Chinese officials expect that the one country, two systems formula will be applied to Taiwan as well as to Hong Kong and the territory of Macao, which, although predominantly populated with Chinese, has had a capitalist system since 1887, established by the Portuguese who settled there in 1557. It is first necessary, however, to examine the origin and development of this one country, two systems concept that forms the core of China's policy toward Hong Kong.

The Origin of the Concept of One Country, Two Systems

Between the late 1970s and 1984, Deng Xiaoping and his followers gradually developed the concept of one country, two systems for the reunification of Taiwan, Hong Kong, and Macao with the Chinese mainland. According to this concept, after China is reunified peacefully the capitalist system and way of life practiced in Taiwan, Hong Kong, and Macao will remain unchanged, and the mainland will continue to adhere to its socialist system (Marxist ideology; Communist leadership; and an economy with different sectors, including state-owned enterprises, collectively owned property, and privately owned property). In other words, socialism and capitalism will coexist under the central authority of the government in Beijing, and Hong Kong, Macao, and Taiwan will be peaceful subdivisions of a reunified China.

The concept of one country, two systems was originally devised to settle the Taiwan issue. Taiwan was politically separated from China's mainland in 1949 and is ruled by Chiang Kai-shek's Nationalists under the title of "Republic of China," the name of China before 1949. Though Chiang was defeated, he announced that his government in Taipei was the only legal government of all China and pledged to return to and recover the mainland. Although he was unable to do so, his government survived with the support of the United States and some other countries. From 1949 until the 1970s, the mainland, ruled by the Communists, and Taiwan, ruled by Chiang's Nationalists, were in a state of war. Governments on each side of the Taiwan Strait were determined to annex each other's territory and to unify the divided nation.

At the end of the 1970s, when Deng Xiaoping reemerged at the center of power, Chinese Communist leaders announced that the mainland would abandon its policy toward Taiwan—the liberation of Taiwan by armed force—and would attempt to settle the Taiwan issue peacefully through negotiations. On New Year's Day, 1979, the Standing Committee of the National People's Congress of the PRC issued a "Message to Compatriots in Taiwan," proposing to end military confrontation and pursue peaceful reunification through negotiations between the Communists and the Kuomintang. The message appealed to the Taiwan authorities' national feelings and asked that if the disunity of China could not be ended soon, "how can we answer our ancestors and explain to our descendants? . . . Who among the descendants of the Yellow Emperor [the respected Chinese ancestor of thousands of years ago] wishes to go down in history as a traitor?"[2] The message further proposed to establish "transportation and postal services between both sides" at an early date and "to have direct contact, write to each other, visit relatives and friends, exchange tours and visits and carry out academic, cultural, sports, and technological interchanges."[3] The appeal to nationalism in the message became a basic strategy in the Beijing regime's campaign for reunification with Taiwan, Hong Kong, and Macao. At the core of the message was the proposal to hold peace talks between the Communists and the Nationalists. This party-to-party talk was Beijing's first proposed step toward reunification and became its consistent policy. For the Beijing authorities, a party-to-party rather than government-to-government talk would avoid the sensitive issue of which government, Beijing or Taipei, would be sovereign during the first negotiations.

On January 9, 1979, eight days after the announcement of the message, Beijing signaled more clearly its reunification policy toward Taiwan. In a meeting with a delegation of the U.S. Senate Military Affairs Committee, Deng Xiaoping said that after peaceful reunification with the mainland Taiwan would maintain its autonomous status and keep its administrative power, military forces, economic and social systems, and way of life.[4]

In June 1979, in his report on government work to the NPC, Premier Hua Guofeng further detailed the mainland's appeal to Taiwan and called for *santong* [three links] and *siliu* [four exchanges]. The three links meant establishment of ties between the mainland and Taiwan in trade, transportation, and postal service; and the four exchanges involved economic, scientific, cultural, and sports relations between the two sides.[5]

This shift in Chinese policy was the result of several events, listed here in order of importance. First, at the Third Plenary Session of the Eleventh Party Central Committee held in December 1978, the Chinese Communist Party, under the direction of Deng Xiaoping, decided to abandon the policy of class struggle proposed by Mao Zedong in the 1960s and to concentrate on economic construction. Second, after thirty years of hostility the People's Republic and the United States, a major supporter of Taiwan, established formal diplomatic relations in 1979. Third, in 1972 China signed a Treaty of Peace and Friendship with Japan, a country with great influence on the Taiwan issue. Before the normalization of the relationship between Japan and the People's Republic, Japan, like the United States, had only recognized Taipei as the legal government of China. Japan was an important supporter of Taiwan in Asia and a major foreign investor in the island.

By the late 1970s and early 1980s, the settlement of the Taiwan issue and the reunification of China were the main items on Beijing's agenda. In several speeches in the early 1980s, Deng Xiaoping proposed three great tasks for China in the 1980s: to speed up socialist modernization, to settle the Taiwan issue and realize national reunification, and to oppose hegemony and safeguard world peace.[6] For Deng, a peaceful settlement of the Taiwan issue and a harmonious international environment were essential for China's modernization.

On September 30, 1981, Marshall Ye Jianying, chair of the Standing Committee of the National People's Congress of the PRC, presented the following "nine-point proposal" for reunification with Taiwan: (1) Talks should be held between the Communist party and the Kuomintang. (2) The two sides should make arrangements to facilitate the exchange of mail, trade, air, and shipping services; family reunions and visits by relatives and tourists; and academic, cultural, and sports exchanges. (3) After reunification, Taiwan would enjoy a high degree of autonomy as a special administrative region and retain its armed forces. The central government would not interfere in the local affairs of Taiwan. (4) Taiwan's current socioeconomic system would remain unchanged, as would its way of life and economic and cultural relations with foreign countries. (5) People in authority and representatives of various circles in Taiwan could serve as leaders in national bodies in Beijing and participate in running the state. (6) When Taiwan's local finance was in difficulty, the central government could subsidize it. (7) Taiwanese people's freedom of entry to and exit from the mainland would be guaranteed. (8) Industrialists and businesspeople in Taiwan would be welcome to invest and engage in various economic undertakings on the mainland; and their legal rights, interests, and profits would be guaranteed. (9) People of all nationalities, public figures of all circles, and all mass organizations in Taiwan would be welcome to make proposals and suggestions regarding affairs of state through various channels and in various ways.[7]

Though the phrase one country, two systems was not used in Ye's proposal, the concept was implicit in it. Ye's appeal included ideas about political autonomy and socio-economic status quo that obviously echoed Deng's position of 1979.[8]

To legalize this new reunification policy, China amended its constitution in December 1982. In Article 31, the new constitution laid the foundation for two systems in one country. Article 31 states:

> The state may establish special administrative regions when necessary. The systems to be instituted in special administrative regions shall be prescribed by law enacted by the National People's Congress in the light of specific conditions.[9]

This attestation marked the first planning in the PRC for establishing a special administrative region in which the social policy might depart from the existing socialist system. In his report on the draft of the revised constitution, Peng Zhen, vice-chair of the Committee for Revision of the Constitution, explained that Article 31 mandated that China's sovereignty, unity, and territorial integrity would be safeguarded, while at the same time the interests and wishes of the people in Taiwan would be fully considered and protected. Peng also indicated that the Hong Kong and Macao questions would be settled according to the same principle.[10]

As will be shown, these radical changes in the Beijing regime's reunification policy were, in fact, products of Deng's ambitious modernization programs. As long as the modernization policy is continued, China's policy of peaceful settlement of the Taiwan issue will be carried out.

The Principle of One Country,
Two Systems and the Hong Kong Question

Though the term was not yet used formally, the concept of one country, two systems that developed toward the end of 1981 applied only to Taiwan. However, although Chinese policy toward Hong Kong and Macao was not yet clear, speeches by the Communist leaders connected the concept with Hong Kong. When modernization became a priority in 1978, China's leaders hoped that Hong Kong would play an important role,[11] and when Hong Kong governor Sir Murray MacLehose visited Beijing in 1979, officials there expressed the position that China welcomed investment from Hong Kong. In a private conversation about the future of Hong Kong, Deng told MacLehose that China had no alternative but to recover Hong Kong, as the question of sovereignty would be raised publicly and China's nationalistic pride would not allow it to lose Hong Kong.[12] However, in public Deng asked the visiting governor to "tell the investors in Hong Kong to put their heart at ease"[13]—a statement widely quoted by scholars. Deng's talk indicated that China would have special policies for protecting the interests of investors in Hong Kong, though Deng did not say what those policies would be. In October 1979, before traveling to Europe, Premier Hua Guofeng told the press that vice-premier Deng Xiaoping made China's position on Hong Kong very clear, and continued, "we think that a good way of settling the question can be sought through consultations. But I think regardless of how the matter is settled, we will take notice of the interests of the investors there."[14]

Obviously, as late as 1979 the Chinese leaders had no clear and concrete plan for settling the Hong Kong question. Deng's and Hua's talks only indicated that China would make a special effort to protect investors in Hong Kong and to maintain Hong Kong's prosperity. There was no sign that the Hong Kong issue would be settled on the basis of the same policy as that announced toward Taiwan. The main reason for this may be that a final settlement of the Hong Kong question was not on Beijing's agenda at that time.

China had no plan to settle the Hong Kong question at any time before 1982. When Deng met with British officials and Hong Kong journalists, he only emphasized Sino-British economic cooperation and indicated that the Hong Kong question would be settled in a way that would benefit China's modernization.[15] Even in Marshal Ye's nine-point proposal of December 30, 1981, in which the idea of one country, two systems was formally outlined, it was clear that the concept was not tied to the Hong Kong issue. Ye said, "We hope that our compatriots in Xianggang [Hong Kong] and Aomen [Macao] and Chinese nationals residing abroad will continue to act in the role of a bridge and contribute their share to the reunification of the motherland."[16]

When the Hong Kong issue was put on the agenda, Chinese policymakers figured out that the Hong Kong and Macao issues could be solved in a fashion similar to their plan for reunification with Taiwan. On February 13, 1982, Hu Yaobang, the general secretary of the Communist Party, made a speech at a forum on the work of Guangdong and Fujian provinces. He said:

> besides the implementation of the open-door economic policy, we will in the
> near future, adopt another method—the method of allowing the existence of

two kinds of social systems in one country—to solve the problems of the reunification with Taiwan and the recovery of our sovereignty over Hong Kong and Macao.[17]

Since Deng Xiaoping himself was directing China's Hong Kong policy at that period, Hu's speech was not his personal opinion. It clearly indicated that at the beginning of 1982, the policymakers in Beijing had determined that their Taiwan policy would apply to Hong Kong. Of course, concrete policies were not made, but Hu's speech may be the earliest document to state that the one country, two systems policy would apply to Hong Kong.

In March 1982, a special committee under the State Council was established to study the Hong Kong question. The committee was headed by Ji Pengfei, a state councillor, and its deputy chiefs were two vice-chairs of the NPC, Liao Chengzhi and Luo Qingchang. Both were leading spokesmen on Hong Kong and Macao affairs. The Chinese authorities also paid attention to various views from the Hong Kong community, and Deng Xiaoping and Premier Zhao Ziyang frequently talked with its prominent members.[18] To strengthen the confidence of the people of Hong Kong, statements about Chinese policy toward Hong Kong were released often, becoming more concrete in mid-1982, before Thatcher's historic September visit to Beijing. According to a report, by July China's position toward Hong Kong included the propositions that:

> —Hongkong, Kowloon and Macau are Chinese territory, over which China should exercise complete sovereignty. The treaties entered into in the past with aggressors are unequal treaties, and the Chinese side cannot acknowledge their legality.
> —Restoring sovereignty over Hongkong and Macau to China is a matter which cannot be postponed to the distant future.
> —The method of one nation, two systems will be used to solve the question of sovereignty over Hongkong and Macau.
> —Hongkong's current system will not change—that is, Hongkong and Macau will be allowed to continue as capitalist societies and capitalism will be allowed to continue to develop in both territories.
> —Hongkong shall remain a free port.[19]

Here the phrase "one country (nation), two systems" was first formally used and clearly defined.[20] In August, the policy was further enriched by a number of propositions: Hong Kong would be a special administrative region whose external affairs and defense would be handled by the central government in Beijing; Hong Kong's domestic affairs, including internal security, would be handled by the SAR; China would not station the People's Liberation Army in the SAR; future chief administrators of the SAR would be resident Chinese, either appointed by Beijing or elected locally; and China would regain Hong Kong's sovereignty in around 1997.[21] In speeches made in September 1982, party leaders Hu Yaobang and Hu Qiaomu made China's policy toward Hong Kong even more concrete:

1. Hong Kong will become a special administrative area.

2. The special feature of this administrative area will be the preservation of a capitalist economic system.

3. The management power of the city will belong to a leading organization comprising Chinese, and the government and the heads of the government will be elected by a popular organization similar to the NPC.

4. There will be no great personnel changes in any departments of the Hong Kong Government.

5. All factories, shops, companies and enterprises will operate and do business as before.

6. Some enterprises, including the enterprises originally of foreign capital, may be leased to interested foreigners.

7. There will be no fundamental changes in the legal system and currency system. However, connections with the British Government will be cut off so as to eliminate the traces left by the British rulers on the currency.

8. Police in the city will be organized by the government and no PLA or people's police-men will be dispatched by China.[22]

These statements, made before Thatcher's visit, outlined the basic Chinese policies toward Hong Kong that were to be clarified in the 1984 Sino-British Joint Declaration. Of course, there were some differences in the declaration, such as the provision about the stationing of the PLA.[23]

The foregoing review indicates that the Beijing regime had already prepared Chinese policy toward Hong Kong under the concept of one country, two systems before the Sino-British negotiations started at the end of 1982, and that in fact this policy was part of the initial Chinese negotiating position. However, the one country, two systems approach was still a general principle. In the following two years, it was developed in greater detail.

In 1983, there was a major development related to the Sino-British negotiations, which was the proposal of the concept of "Hong Kong people ruling Hong Kong." In this year, the negotiations came to deadlock, largely over the issue of sovereignty. When the negotiations began, the Chinese side insisted that China would recover all three territories of Hong Kong and would not engage in further negotiations unless Britain made a concession on sovereignty. Initially the British side was not willing to make such a concession, but then, in May 1983, Prime Minister Margaret Thatcher finally informed Chinese Premier Zhao Ziyang secretly that Britain would accept China's position on sovereignty if agreement could be achieved to insure Hong Kong's stability and prosperity.[24] The next phase of talks focused on the issue of who would administer Hong Kong after China's recovery of sovereignty. As discussed in Chapter 1, Britain proposed the formula of China's sovereignty and Britain's administration. China insisted that it wanted both sovereignty and administrative power, and at the same time proposed the concept of Hong Kong people ruling Hong Kong. This concept not only rejected the British proposal of divided sovereignty, but strengthened the Chinese position in the negotiations. Since 97 percent of the Hong Kong inhabitants were Chinese, the possibility of local people administering Hong Kong's affairs for the first time in 140 years appealed to local nationalistic sentiment against British colonialism. After May 1983, the concept of Hong Kong people ruling Hong Kong quickly became part of the one country, two systems policy. In that same month, a Hong Kong University professor returned from interviewing Chinese leaders with the news that the Hong Kong people were defined as "people who have lived in Hong Kong for seven years, accept Hong Kong as part of China and accept that Beijing is the only legitimate Chinese government." These Hong Kong people would be responsible for the administrative region of Hong Kong, which would have its own constitution.[25] Deng told Ho Ying, chair of the Macao Chamber of Commerce, that Beijing would not send anyone to administer Hong Kong after 1997. The region would be governed by the Hong Kong people who lived there, and not necessarily by Chinese. In other speeches, Deng promised that foreign, and particularly British, investments would be protected after China resumed sovereignty. Deng also mentioned that Hong Kong could issue its own passports and enjoy an independent judiciary, and that Beijing would not intervene in Hong Kong's internal affairs.[26]

In July 1983, a group of Hong Kong students returned from Beijing with a "ten-point plan," which further explained the concept of Hong Kong people ruling Hong Kong and also proved to be the outline of China's policy toward Hong Kong as announced in the joint declaration of 1984 and in the Basic Law. The ten-point plan included the following propositions:

> 1. Except for issues affecting defense or diplomacy, Hong Kong would run its own affairs.
> 2. The territory would be ruled by local government without Beijing's representation. The head of that government would be a "patriot," though not necessarily a socialist, who would be elected by Hong Kong citizens.
> 3. Hong Kong would make its own laws.
> 4. The colony's existing way of life would not be changed.
> 5. Crucial freedoms, including press, speech, assembly, and movement, would be retained.
> 6. Activities of political groups such as the KMT would not be restricted as long as they did not include sabotage.
> 7. The local police force would be responsible for security.
> 8. Hong Kong's capitalist system and status as a free port and financial center would not be altered.
> 9. The Hong Kong SAR would enjoy considerable autonomy from Beijing in its foreign relations and would issue its own travel documents.
> 10. Questions of social reform would be debated by the people of Hong Kong.[27]

In October, Ji Pengfei further offered a complete Hong-Kong-people-ruling-Hong-Kong administrative model. It included a number of concepts: The maintenance of Hong Kong laws and the spirit of the rule of law, excepting those laws that connected with the colonial rule. Hong Kong would have its final appeal court and the judgment of its highest courts would be final. China would be responsible for Hong Kong's defense and external affairs and would not station troops in the region. Hong Kong would have full power in immigration matters and would be allowed to issue identity cards and passports for the free travel of its residents. Hong Kong would manage its own trading relations with other countries. Hong Kong would continue its current economic policy, which included the current free enterprise policy, and residents' property rights would be protected, capital would be allowed to flow freely in and out of Hong Kong, and foreign and Chinese capital would be protected identically. Except for the highest posts, expatriates would be allowed to continue to work in public and private establishments and would enjoy civic rights. Local representative organizations would nominate Hong Kong's governor, who would be appointed by China. The central government would not impose taxes in Hong Kong.[28] The provisions in this Hong-Kong-people-ruling-Hong-Kong model and in the ten-point plan comprised most of the Chinese policy declared in the 1984 agreement.

In October 1984, the editor of *Beijing Review* summarized Deng's talks about the idea of one country, two systems in an article titled "A Significant Concept."[29] The editor simply defined the idea as follows: "in the People's Republic of China, the one billion people on the mainland practice socialism while Hong Kong and Taiwan remain capitalist." The editor asserted that Deng's new idea included four themes, which are as follows: First, the concept of one country, two systems was based on China's historic and current realities, one of which was the need to settle the Taiwan, Hong Kong, and Macao issues peacefully. Deng said:

> How could these issues be settled peacefully? It requires taking into full consideration the history and present conditions of Hongkong and Taiwan. . . . China's present socialist system cannot be changed and will remain in the future. But, if the capitalist system in Hongkong and Taiwan is not guaranteed, stability and prosperity there cannot be maintained and peaceful settlement will become impossible.

Second, capitalism in the SAR would remain unchanged for fifty years after 1997. The reasons for this decision, Deng explained, were that from a legal viewpoint the policy of one country, two systems was not a personal idea but a principle and law adopted by the NPC in the constitution. Therefore, the policy would not be changed. Economically, about fifty to sixty years were necessary to realize the four modernizations, and in fifty years beyond 1997 there would be no great difference between the economies of the mainland and Hong Kong. In addition, Deng argued the correctness of his new modernization drive:

> The key is whether this policy is correct or incorrect; if it is correct, nobody can change it. Otherwise, it should be changed. The flexible domestic policies of opening to the outside world and enlivening economic activities that China has followed since the Third Plenary Session [the Communist Party's session held in 1978] have proved successful in the countryside. Who can alter these

policies now? The living standard of about 80 percent of the Chinese people would decrease if these policies were changed, and in that case, 80 per cent of the party's popularity among the people would be lost.

Third, socialism was dominant. Deng stressed that although capitalism would be allowed in the SARs, the main system in China remained socialism, which had already achieved success. Deng further connected China's policy of reunification with Taiwan and Hong Kong to economic reform. He argued:

> It is a supplement to the development of socialism that China pursues an open policy and allows some methods of capitalism to be introduced. It will benefit the expansion of the forces of production. For example, when Shanghai makes use of foreign capital, this does not mean the entire city is practising capitalism. The same is true of Shenzhen, a special economic zone which still practises socialism. So Shenzhen is different from Hongkong. Shenzhen is not a model of Hongkong in the future, nor is Hongkong a model for Shenzhen today. In China, socialism is dominant.

Fourth, the principle of one country, two systems offered a way of settling international issues peacefully. Deng believed:

> So, if stability is desired, instead of fighting, the only way to settle problems is by the method we have advanced. Using this method we can justify ourselves to the people, stabilize the situation, and neither side is hurt. History is not without such precedents.

A major characteristic underlying Deng's ideas about one country, two systems is, in fact, linkage:[30] a linkage of China's domestic politics with international issues; a linkage of China's modernization with the Hong Kong, Macao, and Taiwanese economies; a linkage of the PRC's socialism with the capitalism of Hong Kong, Macao, and Taiwan; and a linkage of Hong Kong, Macao, and Taiwan in a framework of China's reunification. For Deng, mainland China's ambitious modernization program and socialist system are the core of the one country, two systems structure, without which it would not exist. The success of capitalism in Hong Kong, Macao, and Taiwan would serve the mainland's modernization, and the success of modernization would guarantee those regions' prosperity.

The foregoing review reveals that the idea of one country, two systems was coined by Chinese leaders to settle the Taiwan reunification issue. When the Sino-British negotiations began in 1982, China applied the policy to Hong Kong and Macao and thereafter it became China's reunification policy.

Shortly after the 1984 Hong Kong agreement, the Macao question was settled following the Hong Kong model. On April 13, 1987, the Sino-Portuguese Joint Statement on Macao was announced, according to which Macao would be returned to China in 1999. The Draft Basic Law of the Macao Special Administrative Region was completed in 1993 by a special committee appointed by the NPC, and Macao, like Hong Kong, entered a transition period.

The Hong Kong Model and the Taiwan Issue

As the one country, two systems formula was successfully applied to the Hong Kong and Macao questions, Chinese leaders were further encouraged to believe that both the formula and the negotiation process should be applied to Taiwan. On December 22, 1984, less than three months after the announcement of the Sino-British Joint Declaration, Deng Xiaoping stressed in his speech to the party's Central Advisory Committee that the settlement of the Hong Kong question provided a model for Taiwan. First, he said that "the resolution of the Hong Kong question has a direct impact on the Taiwan policy: Taiwan authorities should be able to accept the 'one country, two systems' concept." Second, "in Taiwan's case, we would adopt an even more flexible policy. By more flexible we mean that, in addition to the policies used to solve the Hong Kong question, we would allow Taiwan to maintain its own armed forces." Third, in the one country, two systems formula, "you won't swallow us up and we won't swallow you up."[31]

In 1986, Li Jiaquan, the mainland's deputy director of the Institute of Taiwan Studies, argued, "Since socialism and capitalism have inhabited the same planet for so long, why should they not be able to operate side by side in one country?" He further appealed to Taiwan with the Hong Kong model: "since the socialist system on the mainland can coexist with Hong Kong's capitalist system why can it not coexist with that of Taiwan?"[32]

On the same day that the Sino-Portuguese Joint Statement on Macao was announced, *Remin Ribao* published Premier Zhao Ziyang's government report to the Fifth Session of the Sixth National People's Congress held on March 26, in which Zhao again appealed to Taiwan with the Hong Kong and Macao models:

> The settlement of the question of Macao is another example of the successful application of the principle of "one country, two systems" to the problem of reunifying the motherland. It represents a major advance towards the ultimate goal of complete reunification. The principle of "peaceful reunification" and "one country, two systems" is also a fair and reasonable one for settling the Taiwan question, and it has been understood as such by a growing number of our Taiwan compatriots.[33]

However, the Taiwanese authorities rejected this proposal for peaceful unification. Taipei interpreted the 1979 New Year's "Message to the Compatriots in Taiwan" from Beijing as the traditional united front propaganda of the Communists. Premier Sun Yun-hsuan asserted that Ye Jianying's nine-point proposal was a "united front offensive." Taiwan's government spokesman commented: "Everyone knows that the communists talk peace and then wage war. So we have been alarmed at the recent escalation of the Chinese Communist smiling offensive."[34] Taiwan also turned down the mainland's proposal of three links and four exchanges and responded with its "three nos" policy—no contact, no negotiation, and no compromise. Chiang Ching-kuo, the late president of the Republic of China and son of Chiang Kai-shek, argued that Beijing's appeal for a peace talk between the Communists and the Nationalists was a conspiracy. He continued that the bitter lessons indicated that "the Communists raise the slogan of 'cooperation' . . . only when they are weak and need to strengthen themselves by clinging to Kuomintang." When the Communists were stronger, they would "lash out once again." Chiang also asserted that differences between the mainland and Taiwan in "the two political philosophies, two systems, and two ways of life . . . shows which is good and which is evil." In addition, Chiang believed that Beijing's appeal for peace talks with Taiwan was intended to "create in the world the false image" that Taiwan refused to talk. But "to talk peace with the Chinese Communists is to invite death," and therefore the Nationalists would never consent to a peace talk with the Communists.[35] Taiwanese authorities maintained that they would continue their efforts toward Chinese reunification under the theory of "Three Principles of People."

Nevertheless, Taiwan, like the mainland, has made great changes politically and economically since the 1980s. Politically, Taipei suffered a major diplomatic setback. Since 1979, the major countries—especially the United States, a long-term supporter of Taiwan—have ceased to recognize the Taipei regime but have extended recognition to Beijing. By the end of the 1980s, only twenty-eight small nations continued official ties with Taipei, while about 130 countries, including all the major powers, maintained formal relations with Beijing. Domestically, the death of Chiang Ching-kuo in 1988 ended forty years of authoritarian rule by the Chiang dynasty, but two years before his death Chiang Ching-kuo initiated several reforms. He accomplished lifting martial law, which had been in force since the Nationalists fled to Taiwan in 1949; legalizing the formation of competitive political parties; reforming the parliamentary structure; and allowing certain freedoms of the press. Since then, Taiwan has made remarkable progress toward political democracy.

Economically, since 1949 Taiwan had been much more successful than mainland China. In 1989, Taiwan's gross national product per capita was US $8,400, fourteen times that of the mainland,[36] and in 1991 Taiwan maintained the world's largest foreign exchange reserve, which had reached over US$84 billion.

As the Taiwanese authorities relaxed their control and allowed Taiwan residents to visit relatives on the mainland (they had been separated since 1949), it became increasingly difficult for Taipei to ignore Beijing's appeal for reunification. Each year, more than one million Taiwanese people visited the mainland, and according to a poll conducted by Taiwan's Bridge Across Straits Foundation in October 1990, 62.7 percent of Taiwan's population opposed Taiwan's independence, compared to only 16.2 percent in favor. The poll also showed that most Taiwanese people favored more exchange between the mainland and Taiwan.[37] In Taiwan, only the Democratic Progress Party, the second largest political party, advocated Taiwan's independence from the mainland.

Despite these pressures, the Nationalists' government continued its policy regarding reunification with the mainland, insisting that the reunification would have to be carried out under Sun Yat-sen's three principles of people.

Since 1986, trade between the mainland and Taiwan has increased substantially, though the Taiwanese authorities have disliked that trend.[38] Taipei has had to face a variety of new issues, such as smuggling, shipping disputes in the Taiwan Straits, unofficial immigration from the mainland to Taiwan, and marriage and inheritance issues that crossed the Taiwan Strait. To handle affairs with the mainland efficiently, Taipei adopted a more flexible policy and established a variety of official and semiofficial institutions and organizations, including the Mainland Affairs Task Force (July 1988); the National Reunification Council (October 1990) under the President's Office; and the Mainland Affairs Council (October 1990). These bodies were mainly responsible for making suggestions on policymaking. To deal more effectively with the mainland on nonpolitical issues, the Straits Exchange Foundation (SEF), an organization that claimed to be nongovernmental but actually was backed by the Taiwanese authorities, was established on November 21, 1990. In response, the mainland established the Association for Relations Across the Taiwan Straits (ARATS), as the counterpart of SEF, on December 16, 1991. SEF and ARATS officials frequently negotiated on issues such as smugglers and fishing disputes. Effectively, Taipei's "three nos" policy was no longer in line with reality.

On April 30, 1991, Lee Teng-hui, the new president of the Republic of China after the death of Chiang Ching-kuo, announced that Taipei would end "the Period of Mobilization for Suppression of the Communist Rebellion," which had first been decreed by Chiang Kai-shek in 1948, when his regime ruled the mainland. Lee also proclaimed that his government was no longer bound by the decree to recover the mainland by military force. In this way Taipei indicated its hope for a peaceful solution to the disputes between Taiwan and the mainland. Under the name of "Chinese Taipei," Taiwan's official delegations also participated in international conferences such as the Asian Development Bank's annual conference held in Beijing. Delegates from quasi-official agencies of both sides visited each other frequently. In 1992, Taiwan further opened its door and for the first time allowed academic personalities and journalists who may have had government positions or be Communist Party members to visit Taiwan. Obviously, a smoother relationship between Taiwan and the mainland was developing, and mutual hostilities were reduced.

The turning point came on April 27, 1993, when Wang Daohan, chair of the ARATS and former mayor of Shanghai, and Koo Chen-fu, chair of the SEF and a member of the KMT Standing Committee, held a historic summit at Singapore. Other leading officials of ARATS and SEF joined the talks, including Tang Shubei, vice-chair of ARATS, and Chiu Cheyne, secretary general of SEF and a close confidant of President Lee Teng-hui. The "Wang-Koo talks" constituted the highest-level formal negotiations between Beijing and Taipei since 1949, though the two parties labeled their talks as nonofficial, economic, functional, and businesslike in nature. Singapore was chosen as the site for this summit to avoid the sensitive issue of which party was the host (and therefore more important) and which was the guest. The Wang-Koo talks were constructive and produced four agreements. One concerned a statement of the purpose of the Wang-Koo talks, and the other three established a regular contact and meeting system of ARATS and SEF, methods to handle and compensate for lost registered mail, and the use of notarial certificates. All the agreements were to go into effect in thirty days. But the real achievement of the talks was the two sides' consensus on strengthening cooperation. They drew up a specific list of issues to be discussed in the coming years, which included repatriation from Taiwan of illegal mainland immigrants; fishing disputes; protection of intellectual-property rights; and efforts to coordinate their different legal systems. The two sides also agreed to discuss cooperation in culture, education, and science, and joint exploitation of natural resources.

However, the two-day Wang-Koo talks failed to find solutions to other, more important issues. The mainland officials tried to initiate discussions on direct shipping, air flights, and postal and telecommunication links; but the Taiwanese seemed to have no interest in these matters. Their priority was to settle the issue of what they considered to be inadequate legal protection of Taiwanese investment in the mainland, which exceeded $10 billion. The SEF delegation asked the mainland officials to sign an accord that was patterned on the bilateral investment agreements made by Beijing with other countries. Such an agreement would strengthen Taipei's claim that the mainland and Taiwan were "equal political entities," a concept that Beijing rejected. The mainland delegation maintained that the bilateral agreement was unnecessary, but conceded to making further improvements in its legal system and environment for Taiwanese investors. Mainland officials also pointed out that Taiwan's request might be considered if Taipei extended reciprocal treatment to mainland investment in Taiwan—which had been banned.[39]

Although both Beijing and Taipei stressed the economic, functional, and businesslike nature of the Wang-Koo talks, obviously both parties were also politically motivated. One of the considerations in Taiwan's request for an agreement protecting its investors on the mainland was that such an agreement would be between two equal political entities, a goal in Taiwan's cause of reunification with the mainland. For the Beijing regime also, direct economic and business links across the Taiwan Strait were significant vis-à-vis negotiations on reunification. However, the Wang-Koo talks revealed the political differences between Beijing and Taipei that hampered settlement of economic and cultural issues. Technically, the mainland and Taipei are still hostile toward each other.

In fact, on the issue of political reunification, differences between Taipei and Beijing have not been reduced. After the 1980s, the new Nationalist leaders continued to criticize Beijing's one country, two systems formula, arguing that reunification could be considered only if Beijing abandoned its socialist system. Taipei also denounced Beijing's threat to settle the Taiwan issue with military force. In his inaugural address on May 20, 1990, President Lee Teng-hui listed three conditions for official contact between Taiwan and the mainland:

> If the Chinese Communist authorities . . . implement political democracy and a free economic system, renounce the use of military force in the Taiwan Strait and [do] not interfere with our development of foreign relations on the basis of a one-China policy, we would be willing, on a basis of equality, to establish channels of communication, and completely open up academic, cultural, economic, trade, scientific, and technological exchange to lay a foundation of mutual respect, peace, and prosperity. . . . When objective conditions are ripe, we will be able to discuss our national reunification, based on the common will of the Chinese people on both sides of the Taiwan Strait.[40]

But in the 1990s, under President Lee's direction, Taiwan's policy toward mainland China became more ambiguous. Though the Lee regime continued to talk about "one China," reunification with the mainland, and acceptance of semi-official talks with Beijing, these policies were being conducted under a new concept: "one China, two governments," or "one China, two political entities." According to this concept, Taiwan and the mainland have been separated under two sovereign governments for over forty years; the Republic of China rules only Taiwan (formerly the Nationalists said the Republic of China was sovereign over all China); and Beijing and Taipei are equally sovereign over the territories they rule. Further, the Lee regime initiated the policy of "pragmatic diplomacy"—meaning that Taipei was ready to establish formal diplomatic relations with all countries, including those who had official ties with Beijing. Lee's purpose was clear—Taiwan and China should be equal in the international arena. In fact, Lee's government had abandoned Taiwan's former mainland policy, and as a result of his new policy the appeal for independence grew on the island. Few nations responded to President Lee's pragmatic diplomacy, however, because Beijing threatened to terminate relations with any country that made official ties with Taipei. Since 1993, Taiwan has worked hard to apply for United Nations membership, supported by a few nations that have diplomatic relations with Taipei. But this effort was also rejected by Beijing as well as by the United Nations. Disappointed by Beijing's Taiwan policy, Lee's government decided to cool down economic connections with the mainland by launching a "Southward Policy," which would promote economic and trade cooperation with Southeast Asian nations and encourage Taiwanese businesses to invest there instead of in mainland China.[41]

In response to President Lee's new policy on the mainland and unification and to the move for Taiwan independence, Beijing released a white paper in August 1993 that rejected Taipei's concept of two political entities within one China. The white paper explained Beijing's Taiwan policy—"peaceful reunification; one country, two systems," which includes:

(1) Only one China. There is only one China in the world, Taiwan is an inalienable part of China and the seat of China's central government is in Beijing.

(2) Coexistence of two systems. On the premise of one China, socialism on the mainland and capitalism on Taiwan can coexist and develop side by side for a long time without one swallowing up the other.

(3) A high degree of autonomy. After reunification, Taiwan will become a special administrative region. It will be distinguished from the other provinces or regions of China by its high degree of autonomy. It will have its own administrative and legislative powers, an independent judiciary and the right of adjudication on the island. It will run its own party, political, military, economic and commercial affairs.

(4) Peace negotiations. It is the common aspiration of the entire Chinese people to achieve reunification of the country by peaceful means through contacts and negotiations.[42]

The White Paper also warned that "The Chinese government is closely following the course of events and will never condone any maneuver for 'Taiwan independence.'"[43] On July 5, 1994, one year after the release of the white paper by Beijing, the Taiwanese government issued its own white paper on relations between Taiwan and China. The Taiwanese white paper summarized Lee Teng-hui's China policy in the statement that the Republic of China on Taiwan "would no longer compete with Beijing for the 'right to represent China' in the international arena." In this way Taipei officially declared it would not be sovereign over China. The white paper also argued that because there are "two political entities" within one China and neither Beijing nor Taipei has jurisdiction over all China, no government should claim sovereignty over the whole country.[44] Taiwan officials argued that the problem of China's reunification should be settled according to the German and Korean models. Both German governments and both Korean regimes had joined the United Nations and had equally established official relations with other countries, with the result, the Taiwanese officials argued, that the two German countries had finally unified.

It was not only Taiwan authorities who rejected the mainland reunification policy. A large number of Taiwan scholars also argued that the principle of one country, two systems was unacceptable. Tao Beichuan, government policy councillor of the president and a member of the National Reunification Committee of Taiwan, pointed out that though the communist leaders promised to allow two systems to coexist in one country, the one country embodied the "four cardinal principles." Therefore, Tao asserted, the people's democratic dictatorship under the leadership of the Communist Party and Marxist-Leninist and Mao Zedong Thought would not allow the people of Taiwan to continue their free, democratic, wealthy life.[45] Lang Kao, whose Ph.D. dissertation concerned Deng's one country, two systems formula[46] and who is now a political scientist at National Taiwan University, may represent the moderates' views on the mainland's reunification policy. Though he concluded in his dissertation that it would be possible to reunify the mainland with Hong Kong, Macao, and Taiwan under one country, two systems, Kao argued in another article that Beijing's reunification policy had three weak points. First, Beijing placed all hopes on the KMT, although the KMT had lost its authority to decide Taiwan's future. Second, Beijing appealed only to Chinese nationalism, but the people of Taiwan also desired other things, such as freedom, happiness, and self-fulfillment. Third, the policy of one country, two systems had no appeal because dealing with the Communists had made the Taiwanese people anticommunist.[47] Kao's view is that the people of Taiwan generally distrust Beijing's reunification formula of one country, two systems.

Taiwanese scholars seemed to favor Taipei's reunification model but also proposed several of their own, including "one China, two separate administrations"; "one China, two governments"; "one China, the federation"; and "one China, the commonwealth of China."[48] Though the names of the proposed models were different, they had two points in common: the insistence that there be only one China; and that Taiwan and the mainland be on equal footing. Thus, these models all rejected Beijing's concept of one country, two systems. It is clear that both the government and the scholars of Taiwan found that formula unacceptable.

Why was it that the concept of one country, two systems could be applied to Hong Kong and Macao (at least as adopted in the Sino-British and Sino-Portuguese Declarations and in the Basic Law of the Hong Kong SAR) but not to Taiwan? The reason is that although the Taiwan and Hong Kong questions have similar aspects, the major differences that distinguish Taiwan from Hong Kong are the crucial ones of sovereignty and military power. Although Beijing rejected the Nationalist government's claim that it is the sovereign government of all China, or at least, of Taiwan, the Communists can do nothing about the fact that the Nationalists do in fact rule Taiwan. However, under Beijing's one country, two systems formula, Taiwan would lose its sovereignty and become a province of the People's Republic. (Taipei also recognized that Taiwan is only a province, but a province of the Republic of China.) Taipei's claim of sovereignty is strengthened by geographical advantage (the Taiwan Strait separates the mainland and Taiwan), its military force, and its official ties with about thirty countries, in particular its semiofficial relations with the United States. These assets make clear that Taiwan can defend its sovereignty militarily. Also, Beijing's one country, two systems formula assures Taiwan that reunification across the Taiwan Strait would be settled peacefully, and military forces would not be used unless Taiwan announced its independence from China. Thus, Taiwan can expect that its status quo will be maintained in the near future.

On the other hand, Hong Kong and Macao are colonies, and as such their governments and citizens lack the independent military power to defend themselves. Therefore, though sovereignty was a key obstacle for settlement in both Hong Kong and Taiwan, the context in which the sovereignty issue operated was different. The Hong Kong case involves a transfer of sovereignty between two major powers, whereas the Taiwan problem is an internal Chinese dispute over legitimacy.

Taiwan scholars have stressed the differences in the issues of Taiwan and Hong Kong and ignored the similarities. For instance, Yu-ming Shaw, director of the Institute of International Relations of Taiwan, argued that Taiwan and Hong Kong are "absolutely different in status." Taiwan "has been active in the international arena as a political entity with national sovereignty as well as independent defense capability." But Hong Kong is a British colony "without sovereignty, with no military forces of its own to defend itself." Shaw concluded that Taiwan and Hong Kong "cannot be put on a par with each other."[49]

However, historically both Hong Kong and Taiwan were regions of China (even the Taiwan authorities recognize that Taiwan was a province of the Republic of China); and both practice capitalism. Taipei has been waiting to see what will happen in Hong Kong after 1997. If Hong Kong's capitalism and prosperity are maintained, it is possible that the one country, two systems formula and the Hong Kong model will then appear relevant to Taiwan. In his press conference in May 1991, President Lee Teng-hui made it clear that his government would be watching how the Beijing authorities handle Hong Kong after 1997, given the huge difference between mainland and Hong Kong residents' incomes.[50] However, if the practice of one country, two systems is not an economic success and the Hong Kong SAR becomes socialist, the people of Taiwan most probably will not accept the formula. Thus, Hong Kong will be a showcase of Deng's one country, two systems for Taiwan.

It is not clear how the stalemate between Beijing and Taipei will be broken. However, a settlement of the Taiwan sovereignty issue (Beijing's claim over all of China and the Nationalists' actual rule over Taiwan) would be facilitated by the establishment of a successful Hong Kong SAR under the one country, two systems formula. Conversely, a statement of the Taiwan issue under that formula would increase the confidence of the Hong Kong people after 1997. As previously noted, under the one country, two systems formula Taiwan's military forces will be maintained if the mainland reunifies with Taiwan. As a consequence, if the Beijing regime tried to change its policy in order to impose the socialist system on Hong Kong, Macao, and Taiwan, those three SARs, and particularly Taiwan, which would retain its military forces, could unite to reject any policy harmful to them. Such a confrontation would not be in the interests of the central authorities. Moreover, if the Taiwan issue cannot be settled according to the Hong Kong model, difficulties will arise because there are no apparent feasible alternatives. Beijing will not give up its status as the sovereign government of all China. Nor will it abandon its socialist system and thereby deny the Communists' rule on the mainland. Therefore, the Beijing regime can be expected to attempt to persuade Taiwan to accept the Hong Kong model, and that appeal will depend on success and prosperity in the Hong Kong SAR.

Notes

1. David J. Clark proposed such an assumption. Based on "China's domestic record of noncompliance with its own law," Clark listed, among seven of his "operating assumptions about the Chinese political and legal system," the point that "China does not really intend to maintain Hong Kong unchanged for fifty years after July 1, 1997, nor does it desire to preserve fully Hong Kong's capitalist system and life-style, whatever the 1984 Sino-British Joint Declaration (JD) may say on the matter (Article 3 (2)). The JD is an expedient or tactic employed to achieve a strategic objective, that is, a unified country under one system, that is socialism." See David J. Clark, "The Basic Law: One Document, Two Systems," in Ming K. Chan and David J. Clark, *The Hong Kong Basic Law: Blueprint for "Stability and Prosperity" under Chinese Sovereignty?* (Armonk, N.Y.: M. E. Sharpe, 1991), 36–38.

2. The NPC Standing Committee, "Message to Compatriots in Taiwan," *Beijing Review* 22, no. 1 (5 January 1979): 16.

3. Ibid., 17.

4. See Joseph Y. S. Cheng, "The Future of Hong Kong: A Hong Kong 'Belonger's' View," *International Affairs* 58 (Summer, 1982): 486. An-chia Wu suggested that the principle of one country, two systems was put forth by Ye Jianying, the then chair of the Standing Committee of People's Congress, in his September 1981 "nine-point proposal" of peaceful reunification with Taiwan. This chapter discusses Ye's proposal later. See An-chia Wu, "'One Country, Two Systems': A Model for Taiwan?" *Issues and Studies* 21, no. 7 (July 1985): 33–34. In fact, Deng's offer to Taiwan was the same as Ye's but was made two years earlier.

5. Hua Guofeng, "Zai Diwu Jie Quanguo Renmin Daibiao Dahui Di'er Ci Huiyishangde Gongzuo Baogao" [Report on the Work of the Government Presented at the Second Session of the Fifth National People's Congress], *Hongqi* [Red Flag], no. 7 (3 July 1979): 27.

6. See Deng Xiaoping, "Muqian de Xingshi he Renwu" [The Present Situation and Tasks], in *Deng Xiaoping Wenxuan, 1975–1982* [Selected Works of Deng Xiaoping, 1975–1982] (Beijing: Renmin Chubanshe, 1983), 203–205; "Three Great Missions for the 1980s," *New China News Agency (NCNA)*, 1 September 1982, 1; and "Deng Congress Speech Hints Hong Kong Reunification," *The Standard*, 4 September 1982, in FBIS, 1 September 1982, W3–4.

7. "Chairman Ye Jianying's Elaborations on Policy Concerning the Return of Taiwan to Motherland and Peaceful Reunification," *Beijing Review* 24, no. 40 (5 October 1981): 10–11.

8. Concerning this concept, see Chapter 4.

9. *Constitution of the People's Republic of China* (1982), in *Beijing Review* 25, no. 52 (27 December 1982): 16.

10. Peng Zhen, "Report on the Draft of the Revised Constitution of the People's Republic of China," *Beijing Review* 25, no. 50 (13 December 1982): 20.

11. See Chapter 1.

12. See Joseph Y. S. Cheng, "The 1985 District Board Elections in Hong Kong," in Joseph Y. S. Cheng, ed., *Hong Kong in Transition* (Hong Kong: Oxford University Press, 1986), 67.

13. Ibid.; also see *Asia Yearbook, 1980* (Hong Kong: *Far Eastern Economic Review,* 1980), 160.

14. "Premier Hua Guofeng Holds Press Conference," *Beijing Review* 22, no. 41 (12 October 1979): 11.

15. "Hong Kong Newspaper President Visits Beijing: Meets Deng Xiaoping," *Xinhua,* 18 July 1981, in FBIS, 22 July 1981, E5.

16. "Chairman Ye Jianying's Elaborations on Policy Concerning the Return of Taiwan to the Motherland and Peaceful Reunification," *Beijing Review* 24, no. 41 (5 October 1981): 11.

17. Luo Ping, "Hu Yaobang on Hong Kong-Macao Policy," *Cheng Ming*, 1 August 1982, 8–11, in FBIS, 5 August 1982, W6.

18. "PRC Forms Committee to Study 1997 Question," *South China Morning Post*, 10 July 1982, 6, in FBIS, 21 July 1982, W5.

19. Robert Delfs, "Hongkong: 1997 and All That," *FEER*, 16 July 1982, 15.

20. Lang Kao, in contrast to this analysis, dates the first mention of the one country, two systems approach to a February 1984 meeting between Deng Xiaoping and a delegation from the Center of Strategic and International Studies of Georgetown University led by Zbigniew Brzezinski. See Lang Kao, "One Country, Two Systems: Its Theory, Practice, and Feasibility" (Ph.D. Diss., University of Maryland, 1988), 82.

21. Teery Cheng, "China Leaking Lease Plans," *Standard*, 11 August 1982, 1, 16, in FBIS, 11 August 1982, W4.

22. Lo Ping, "CPC Brain Trust's Plans for Post-1997 Hong Kong," *Cheng Ming*, 1 September 1982, 14–15, in FBIS, 7 September 1982, W2.

23. The two party leaders' speeches stated that the PLA would not be sent to Hong Kong after 1997. However, the 1984 agreement provides that the PLA will be stationed in the Hong Kong SAR.

24. "*South China Morning Post* on Sovereignty Question," FBIS, 18 May 1983, W3–4.

25. *South China Morning Post*, 26 December 1983, 8, cited in Lane, *Sovereignty and the Status Quo*, 94.

26. "Peng Says PRC Policy on Hong Kong Unchanged," *Xinhua*, 25 June 1983, in FBIS, 6 July 1983, E1; "CPPCC Delegate Gives Deng's Views on Hong Kong," *AFP*, 27 June 1983, in FBIS, 28 June 1983, E1; and "Hong Kong Gets Same Status as Macao After 1997," *AFP*, 7 July 1983, in FBIS, 8 July 1983, E1.

27. See Lane, *Sovereignty and the Status Quo*, 95.

28. "Self-Rule 'To Be Assured'," *South China Morning Post*, 15 October 1983, 1, 8, in FBIS, 17 October 1983, W1–2.

29. "A Significant Concept," *Beijing Review* 27, no. 44 (29 October 1984): 16–17. The following quotations from Deng are all from this article. Concerning this concept, see also Deng Xiaoping, "One Country, Two Systems," in his *Speeches and Writings*, 2nd ed. (Oxford: Pergamon Press, 1987), 91–94.

30. Concerning the theory of linkage, see James N. Rosenau, ed., *Linkage Politics* (New York: The Free Press, 1969).

31. "'One Country, Two Systems' Born of Reality," *Beijing Review* 28, no. 5 (4 February 1985): 15.

32. Li Jiaquan, "Mainland and Taiwan: Formula for China's Reunification," *Beijing Review* 29, no. 5 (3 February 1986): 21.

33. *Renmin Ribao*, 13 April 1987, quoted in C. L. Chiou, "China's Reunification Policy: No 'Mousetrapping' of Taiwan," in Joseph Y. S. Cheng, ed., *China: Modernization in the 1980s* (Hong Kong: The Chinese University Press, 1989), 222–223.

34. "Premier Reiterates to Talk with PRC," *Taipei International Service*, 10 October 1981, in FBIS, 13 October 1981, V2; and "Spokesman Comments on CCP 'Peace Offensive,'" *Taipei CNA*, 10 October 1981, in FBIS, 13 October 1981, V2–3.

35. Chiang Ching-kuo, "Bitter Lessons and a Solemn Mission," in Hung-mao Tien, ed., *Mainland China, Taiwan, and U.S. Policy* (Cambridge, Mass.: Oelgeschlager, Gunn & Hain, 1983), 241–245.

36. *Asia 1990 Yearbook* (Hong Kong: Review Publishing Company, 1990), 6–7. In 1994, GNP per capita in Taiwan surpassed the US$10,000 level. See "Republic of China

on Taiwan in the Global Community," *Foreign Affairs* 73, no. 5 (September–October 1994): advertising section.

37. "Majority Favor More Links with Mainland," *China Post*, 10 October 1990, 12.

38. For details of the economic exchanges between Taiwan and the mainland, see Chapter 6.

39. Concerning the Wang-Koo talks, see Nicholas D. Kristof, "Starting to Build Their First Bridge, China and Taiwan Sign 4 Pacts," *The New York Times*, 30 April 1993, A7; Jeremy Mark, "Taiwan and China Fail to Resolve Investment Dispute," *The Wall Street Journal*, 29 April 1993, A10; Julian Baum, "The Narrowing Strait: Taipei and Peking Prepare for Unofficial Talks," *FEER*, 29 April 1993, 13; id., "The Stumbling Block: Investment Guarantees a Hurdle at Singapore Talks," *FEER*, 6 May 1993, 11–12; Xie Liangjun, "Rapport Is Reached at Historic Meeting," *China Daily*, 28 April 1991, 1; and id., "'Historic' Strait Agreements Signed," *China Daily*, 30 April 1993, 1.

40. "Lee Tenghui Gives Inaugural Speech," FBIS, 21 May 1990, 61–63.

41. Concerning President Lee's new policy on mainland China, see Fredrick F. Chien, "UN Should Welcome Taiwan," *FEER*, 5 August 1993, 23; Yvonne Yuan, "A Pragmatic Vision," *Free China Review* 43, no. 2 (February 1993): 16–20; "Building Better Relations," *Free China Review* 43. no. 2 (February 1993): 4–15; Julian Baum, "Divided Nations," *FEER*, 16 September 1993, 10–11; Julian Baum, John Mcbeth, and Rodney Tasker, "In His Private Capacity: President Lee Scores Points in Holiday Diplomacy," *FEER*, 24 February 1994, 18–19; Philip Liu, "Golf Ball Diplomacy," *Free China Review* 44, no. 5 (May 1994): 30–37; "Taiwan: The Outsider," *The Economist*, 2 July 1994, 17–19; and "Republic of China on Taiwan in the Global Community," *Foreign Affairs* 73, no. 5 (September–October 1994): advertising section.

42. Taiwan Affairs Office and Information Office State Council of the People's Republic of China, "The Taiwan Question and Reunification of China," *Beijing Review* 36, no. 36 (12 September 1993): I–VIII.

43. Ibid.

44. See Frank Ching, "An About-Turn by Taiwan," *FEER*, 4 August 1994, 30.

45. Tao Beichuan, "Jianli Zhonghua Gongtongti, Micheng Gouhe Shen Mou Tongyi" [On the Establishment of the Chinese Commonwealth and Ending the Dispute for Reunification], *Zhongyang Ribao* [Central Daily News], 24 October 1991, 1.

46. Lang Kao, "One Country, Two Systems: Its Theory, Practice, and Feasibility" (Ph.D. Diss., University of Maryland, 1988).

47. Lang Kao, "A New Relationship Across the Taiwan Strait," *Issues and Studies* 27, no. 4 (April 1991): 62–63.

48. Wen-hui Tsai, "Convergence and Divergence Between Mainland China and Taiwan: The Future of Unification," in *Issues and Studies* 27, no. 12 (December 1991): 11–12.

49. Yu-ming Shaw, "An ROC View of the Hong Kong Issue," *Issues and Studies* 22, no. 6 (June 1986): 26.

50. "Li Denghui Zongtong Juxing Jizhe Hui" [President Lee Teng-hui Holds Press Conference], *Zhongyang Ribao*, 2 May 1991, 3.

3

The Formation of the SAR's Political System in the Basic Law

According to the 1984 Sino-British Joint Declaration, the Chinese policy toward Hong Kong stated in that document was to serve as a groundwork for a Basic Law of the Hong Kong Special Administrative Region under Chinese sovereignty. After a five-year drafting process, the Basic Law was finally completed on April 4, 1990. This legislation defined the Chinese policy toward Hong Kong in detail. Both the declaration and the Basic Law are legal formulations of the Chinese policy toward Hong Kong, with the major difference that the declaration is an international document while the Basic Law is Chinese legislation. However, the Basic Law proved more controversial than the declaration. Several studies have described how the drafters from the mainland and Hong Kong disputed each article, each term, even each word of the law.[1] This chapter will focus on two questions: (1) What conditions affected the formulation of the political system of the Hong Kong SAR and Hong Kong's process of democratization?[2] (2) Whose interests, in terms of social groups in Hong Kong, are represented by the Basic Law? These two issues, involving the democratization of Hong Kong and the composition of the government of the SAR, were the ones that created the most controversy.

In the 1984 Joint Declaration, the Chinese government announced that Hong Kong's social and economic systems and way of life would remain unchanged until 2047. The Basic Law further confirms this promise: "the previous capitalist system and way of life shall remain unchanged for 50 years" after 1997 (BL 5). Though the declaration and the Basic Law do not mention Hong Kong's present political system under British colonial rule, the two documents hammer out the new political system of the SAR, indicating that the present one will be greatly changed.[3] This chapter will show that the current British colonial system was an important factor affecting establishment of a new political system in the SAR. To gain an understanding of alterations that will be made in Hong Kong's political system in 1997, it is first necessary to review Hong Kong's current political system.

Hong Kong's Current Political System:
Its Constitution and Practice

Hong Kong's current political system is a product of British colonial rule. After Hong Kong was ceded to Great Britain in the 1842 Nanjing Treaty, the British Crown issued Henry Pottinger, the first governor of the British colony of Hong Kong, two important documents. The Letters Patent of April 5, 1843, and the Royal Instructions, issued on the following day, regulated the political system of the new colony and consequently became the constitution of the British colony of Hong Kong for over 150 years. Though both the Letters Patent and the Royal Instructions were amended many times,[4] their main content has not been changed. As N. J. Miners wrote in 1977:

> Indeed, if the first British governor of Hong Kong, Sir Henry Pottinger, were to return to the colony today practically the only things he would recognize would be the outlines of the Peak and the system of government, which has hardly changed in 130 years.[5]

The Letters Patent stipulate the relationship between Hong Kong and London as well as the colony's internal political system. The core of Hong Kong's political system is the governor, who is appointed by the Queen of the United Kingdom and is the representative of the British Crown in Hong Kong. The governor is not only the highest authority of the colony, but also the commander-in-chief of British military forces in Hong Kong. He possesses the power to make laws for the colony.

The Letters Patent created an Executive Council (Exco) and a Legislative Council (Legco), both of which are only consultative bodies to the governor. In addition to the governor, there were three other members of the first Legco, but it was later expanded in amendments to the Royal Instructions. In 1984, when the Sino-British Joint Declaration was concluded, the Hong Kong government decided to introduce a representative system to the Legco, which resulted in a newly established Legco of 1985 composed of fifty-six seats: thirty-two were official or nominated seats, while twenty-four were held by members indirectly elected by functional constituencies[6] and by an electoral college composed of the members of the District Boards, the Urban Council, and the Regional Council.[7] In 1989, based on the amended Letters Patent, there were fifty-seven members in the Legco, including the governor, who was the president; three ex-officio members (the chief secretary, the financial secretary, and the attorney general); seven other official members (other heads of the departments); twenty appointed members; and twenty-six indirectly elected ones. The official and appointed members were chosen by the governor and were approved by the secretary of state in London.[8] This was the arrangement of Hong Kong's legislature when the drafting of the Basic Law was in process. This section will show how the composition of the Legco affected the formulation in the Basic Law of the first Legislative Council of the SAR.

The earliest Executive Council also consisted of the governor and three members who were nominated by the governor and appointed by the Queen. The governor was the president of the Exco and had the power to veto proposals by any other members. Later the Exco also was enlarged. In 1989 it consisted of four ex-officio members—the chief secretary, the commander of British forces, the financial secretary, and the attorney general—and ten appointed members.[9]

As president of both the Executive and the Legislative Councils, the governor possesses the power to dismiss or to discipline other members, to make final decisions for all important matters of the colonial government, and to veto laws passed in the Legco. Norman Miners commented that "The governor's legal powers are such that if he chose to exercise his full authority he could turn himself into a petty dictator."[10]

The foregoing discussion outlines the constitutional basis for Hong Kong's colonial government and for the relationship between London and Hong Kong. But the word "constitution" does not actually describe the way in which this region is governed. In practice, Hong Kong in the last decades has had much more power independent of London than the Letters Patent and Royal Instructions bestowed. Also, the governor has not fully used the absolute powers authorized by those two documents. For a better understanding of Hong Kong's current politics, it is necessary to see how Hong Kong's constitution is manifested in actual practice.

The royal government in London is the highest and final authority over the affairs of Hong Kong. London retains the power to appoint the governor, the officers of the Exco, the members of the Legco, and the judges of the colony, based on the nomination of the governor. Moreover, London maintains the power to make law for Hong Kong and to veto legislation passed in the Legco. In the early years, the British authorities in London did use this veto power to reject ordinances passed by Hong Kong's Legislative Council and approved by the governor. From 1842 to 1913, the British authorities in London exercised this power fifteen times.[11]

However, in the last decades Hong Kong has enjoyed much more autonomy in its internal affairs than is strictly provided by its constitution. The British Crown has not exercised its right to veto laws passed by the Legco since 1913. The Crown has the power to instruct the governor not to allow any bill to pass, but that power was only exercised once in Hong Kong's history, in 1946. The British Parliament has restricted its use of the power to pass laws applicable in Hong Kong to matters involving the colony's external affairs, such as defense, air navigation, treaties, and national citizenship. In conclusion, London has rarely intervened in Hong Kong's affairs or vetoed the Hong Kong government's decisions.[12]

Economically, Hong Kong has been free to decide its dollar's exchange rate since the 1960s and to invest its reserves in any currency since the 1970s. Hong Kong's financial and monetary systems have also functioned without

British interference. Since 1969, the colony has been allowed to independently conduct bilateral commercial agreements and since 1973 to negotiate external multinational trading treaties as well. Hong Kong officials have sat as part of the British delegation in international economic conferences, such as the General Agreement on Tariffs and Trade (GATT), but have represented their region independently. Indeed, their positions on trading issues sometimes differed from those of British officials.[13] The colony's exercise of autonomous economic status, which was established in the last decades, actually set up a pattern for the relationship between China and the Hong Kong SAR in economic, financial, and monetary systems after 1997. The 1984 Joint Declaration and the Basic Law maintain Hong Kong's autonomous status in these areas.

However, Hong Kong was, after all, a British colony. Britain's sovereignty could be perceived in the appointment of the governor and major government officials and in the colony's foreign affairs and defense. Hong Kong had no independent diplomatic relations with any states. Its external relationships and negotiations were conducted on its behalf by Britain, and its security was protected by British military forces stationed in Hong Kong. More importantly, the governor was sent to the colony to implement British policy.

As for the colony's internal politics, although the Letters Patent and Royal Instructions authorize the governor to wield tremendous executive, legislative, and judiciary powers, in practice he usually did not fully exercise these powers. The governor typically made decisions based on consultations with other officials of the Exco. Also, the governor never vetoed a bill in the Legco.[14] The current system of the Legco almost guaranteed the governor's proposals to be adopted, because a majority of the seats were taken by official or appointed members who were the governor's representatives. Even after 1985 over thirty of fifty-five were still official or appointed members who were expected to support the governor's motions. Only after 1990, when political parties emerged, did representatives in the Legco begin to challenge the governor. For instance, a majority of Legco members rejected the British authorities' decision on the establishment of Hong Kong's Court of Final Appeals (as will be discussed in Chapter 7).

Another phenomenon of Hong Kong's colonial system was that although in the last decades Hong Kong people have enjoyed Western-style political freedoms—freedom of speech, freedom of the press, freedom of religion, and freedom of assembly—there was no Western-style democracy characterized by representative government and competitive political parties. The governor was not elected by the people, he had constitutional power to control the government, and he was responsible only to London. Before the Sino-British negotiations on Hong Kong began in 1982, elections had been introduced only for the Urban Council. Yet the franchise was highly restricted to voters who qualified in one of twenty-three categories by standards of education, tax paying, or membership in professional bodies. Of the estimated 440,000 eligible voters in a city of over five million, only 35,000 registered; and 6,195 actually voted.[15]

Slow progress was made toward representative government in the 1980s. In this decade, elections were introduced to the Regional Council and District Boards. Even so, most of the members of the Urban Council, the Regional Council, and the District Boards were not directly elected. Moreover, all members of the Exco and most members of the Legco were appointed by the governor and approved by the secretary of state in London. During the 150 years the British ruled Hong Kong, no member of the Legislative Council was elected directly by the people until 1991.

This system of appointment, rather than election, of local representatives gave rise to the specific problem of the exclusion of ethnic Chinese from the colonial government. Although ethnic Chinese accounted for 98 percent of the colony's population, few were appointed to higher-level administrative offices. Because all government officials were appointed and no Legco members were elected directly through geographical constituencies before 1991, the absence of locally born Chinese in high-level positions became a distinct issue in the move toward representative government. Between 1947 and 1960 the colonial government appointed only seven Chinese as administrative officers, compared to forty-one expatriates. In the following decades, the proportion of Chinese in the directorate class (heads of government departments, senior professional officers, and other positions of similar status) was slowly increased. By 1970, Chinese comprised 19 percent of the directorate class; by 1980, 39.2 percent; and by 1985, 52.5 percent.[16] Despite these increases, one can only conclude that two political systems were operating under British rule: in the British homeland, there was a democratic political system, but in Hong Kong democracy had been ignored.

The foregoing review of the theory and practice Hong Kong's constitution reveals that in recent decades the colony has been autonomous in its social and economic affairs. Also, within the context of colonial government, the governor generally consulted appointees in the Exco and Legco before making decisions regarding everyday operations. However, it should be noted that under the Letters Patent, the British government in London had continued to use its power exclusively in the crucial decisions concerning selection of the governor and the major local officials. Also, the governor alone made the final decisions as to the appointment of Legco and Exco members. As will be further discussed in Chapter 7, the political development in the early 1990s demonstrated that the British authorities in London and Hong Kong still exercised unchallenged power in important matters. For instance, in 1992, in order to implement its new Hong Kong policy London replaced Governor David Wilson with Christopher Patten. Also, even though local political groups competed for seats in the Exco and Legco, both Governors Wilson and Patten appointed their favored persons. Moreover, in 1991 British authorities in both London and Hong Kong rejected the Legco's resolution on the Sino-British agreement concerning the establishment of Hong Kong's Court of Final Appeal.

In conclusion, there were three major characteristics of Hong Kong's existing system of government that significantly affected the establishment of the

SAR's political system in the Basic Law: a strong and unchallenged executive; a lack of representative government; and, by 1989, a lack of political parties. As will be shown, Chinese officials and the mainland's Basic Law drafters perceived Hong Kong's current system as efficient, workable, and necessary to the region's political stability and economic growth. The Chinese insisted that except in the area of sovereignty the system must not be changed dramatically after 1997, because any radical change might result in political unrest.

Hong Kong Divided on Democratization and the SAR's Political System

After the 1984 Sino-British Joint Declaration was announced, the democratization of Hong Kong became a controversial issue over which disputes arose that affected the making of the Basic Law. During the Basic Law drafting process, prodemocracy liberals headed by Martin Lee and Szeto Wah—mainly the younger generation of intellectuals, grass-roots leaders, social workers, religious people, and lawyers—appealed for radical democratization. Lee and Szeto were appointed to the Basic Law Drafting Committee (BLDC) by China's NPC where they participated in the subgroup on political structure. Fearing that the chief executive and the government of the SAR would be controlled by Beijing, prodemocracy radicals asked for universal suffrage in the election of the chief executive and the Legco of the SAR. These liberals suggested that the Legco should possess sufficient power to supervise and check executive authority and should "be elected by direct election."[17] They also argued that under the joint declaration, the Central People's Government was to be responsible only for defense and foreign affairs and that in local affairs the central authorities could not intervene. Otherwise, the principle of Hong Kong people ruling Hong Kong would not be guaranteed. However, the Beijing Authorities insisted that because the SAR would still be under Chinese sovereignty, the autonomy expressed in Hong Kong people ruling Hong Kong did not mean that the SAR would be entirely independent of the central government. In addition to its powers in foreign affairs and defense, the central government's NPC Standing Committee had the authority to interpret the Basic Law. But the liberals believed that because the Communist regime had not made a serious effort to implement laws, the Communist leaders in Beijing could not be trusted and only an elected government could safeguard the freedom of the people and the autonomy of the region. These radicals appealed to the Hong Kong government to introduce direct election to the Legco in 1988 and to establish a solid representative government before 1997. However, in February 1988 Governor Wilson's government issued a white paper that stipulated that in 1991 only ten of fifty-six Legco seats were to be elected directly by geographical constituencies. The white paper explained that polls showed there was no clear opinion in the community as to when and how the proposed direct election should be introduced. The introduction of direct election was an important step toward democratization for the Hong Kong government, but the radicals were angered by the government's hesitation. In their open letter to the British government, eight Legco members, included Martin Lee, requested that direct elections be introduced immediately. They argued that without democracy, there was no hope that the government of the SAR would be able to defend the rights and freedoms of Hong Kong citizens and protect local interests in situations of conflict with the central government. The letter also said that without democracy, the policies of one country, two systems and Hong Kong people ruling Hong Kong would be doomed to fail.[18] In a Legco meeting, Lee, representing the views of the liberals, explained why a rapid democratization was necessary after over 100 years of British colonial rule and why Beijing could not be trusted:

> The answer is simple. It is not due to the Hong Kong Colonial Government that our freedoms are safeguarded; rather, it is due to the British Government, which is itself a democratic one. Thus, if people were to be imprisoned in Hong Kong without trial, questions would be raised in Britain's Parliament. And if Hong Kong were not run to the satisfaction of the British people, it could even result in a change of government at home. In short, we owe the protection of our rights and freedoms not to the Hong Kong Government but to a democratically elected British Government that acts as a watchdog over local authorities. The question is, with the changes come 1997, can we still entrust the preservation of our freedom and rights in the same way to the National People's Congress, which operates under the Communist system? The Chinese Constitution is a marvelous document on paper, yet there are still many people imprisoned in the People's Republic of China without any trial. And no question has ever been asked in the National People's Congress about this.[19]

Lee's statement expressed the fundamental difference between the prodemocracy liberals and the Beijing authorities on political ideology and governmental system. During the transition period, disputes concerning Beijing's one country, two systems, the forming of the SAR government, the relationship between the central authorities and the SAR, and the democratization of Hong Kong can all be traced to this difference in belief and perception. In short, an incompatible difference had emerged.

The business and professional communities, however, generally favored maintaining the status quo. They believed that Hong Kong's economic miracle proved that the current system was efficient, and that dramatic changes were not only not necessary but that democratization would jeopardize the achievements of the system. Helmut Solmen, son-in-law of the late Sir Pao Yue-kong and a Legco member elected from the business community, argued:

> As happened in other countries, professional and full-time politicians will gradually replace the part-time legislators coming from a variety of backgrounds and bringing balanced and objective views to bear on the solution of prob-

> lems. Hong Kong will be the poorer for it. . . . We shall be sacrificing prag-
> matic sense and the chance to refine and strengthen our peculiar Hong Kong
> institutions—which have been so successful in good and bad times—on the
> altar of expediency to achieve what is probably a misplaced feeling of greater
> security in facing the future.[20]

Ronald Li, former chair of the Hong Kong Stock Exchange, further expressed
the view of the conservative business community: "Hong Kong is a colony. It is
a dictatorship, although a benevolent one. It is and has been a British colony,
and it is going to be a Chinese colony, and as such it will prosper. We do not
need elections here."[21]

Why did the business community dislike radical reform? They feared that
radical change would lead to political unrest and economic decline such as
Hong Kong had experienced in the last decades. In 1967, Hong Kong Chinese,
instigated by China's Cultural Revolution, rebelled against the British colonial
authorities. The turmoil resulted in fifty-one deaths, 800 injuries, and 5,000
arrests for violence, and cost millions of dollars in property and economic damage.[22] In the early 1980s, when the future of Hong Kong was uncertain and
Sino-British negotiations on Hong Kong were in a deadlock, the Hong Kong
dollar fell versus the U.S. dollar from HK$5.9 (US$1) in January 1982 to
HK$9.55 in September 1983. The slumping value of the Hong Kong dollar
shocked the Hong Kong community.[23] Also, the business and professional communities were heavily represented in the Executive and Legislative Councils,
and they feared that in direct elections they might lose their seats and their
influence. The business community accepted China's one country, two systems
policy, and a large portion of the Hong Kong Basic Law drafters came from that
community. The most influential figures of the business community—such as
Pao Yue-kong, Ann Tse-kai, Li Kang-sheng, and Henry Fok Ying-tung—had
personal friendships with Chinese leaders. Their views certainly affected the
forming of the SAR's political system during the drafting of the Basic Law.

Early in August 1986, the businesspeople and professionals who comprised
one-third of the 180-member Basic Law Consultative Committee called for the
preservation of "the good aspects of the present system." These aspects included efficient executive authority, the absence of party politics, and an independent judicial system. Their plan was described thus:

> The chief executive—with a role similar to that of the present Governor but
> not chairing the legislature—to be chosen by an electoral college for over 600
> people, including law-makers, members of District Boards, the Urban and
> Regional Councils and representatives of various functional constituencies.
>   A group of advisers responsible only to the chief executive to form the
> Chief Executive's Council. Members would be officials and unofficials ap-
> pointed by the chief executive or through a process of nomination.
>   The legislature to be composed of approximately 80 members, with half
> of the seats held by functional constituencies, a quarter elected by the elec-
> toral college and the rest directly elected.[24]

Obviously, the conservatives' ideal model was a copy of the existing system with limited changes. A comparison of the system proposed by the business community with the current British system reveals only two small differences. One was that the chief executive of the SAR would not preside over the Legco, as the British governor did. The other was that a quarter of members of the Legco would be elected directly by geographical constituencies, compared with the situation in the 1980s when no single member of the Legco was elected directly. For the conservatives, these two points might have constituted progress toward democracy. However, the conservatives also suggested that candidates for directly elected seats be nominated by members of the Legislative, Urban, and Regional Councils and the District Boards, and not by political parties. Therefore, there would actually be no great reform in terms of representative government. Yet the conservatives' proposal contained three important concepts about the structure of the political system that were later adopted in the Basic Law: the chief executive would be chosen by an electoral college with hundreds of members; the Exco members would be appointed by the chief executive; and finally, the overwhelming majority of members of the Legco would be selected by functional constituencies and by an electoral college.

On September 28, 1987, a joint statement rejecting the liberals' demand that directly elected seats be introduced in the 1988 Legco election was issued by eighty-four business organizations, including the pro-China Chinese General Chamber of Commerce, the Federation of Hong Kong Industries, and the Chinese Manufacturers' Association. The statement warned that any political unrest would result in an economic recession, as previous experiences had demonstrated. The statement also suggested that the Legco direct election be introduced after 1990, when the Basic law was promulgated.[25]

To end the conflict between liberals and conservatives, Louis Cha, publisher of local *Ming Pao* and a co-convener of the BLDC's subgroup on political structure, submitted in November 1988 a compromise proposal for gradual democratization, which later became known as the "mainstream proposal." Cha suggested that the proportion of directly elected seats of the Legco of the SAR be increased to 50 percent over the course of four terms, or twelve years. The chief executive would be elected by a grand electoral college with 800 members for the first three five-year terms, after which a referendum in Hong Kong would be held to make a determination on universal suffrage. Cha's proposal immediately passed the BLDC's subgroup on political structure, although the plan was opposed by liberal members such as Martin Lee and Szeto Wah, who argued that the mainstream proposal was too slow. They launched a hunger strike to protest the BLDC's adoption of Cha's proposal and burned the draft Basic Law. Conservative members, on the other hand, generally supported the mainstream proposal but argued that the pace of democratization was still too radical. Ngai Shiukit, a famous figure in the Hong Kong industrial and commercial circle and a Legco member, argued: "'the mainstream program' is in line with the principle of proceeding in an orderly way, step by step, and steadily marching toward democracy." However, he thought that the move toward democratic government was still too fast.[26]

Hong Kong government officials opposed radical political reforms. Sir Chung Sze-yuen, a senior member of the Exco, rejected the idea of direct elections and said that the successful functioning of Hong Kong's political system in the last forty years demonstrated that Hong Kong needed no political reform. He also maintained that the structure of the government, which since 1976 had featured an executive and a legislature that were neither separated nor united, was unique: some members were sitting on the Exco and the Legco simultaneously. He stressed that the urgent issue for the future was the question of the separation of the executive, legislative, and judicial organs, not direct elections.[27] However, Chung failed to explain why he held this priority, and also why he opposed a separation of the executive and legislative functions before 1997 but favored a final separation of the judicial, executive, and legislative functions thereafter. Lydia Dunn, an influential senior Exco member, also favored limited democratization. She said that the mainstream proposal was in accordance with the Hong Kong people's political consciousness and social demands. She pointed out that half of the members of the SAR's Legco would be elected by direct vote within six years after 1997, a step that could not be regarded as conservative, but progressive.[28] Lydia Dunn was a career businesswoman, director of the Swire Group, and the chair of the Hong Kong Trade Department Council. Clearly, one of the reasons that Chinese officials in the Hong Kong government opposed radical reform was that most of them were also from the business community, and their views reflected the interests of that community.

China's Position on Hong Kong's Democratization and the SAR's Political System

The drafting of the Basic Law tested China's ability to handle the complicated situation in Hong Kong after 1984. For the Beijing authorities, it was not only the final draft of the Basic Law that was important. The drafting process itself was an opportunity to show China's willingness to let Hong Kong people rule Hong Kong. However, the situation was difficult and produced contradictory responses. On the one hand, China insisted that drafting the law was China's internal affair and rejected any British attempt to influence the process. On the other hand, China reassured Britain and the Hong Kong people that the Basic Law would accord with the joint declaration, and also asked Britain to arrange for Hong Kong's reforms before 1997 to link up with the SAR's political system.

The Chinese government partially shared the views on political reform of Hong Kong's conservative business community. Communist Chinese officials did not want a radical change of the current system before 1997, nor did they think that rapid democratization was necessary. They perceived Western-style democracy with Marxist-Leninist views, maintaining that it was a bourgeois, financially based democracy in which only the wealthy would be elected. They also distrusted Western party politics and objected to the introduction of organized competitive political parties in Hong Kong. Li Hou, deputy director of the Hong Kong and Macao Affairs Office at the State Council, indicated in discussions that the central government would not like to see Western-style party politics in the SAR.[29] Lu Ping, director of the same office, stated that it was "better for Hong Kong that party politics do not emerge. . . . One political party comes to power today and another will come to power tomorrow. This is detrimental to Hong Kong's stability."[30] The Beijing authorities' perception of democracy mainly focused on the results of governmental decisionmaking rather than on the process, which involved competition between political parties, and on compromise among the elites rather than on massive participation in elections. Therefore, Chinese officials and the mainland drafters favored an electoral college, rather than direct elections, for the selection of SAR officials and legislators. This was one reason why Hong Kong's business community and professionals supported China's views on political reform.

Furthermore, the Beijing authorities believed that the British Hong Kong government had managed the region's economy efficiently and that radical political reform would jeopardize it. An article published in one of China's leading newspapers in 1985 argued:

> Hong Kong's economy is rather fragile and cannot stand much turbulence. If there is a sudden change in the political system in Hong Kong, accomplished by a violent upheaval in its social structure, the international society will lose faith in Hong Kong and refrain from making investment and engaging in commerce and finance in Hong Kong, and the city will soon suffer from an economic depression. Therefore, the maintenance of Hong Kong's stability is of special significance in promoting the economic prosperity of Hong Kong.[31]

The Chinese government attributed the success of Hong Kong's economy in part to the colonial political system, with its authoritarian government and lack of competitive political parties. Deng Xiaoping favored the model of strong government coupled with a free market economy and insisted that Western-style democracy could not work in Chinese society.

Finally, Chinese leaders expected that Hong Kong's governmental power would pass to persons who could be trusted by Beijing. For this reason the Chinese officials insisted that candidates for the office of chief executive and other major officials of the SAR, although selected locally, would be appointed by the Central People's Government. The Chinese leaders feared that this projected arrangement might be damaged if radical reforms like direct elections were introduced. Deng Xiaoping argued:

> Our opinion is that the people who manage Hong Kong affairs should be those Hong Kong people who love both the motherland and Hong Kong. Can general elections guarantee that such people will be selected?[32]

As they rejected Hong Kong's rapid democratization, the Communist leaders applied traditional united front tactics to gain support from social groups and personalities in various sectors of the community—business, government, labor, religion, finance, and education. They established good relationships with elites of the Hong Kong community, particularly in the business and professional groups. Leading Hong Kong business leaders like Sir Pao Yue-kong (who died in 1991), Ann Tse-Kai, Li Ka-sheng, Gordon Wu, and Henry Fok Ying-tung were distinguished friends of Beijing. Business magnates like Henry Fok Ying-tung, well-known professionals like the lawyer Liu Yiu-chu, and the president of the independent newspaper *Ching Pao*, Xu Ximin, were Hong Kong deputies to the NPC or members of the Chinese People's Political Consultative Conference (CPPCC). Most were members of the BLDC, and Ann Tse-kai and Sir Pao Yue-kong were the vice-chairs. Most probably, wealthy businesspeople and professionals like these will participate heavily in the SAR's first government.

Chinese officials were dissatisfied with the liberals in the BLDC because they did not compromise with the other drafters. In November 1988, in response to liberal criticism of the SAR's political system as drafted by the BLDC, Lu Ping said: "I cannot agree with their comment that the system is undemocratic" and he continued, "there are different understandings over democracy. The issue now is just a matter of the pace. You can't say the system the political sub-group has decided on is undemocratic."[33] After the 1989 Tiananmen incident, liberal members Martin Lee and Szeto Wah were dismissed because they supported Beijing students.

From the Beijing authorities' perspective, the Basic Law drafting process was indeed democratic: almost half the members in the drafting committee were from various walks of life in Hong Kong. The draft was revised three times, based on opinions of Hong Kong people solicited by the BLCC over the course of five years. Moreover, both liberals and conservatives were represented in the drafting committee. Finally, for final approval of the Basic Law each article had to be passed by a two-thirds majority of all BLDC members on the basis of one person, one vote, a system which gave the Hong Kong drafters enough votes to block any articles with which they were dissatisfied.

Britain's Influence and Sino-British Compromise

Britain's involvement also affected the political formation of the SAR in the drafting of the Basic Law. Since 1984, London and Beijing have held different views on the issue of democratization. Before 1984, the British government had not introduced representative government to Hong Kong because it was perceived as a threat to colonial control. For instance, in 1946, one year after Britain recovered its colony from four years of Japanese occupation, Sir Mark A. Young returned to his governorship of Hong Kong and proposed to reform

Hong Kong politics by introducing limited representative government. He announced that the British government intended to grant the inhabitants of Hong Kong "a fuller and more responsible share in the management of their own affairs." This goal was to be achieved by "handing over certain functions of internal administration, hitherto exercised by the Government, to a Municipal Council constituted on a fully representative basis."[34] The governor's proposal became known as the "Young plan." Later, Governor Young further proposed that the Municipal Council administer the urban areas and fully control its own finance. To encourage the development of representative government, two-thirds of the Municipal Councillors would be elected and the Legco would be reformed by adding one unofficial member and retiring two official ones.[35] Through these reforms, Young hoped that the Hong Kong Chinese would become loyal British subjects.

However, Sir Alexander Grantham, Young's successor as governor from 1947 to 1957, criticized the Young plan as unrealistic. He argued that since Britain had only leased the New Territories for ninety-nine years and was to return Hong Kong to China in 1997, Hong Kong was unique among the British colonies and should not follow the pattern of self-government of other colonies. The British secretary of state, Creech Jones, and the Colonial Office supported Grantham's view. They feared that representative government introduced before the fall of 1948 would result in the infiltration into the Hong Kong government of Kuomintang members, and of Chinese Communists after 1948. Moreover, the British officials also suspected that popular election would result in Chinese domination of local politics.[36] Consequently, the Young plan was abandoned. It was the only British attempt to introduce representative government between 1842 and the 1970s.

Furthermore, Hong Kong has been at the doorstep of its powerful neighbor, the People's Republic of China, since 1949. The Hong Kong government has usually been attentive to Beijing's position when handling sensitive issues in both internal and external affairs. For instance, the Hong Kong authorities banned any anti-China activities by the Kuomintang and Soviet agencies located in the colony. Before the 1980s, colonial authorities also paid attention to Beijing's position on issues of Hong Kong's political reform. Sir David Trench, governor of Hong Kong from 1964 to 1971, said in 1971 that "China has made it pretty clear that she would not be happy with a Hong Kong moving toward a representative system and internal self-government." Lord Shepherd, a minister of state responsible for Hong Kong at the Foreign and Commonwealth Office from 1967 to 1970, supported Governor Trench's view and asserted that Hong Kong should retain its current system because of the China factor.[37] For all these reasons, a representative system was not introduced before 1984.[38]

After the 1984 Sino-British agreement, because Hong Kong would cease to be a colony British policymakers no longer feared either Chinese pressure or confrontation with the people of Hong Kong if democracy were introduced. From the British perspective, the introduction of representative government was an important step in the preparation of Hong Kong people ruling Hong Kong after the return of the colony to China.[39] From 1984 to 1991, the colonial government increasingly introduced limited representative systems in Hong Kong. On July 18, 1984, two months before the Sino-British Joint Declaration was announced, the government issued a green paper entitled "The Further Development of Representative Government in Hong Kong," and asked the people of Hong Kong to comment on it. According to the green paper, the aim of the government was

> to develop progressively a system of government the authority for which is firmly rooted in Hong Kong, which is able to represent authoritatively the views of the people of Hong Kong, and which is more directly accountable to the people of Hong Kong.[40]

The most significant progress delineated in the 1984 green paper concerned the electoral college and functional constituencies, which would introduce indirectly elected seats to the Legco for the first time. The green paper proposed that both the electoral college and functional constituencies would elect six Legco members in 1985 and twelve in 1988. In addition, the number of appointed unofficial members would be reduced progressively to twenty-three in 1985 and sixteen in 1988, and official members would be reduced to thirteen in 1985 and ten in 1988.[41]

The creation of functional constituencies and the electoral college was the first step in reforming the Legco from a council composed entirely of the governor's apointees to a local legislature representing professional and occupational groups. The long-term target was direct election of all Legco members through universal suffrage. But in the short-term transitional period, the concepts of functional constituencies and electoral college played important roles in determining the composition of the Legco and the content of the Basic Law. The Chinese government and Hong Kong conservatives both favored the concepts of the functional constituencies and electoral college over the concept of direct elections.

In its white paper published on November 21, 1984, the Hong Kong government made a proposal, based on the responses of the people of Hong Kong to the green paper, to increase the number of indirectly elected seats and to reduce the official and appointed seats in the Legco in the following year. According to the white paper, Legco members returned by both electoral college and functional constituencies would be increased to twelve, six more than were proposed by the green paper. At the same time, official members would be reduced to ten from the proposed thirteen and appointed members would be reduced to twenty-two from twenty-three.[42]

When the first elections to the Legco were held in September 1985, the reform plan announced by the 1984 white paper was carried out. Of the fifty-six Legco members, twelve were elected by nine functional constituencies and twelve by electoral college. The nine functional constituencies were defined as commercial, industrial, financial, labor, social services, medical, education, legal, and engineers and associated professions. The commercial, industrial, and labor constituencies each elected two members to the Legco while the other six returned one seat each. The electoral college was composed of all members of the District Boards, the Urban Council, and the Regional Council. There were nineteen District Boards with a total of 426 members, thirty members in the Urban Council, and thirty-six in the Regional Council.

In May 1987, the Hong Kong government issued another green paper aimed at soliciting public opinion on the further development of a representative democracy. This paper clearly proposed to introduce directly elected seats to the Legco.[43] According to a white paper issued in February 1988, of all the questions raised, the Hong Kong community demonstrated greatest interest in the subject of direct election of the Legco. Nevertheless, the government decided that direct election would not be introduced until 1991, and that in that year ten Legco members would be elected directly. Why was direct election postponed in 1988? The white paper explained that government surveys showed that the people of Hong Kong were "sharply divided" on the matter. It also stated that stable government had always been crucial to the success of Hong Kong and was essential to the development of representative government as well. In addition, the white paper stated that for a smooth transfer of government in 1997, the deliberations of the BLDC over how the provisions for a representative system would be arranged in the Basic Law had to be taken into account.[44]

Obviously, on the one hand the Hong Kong government tried to introduce representative democracy before 1997. In the four years from 1984 to 1988, it initiated indirect election to the Legco and proposed direct election. These were significant changes in Hong Kong's history. On the other hand, the colonial government was committed to cooperating with China in reforming the current system, in order to ensure that "the system in place before 1997 should permit a smooth transition in 1997 and a high degree of continuity thereafter."[45]

The Chinese government favored maintaining the existing system and opposed any dramatic changes on the grounds that political unrest and economic decline could result. When the green paper on representative government was issued in 1984, the Chinese foreign minister responded that his government undertook no obligation to it.[46] Xu Jiatun, director of the Xinhua News Agency Hong Kong Branch, asserted that the British government had been "pushing the representative system in Hong Kong," and argued that radical political reform would be inconsistent with the 1984 agreement.[47] The proposal of the 1988 white paper to introduce ten directly elected seats in the Legco in 1991 also raised the objection of Beijing authorities, who argued that democratization must "converge" with the Basic Law, which would be finished by 1990.[48]

However, after the 1989 Tiananmen incident a large number of Hong Kong citizens urged London to accelerate the democratization process and to take measures to protect the freedoms of the Hong Kong people. In response, the

British government decided to grant 50,000 heads of Hong Kong households (with about 225,000 family members altogether) full British citizenship and to introduce a Bill of Rights in Hong Kong.[49] In addition, Britain dealt seriously with China on the issue of democratization. In order to have an effect before the draft Basic Law was finally adopted by the BLDC and then by the NPC, London proposed several suggestions on the formation of the SAR's Legco and on the relationship between political reform before 1997 and the systems of the SAR. Secret documents, including seven letters exchanged by British Foreign Minister Douglas Hurd and his Chinese counterpart Qian Qichen in January and February 1990,[50] later revealed that Britain was directly involved in the design of the Basic Law. The letters showed that the two governments tried to link the reforms before 1997 with the system provided by the Basic Law. However, London and Beijing differed on two key issues: the number of directly elected seats of the SAR's Legco and the composition of the Election Committee that would select the SAR's chief executive and some of the members of the Legco. Regarding the number of directly elected seats in the SAR's Legco, China adopted the proposal of twenty of sixty (33.3 percent) in 1997. (China originally wanted eighteen directly elected seats, but drafters from Hong Kong insisted that there should be twenty.) The Chinese government also proposed that twenty-four (40 percent) be filled by direct election in 1999, and thirty (50 percent) in 2003. The Chinese foreign minister further suggested that if Britain accepted this plan, China would accept the British proposal that the Legco have eighteen directly elected seats in the 1991 election (three more than the former proposal). However, Douglas Hurd said that the SAR's directly elected seats should be twenty-four (40 percent) in 1997, a target that had been set by the Chinese for 1999. Hurd's proposal included eighteen directly elected seats in the Hong Kong Legco's first election in 1991 and twenty-four in the 1995 election. In addition, Hurd proposed that for a smooth transfer of government the last Legco, which was to be determined in the 1995 election, should automatically become the SAR's first Legco and serve until 1999. This arrangement was known as the "through train" proposal—meaning that all members of the last colonial Legco would stay on board into the new SAR Legco.

Another major difference between China and Britain concerned the composition of the first SAR government's Election Committee. Britain proposed that the committee should consist of four social groupings, each of whose members would hold one-fourth of the seats. These collectivities were to include (1) industrial, commercial, professional, labor, social service and religion sectors; (2) senior political figures, including former members of the Exco and Legco; (3) members of the Urban and Regional Councils; and (4) all representatives of consultative committees. Obviously, the last three groupings would be mainly pro-Britain personalities. China rejected the British proposal and insisted that the composition of the Election Committee had already been set by the BLDC and could not be changed.

Subsequently, a tentative agreement on the China-drafted Basic Law was reached between Britain and China. The two countries compromised on the issue of directly elected seats in the Legco from 1991 to 2007, though Britain reiterated that the increase of directly elected seats in China's plan was much slower than the people of Hong Kong expected.[51] Britain also gave tacit consent to the principle of the Chinese plan for the composition of the Election Committee, but maintained that the actual composition of the committee should be further discussed. Although the secret letters between British and Chinese ministers were not published until October 1992, London's deal with Beijing on the draft Basic Law was reported on February 15, 1990, and aroused strong criticism in Britain and Hong Kong. Douglas Hurd argued in Britain's defense that although the rate of progress toward full direct election was not as rapid as many people wanted, considerable improvement had been made and it was possible that full direct election would be introduced in 2007.[52] Governor David Wilson was also an important policymaker in the compromise in 1990, and he was convinced that for the protection of Hong Kong's capitalism and autonomy under the Basic Law and the one country, two systems policy, Sino-British cooperation was crucial and confrontation must be avoided.[53]

In return, China conceded to Britain on several issues. First, China accepted Britain's suggestion that motions and bills in the SAR's Legco be passed by a simple majority vote. According to this scheme, the simple majority would include both sectors of the Legco—members returned by functional groupings and members returned by direct election. Obviously, China's original plan had been devised to prevent the directly elected sector from dominating and to empower functional groupings, which were more supportive of China's policy. Second, China conceded to Britain on the percentage of foreign nationals (who are permanent residents in Hong Kong) in the Legco. China's former plan was that the number of seats for foreign nationals could not exceed 15 percent, a figure that Britain opposed on the grounds that it was inadequate. China accepted Britain's position, and it became the policy of the final Basic Law that permanent residents of Hong Kong who are not of Chinese nationality or who have a foreign passport may be elected to the Legco but may not hold more than 20 percent of the seats. Third, China accepted the British proposal that the last Legco constituted in 1995 be linked with the SAR's first. The Chinese, however, revised the through train model, arguing that its link to the period of colonial government meant that it would be the British, not the Chinese, who would establish the SAR's first government. Instead, the Chinese proposed the "Luohu solution." Luohu is a mainland China–Hong Kong border station, where passengers on trains traveling to and from the two regions must get off, clear Customs, then walk across the border—the Luohu Bridge. According to the Luohu solution, if the 1995 Legco members are qualified to be members of the SAR's Legco and will take an oath of allegiance to the Basic Law and the SAR, they may continue to serve in the SAR's first Legco. According to the Basic Law, the China-dominated Preparative Committee for the establishment of the first government of the SAR will be the agency to decide which Legco members can walk across the "Luohu Bridge." The Luohu solution expressed two Beijing positions. First, only when Hong Kong's last Legco, created in 1995, accords with the Basic Law would its members be allowed to take the through train into 1997. Second, Chinese sovereignty over Hong Kong would not be eroded when the government of Hong Kong is transferred.

Consequently, the Basic Law finally was adopted by the BLDC, in which an overwhelming majority were conservatives from the mainland and Hong Kong. As a result, although the Basic Law promises to continue political reform in Hong Kong instituted since the 1980s, the progress toward democracy will be limited because the majority of the drafters were conservative. Both the chief executive and the members of Legco of the SAR will be elected. The chief executive will be elected by an Election Committee, which has many members and will consist of permanent residents of Hong Kong from many different social groups. The first chief executive will be elected by a Selection Committee of 400 members, with 100 members in each of four sectors, including (1) industrial, commercial, and financial sectors; (2) the professions; (3) labor, grass-roots, religious, and other sectors; and (4) Hong Kong's deputies to the NPC and representatives of Hong Kong membership in the National Committee of the CPPCC. The second and subsequent chief executives will be elected by an Election Committee of 800 members with 200 members in each sector, and the division of the sectors will be as same as in the first Election Committee.

Beijing took three measures to ensure the selection of a chief executive who would not be too independent of the Central People's Government. First, members of the Selection Committee will be recommended by a Preparative Committee appointed by the NPC. Second, three of the four constitutive sectors of the Selection Committee—business, professions, and Hong Kong deputies and representatives to the NPC and the CPPCC—generally support China's policy. Even in the labor, social services, and religious sector, some local leaders, such as the influential union leader Tong Yat-chu, support Chinese policy. Finally, Beijing has the power either to appoint or veto the candidate for chief executive who is recommended by the local Selection Committee.

The most obvious reform instituted by the Basic Law is that members of the Legco of the SAR will no longer be appointed. However, on the major issue—the introduction of direct election—the conservatives' views prevailed. The increase in directly elected seats was, in fact, arranged by those confidential letters between the British and Chinese foreign ministers. As China promised to Britain, in the first term of the Legco of the SAR (1997–1999)[54] only twenty of the sixty members will be returned by geographical constituencies through direct election. Ten members will be returned by an Election Committee and thirty by functional constituencies. In the second term (1999–2003) and the third term (2003–2007), the directly elected members will be increased to twenty-four and thirty respectively, while the number of members returned by the Election Committee will decrease and then disappear. Nevertheless, the ratio of members selected by the functional constituencies will remain at 50 percent (thirty of sixty) in 2007. Since the majority of the functional sector consists of businesspeople and professionals who support China's policy, the Legco will not be in conflict with the Central People's Government. The Basic Law arranges for a gradual and conservative reform. Table 3.1 shows the arrangement between London and Beijing for the composition of Hong Kong's Legislative Council from 1991 to 2007.

Table 3.1   The Composition of Hong Kong's Legislative Council, 1991–2007

	1991–1995	1995–1999	1999–2003	2003–2007
Direct election	18	20	24	30
Functional constituencies	21	30	30	30
Election Committee	0	10	6	0
Total number of seats	60[a]	60	60	60

Source: Basic Law of the Hong Kong SAR.
Note: a. Beijing and London did not discuss nondirect election seats. The colonial government alone arranged that twenty-one seats would be for functional constituencies and three seats would be for government officials, while eighteen seats were to be appointed by the governor for the 1991–1995 Legco. See Miners, The Government and Politics of Hong Kong, 5th ed., 116. However, Beijing and London agreed that government official seats and appointed seats would be abolished in the 1995–1999 Legco.

In conclusion, the major disputes on Hong Kong's reforms focused on one issue: how many members of the Legislative Council should be returned by geographical constituencies through direct election. Liberals appealed that 50 percent of the seats of the SAR's first Legco should be elected directly, while the conservative business community thought that number too radical. Chinese officials planned to arrange eighteen of sixty members to be elected directly. However, under pressure from the British government and from Hong Kong's massive demand for greater democracy after the Tiananmen incident, the Chinese authorities decided to permit twenty directly elected seats. But in fact, China's concession did not change the essential composition of the Legco. The conservatives will continue to be overwhelmingly represented in the SAR legislature as well as in the executive. The political structure of the Hong Kong SAR, as regulated by the Basic Law, was a compromise between Hong Kong's conservative business communities and the prodemocracy liberals, but the law favored business. The Beijing authorities perceived that a gradual political reform mandated in the Basic Law would guarantee Hong Kong's political stability. In addition, Chinese officials believed that under the Basic Law, Hong Kong's capitalists would continue to make a great contribution to China's modernization and the SAR's prosperity.

Changes in the Political System

The Basic Law explicitly indicates the changes that will occur in Hong Kong's political system in 1997, most of which relate to the transfer of sovereignty. First, the Basic Law stresses China's sovereignty over the SAR. Hong Kong's status after 1997 will be that of a local and special administrative region of the PRC. Chapter 5 will discuss sovereignty in more detail. The locally selected public figures, including the chief executive and the major officials of the Exco, must be finally approved by the Central People's Government, but only permanent, local Chinese residents are qualified to take leading public posts, including those of chief executive, the major Exco officials, over 80 percent of the membership of the Legco, the chief justice of the Court of Final Appeal, and the chief judge of the High Court of the SAR (BL 45, 48, 55, 67, 90).

The Basic Law also introduces checks and balances among the executive, legislative, and judiciary branches: (1) the chief executive will have much less power than the previous British governor; (2) the Legco will enjoy independent legislative power; and (3) the judiciary will be independent. It is necessary to discuss these points in more detail.

The office of chief executive of the SAR will be fundamentally different from the British governorship. The argument that the function of the chief executive of the SAR resembles that of the British governor of Hong Kong[55] cannot be proved by the Basic Law. Though the chief executive will be appointed by the Central People's Government, that appointment must be based on local selection through election and consultation. Moreover, the chief executive will represent the Hong Kong people, not the central authorities.[56] In contrast, the Hong Kong governor is appointed directly by the British Crown and represents the British government, not the Hong Kong people.

The chief executive will be less powerful than the British governor. He or she will neither be a member of nor preside over the Legco. His or her role in the legislative process is to "sign bills passed by the Legislative Council and to promulgate laws" (BL 48). Moreover, unlike the British governor, the chief executive will not appoint members to the Legco. Most importantly, the Basic Law makes the executive accountable to the Legco. The legislation states:

> The Government of the Hong Kong Special Administrative Region must abide by the Law and be accountable to the Legislative Council of the Region. It shall implement laws passed by the Council and already in force; it shall present regular policy addresses to the Council; it shall answer questions raised by members of the Council; and shall obtain approval from the Council for taxation and public expenditure (BL 64).

The term "government of the SAR" includes the chief executive; the major governmental officials nominated by the chief executive and appointed by the Central People's Government; and all the agencies of the Exco. They must all be accountable to the Legislative Council.[57]

Compared with the current Legco, the power of the SAR Legco will be greatly increased. All its members will be elected directly or indirectly and it will enjoy the power to enact, amend, and repeal laws; to examine and approve budgets; to question and supervise the government; to impeach the chief executive; and to endorse the appointment and removal of high-ranking judges. These are the most important changes in the Legco (BL 73).

The real change in the judiciary is that London is no longer the supreme authority, and neither will Beijing have the power of final adjudication after 1997. The SAR will have its own adjudication and the Court of Final Appeal will be its highest judicial system.

The Systems That Remain Unchanged

In contrast to the dispute over democratization, there was little difference between China and Britain and between the Chinese central authorities and the Hong Kong community on the issue of social and economic systems. Hong Kong's private ownership and free market, the core of Hong Kong's economy, remain unchanged in the Basic Law. Hong Kong will continue to have independent financial and monetary systems and the Central People's Government will not levy taxes. The Hong Kong dollar, as the legal tender of the SAR, will continue to circulate and to be freely convertible, and Hong Kong will remain a free port. The next chapter will discuss these systems.

In addition, some aspects of the political system also will remain unchanged. Hong Kong's current executive-led system will be preserved. Under the British system, the governor is the sole authority; and the Executive and Legislative Councils are only consultative bodies. Under the Basic Law, the chief executive of the SAR, like the British governor, will appoint all members of the Exco. The difference is that the governor's appointment must be approved by London, but the choice of chief executive will be a final decision. Also, in the SAR as in the colonial system some members of the Exco may come from the Legco, and the Exco will be only an advisory body and "an organ for assisting the Chief Executive in policy-making" (BL 54, 55). Like the British governor, the chief executive will have dominant power within the Exco and will be authorized to appoint and dismiss members. The Beijing authorities insisted that the authoritarian British Hong Kong government was efficient and that the current executive-led system should be preserved.

The legal and judicial systems will remain basically unchanged except for those aspects related to sovereignty. Hong Kong laws, including the common law, rules of equity, ordinances, subordinate legislation, and customary law, will continue to be in force after 1997 unless they contravene the Basic Law. Therefore, laws that will be in force in the SAR will include the Basic Law, laws previously in force in Hong Kong, and laws that will be enacted by the SAR's Legco. Chinese officials recognized that Hong Kong's current legal system has played an important role in the progress and prosperity of Hong Kong[58] and that the Hong Kong people are used to it. Further, except for the change in the Court of Final Appeal Hong Kong's judicial system will be unchanged. The court of the SAR will exercise judicial power independently, free from any interference, and the principle of trial by jury in criminal and civil proceedings will be maintained. The previous system of appointment and removal of members of the judiciary other than judges will also be maintained. Previous judges and other members of the judiciary may remain in employment (BL 85, 86, 91, 93).

Finally, Hong Kong's civil service system, which was introduced from Great Britain, will remain basically as it is. The main characteristic of this system is that the recruiting, appointment, promotion, and discipline of public servants are based on their qualifications, experience, and ability. Even those "British and other nationals previously serving in the public service" may continue to be employed in "government departments at all levels," except the following posts: secretaries and deputy secretaries of departments, directors of bureaus, Commissioner Against Corruption, Director of Audit, Commissioner of Police, Director of Immigration, and Commissioner of Customs and Excise (BL 101).

From the Declaration to the Basic Law

Here it is necessary to discuss further whether the Basic Law accords with the joint declaration—a question that aroused disputes during the Basic Law drafting process. Obviously, as there was little dispute on the SAR's social and economic systems, there will be no changes on these matters in 1997. However, there have been disputes over the SAR's political system as well as the relationship between the Central People's Government and the SAR. In the joint declaration, the Chinese government only outlined the political system of the SAR:

> The Government and Legislature of the Hong Kong Special Administrative Region shall be composed of local inhabitants. The chief executive of the Hong Kong Special Administrative Region shall be elected by election or through consultations held locally and be appointed by the Central People's Government. Principal officials (equivalent to Secretaries) shall be nominated by the chief executive of the Hong Kong Special Administrative Region and appointed by the Central People's Government. The legislature of the Hong Kong Special Administrative Region shall be constituted by elections. The executive authorities shall abide by the law and shall be accountable to the legislature.[59]

Discussions in this chapter have shown that in principle the Basic Law indeed follows the declaration. The Basic Law clarifies that the chief executive as well as all members of the Legco will be elected by the Hong Kong inhabitants. However, the joint declaration does not state how these elections will be held, and how social groups will be represented in the Legco. As discussed in this chapter, China and Britain as well as Hong Kong's liberals and conservatives disputed these issues.

Another question concerns the relationship between sovereign China and the autonomous Hong Kong SAR. The joint declaration also states this matter very simply by saying that the SAR will have a high degree of autonomy: except in foreign affairs and defense, which will be the responsibility of the Central People's Government, the SAR will have executive, legislative, and independent judicial power, including that of final adjudication.[60] However, serious disputes occurred when the two concepts, the SAR's "high degree of autonomy" and China's sovereignty, were discussed during the Basic Law drafting process. The mainland Basic Law drafters and the Hong Kong liberals interpreted those concepts differently. Chapters 4 and 5 will discuss these issues.

Notes

1. See *Jibenfa de Dansheng* (Hong Kong: Wen Wei Publishing); Lau, "The Early History of the Drafting Process," in Wesley-Smith and Chen, eds., *The Basic Law and Hong Kong's Future*; Lane, *Sovereignty and the Status Quo*, 119–135; and McGurn, ed., *Basic Law, Basic Questions*.

2. Questions of Hong Kong's democratization mainly focused on the process of popular participation in the direct election of Hong Kong's Legislative Council before and after 1997. In other words, how many members of the Legco should be elected directly by geographical constituencies, and should the progress toward general election of the Legco be slow or fast? Conservatives and liberals answered this question differently.

3. Some scholars have asserted that there will be no political change in Hong Kong in 1997. That assumption obviously seems inaccurate. See Denis Cheng, "Toward a Jurisprudence of the Third Kind—One Country, Two Systems," *Case Western Reserve Journal of International Law* 20, no. 1 (Winter, 1988): 105; and Kao, "One Country, Two Systems: Its Theory, Practice, and Feasibility," 141.

4. Norman Miners, *The Government and Politics of Hong Kong*, 2nd ed. (Hong Kong, Oxford University Press, 1977), 258, 263.

5. Ibid., xv.

6. Functional constituencies refer to the economic and professional sectors of Hong Kong society. The sectors chosen by the government were commerce, industry, labor, finance, social services, education, and the legal, medical, and engineering professions. The government stressed that these sectors "are essential to future confidence and prosperity." See Norman Miners, *The Government and Politics of Hong Kong*, 4th ed. (Hong Kong: Oxford University Press, 1986), 119–120. Those Legco members from functional constituencies were usually prominent figures of the business and professional communities.

7. The Urban Council is a statutory council with responsibilities for the provision of municipal services to people in the districts of Hong Kong Island and Kowloon. These services include street cleaning, public health, recreation, and culture. The Regional Council is a body in the New Territories that carried out functions similar to the Urban Council. A District Board is a statutory body that provides a forum for public consultation and participation in the administration of the district. The function of the

District Board is to advise the government on matters affecting the well-being of the people of the District.

8. David Roberts, ed., *Hong Kong 1990* (Hong Kong: Government Printer, 1990), 25.

9. Ibid., 24.

10. Norman Miners, *The Government and Politics of Hong Kong*, 2nd ed., 64.

11. Norman Miners, *Hong Kong Under Imperial Rule, 1912–1941* (Hong Kong: Oxford University Press, 1987), 74.

12. In a few cases, London intervened in Hong Kong's internal affairs. In 1973, the British government granted a reprieve to a convicted murderer, vetoing the governor's decision that the murderer be hanged, as advised by the Executive Council. London's decision aroused strong local protest. In 1974, the British Labour government pressured the Hong Kong government to introduce comprehensive social insurance and more progressive tax policies. Miners, *The Government and Politics of Hong Kong*, 4th ed., 221–222, 228–229.

13. For details of the relationship between Britain and Hong Kong, see ibid., 219–231.

14. Roberts, *Hong Kong 1990*, 24; also see Miners, *The Government and Politics of Hong Kong*, 2nd ed., 64–67.

15. Miners, *The Government and Politics of Hong Kong*, 4th ed., 168.

16. Ibid., 98–100.

17. Martin C. M. Lee, "How Much Autonomy?" in William McGurn, ed., *Basic Law, Basic Questions* (Hong Kong: Review Publishing Company 1988), 42.

18. Kevin Rafferty, *City on the Rocks: Hong Kong's Uncertain Future* (New York: Viking, 1990), 452.

19. Lee, "How Much Autonomy?" in McGurn, ed., *Basic Law, Basic Questions*, 39.

20. Rafferty, *City on the Rocks*, 446–447.

21. *South China Morning Post*, 17 June 1987.

22. J. P. Jain, *China in World Politics: A Study of Sino-British Relations, 1949–1975* (New Delhi: Radiant Publishers, 1976), 177–178.

23. Philip Bowring, "Down in the Dumps," *FEER*, 29 September 1983, 146–147; and Teresa Ma, "No News Is Bad News," *FEER*, 6 October 1983, 18–20.

24. Lulu Yu, "Basic Law Body: Businessmen Propose 'Blueprint,'" *South China Morning Post*, 22 August 1986, 2, in FBIS, 25 August 1986, W3–5.

25. Stanley Leung, "Businesses Oppose Elections," *South China Morning Post*, 29 September 1987, 2, in FBIS, 29 September 1987, 37.

26. Zhao Yuanguang, "'Mainstream Program,' Drawbacks Discussed," *Zhongguo Tongxun She*, 28 December 1988, in FBIS, 28 December 1988, 74.

27. "Council's S. Y. Chung Opposes Political Reform," *South China Morning Post*, 4 May 1987, 1, in FBIS, 5 May 1987, W3.

28. "Commentator on Reaction to Basic Law Proposal," *Ta Kong Pao*, 1–7 December 1988, 16, in FBIS, 1 December 1988, 43.

29. Stanley Leung and C. K. Lau, "Li Hou Discusses Party Politics," *South China Morning Post*, 3 June 1986, 14, in FBIS, 4 June 1986, W5–7.

30. "Lu Ping Views Hong Kong Law, Election," *Hsin Wan Pao*, 2 July 1986, 2, in FBIS, 9 July 1986, W5.

31. Xu Bing, "The Necessity and Feasibility of 'One Country, Two Systems' from the Perspective of Economic Development," *Zhongguo Fazhi Bao* [China Legal News], 25 January 1985, in FBIS, 4 February 1985, E3.

32. *Ta Kung Pao*, 20 September 1987, quoted in Rafferty, *City on the Rocks*, 450–451.

33. Chris Yeung, "Two Law Drafters Claim Majority Wishes Ignored," *South China Morning Post*, 21 November 1988, 1, 6, in FBIS, 23 November 1988, 71.

34. See G. B. Endacott, *Government and People in Hong Kong 1841–1962: A Constitutional History* (Hong Kong: Hong Kong University Press, 1964), 182.

35. Ibid., 185.

36. Steven Yui-sang Tsang, *Democracy Shelved: Great Britain, China, and Attempts at Constitutional Reform in Hong Kong, 1945–1952* (Hong Kong: Oxford University Press, 1988), 123, 183–214.

37. Miners, *The Government and Politics of Hong Kong*, 4th ed., 45, 40–41.

38. In the 1990s, when China and Britain conflicted over the development of Hong Kong's representative system, the British government explained why democracy had not been introduced to Hong Kong. A white paper of the British government wrote: "why did Britain not introduce democracy to Hong Kong much earlier? The short answer is that for many years the community had other priorities. There was a deep-seated concern that the introduction of politics could lead to open clashes between Nationalists and Communists, and that this could lead China to invoke its claim to sovereignty over Hong Kong." The white paper continues: "Some constitutional development was again considered in the mid-1960s. But the Cultural Revolution in China caused disruption and uncertainty in Hong Kong. Many in the Community feared that elections would have put at risk the stability of Hong Kong (there had been Nationalist-inspired riots in Hong Kong in 1956, and Communist-inspired riots in the 1960s). Local attitudes were also influenced by the knowledge that China was opposed to the introduction into Hong Kong of party politics and elections on western lines. There was no wish to provoke China into challenging the *status quo* in pursuit of her standing claim to sovereignty over Hong Kong." See *White Paper: Representative Government in Hong Kong* (Hong Kong: The Government Printer, February 1994), 3–4, 6.

39. See Miners, *The Government and Politics of Hong Kong*, 4th ed., 41.

40. *Green Paper: The Further Development of Representative Government in Hong Kong* (Hong Kong: The Government Printer, July 1984).

41. Ibid.

42. *White Paper: The Further Development of Representative Government in Hong Kong* (Hong Kong: The Government Printer, November 1984).

43. *Green Paper: The 1987 Review of Developments in Representative Government* (Hong Kong: The Government Printer, May 1987).

44. *White Paper: The Development of Representative Government: The Way Forward* (Hong Kong, The Government Printer, February 1988).

45. Ibid.

46. Emily Lau, "Hong Kong: A Question of Semantics," *FEER*, 23 August 1984, 17.

47. "Xu Jiatun Hong Kong Remarks," *Ta Kung Pao*, 28 November 1985, in FBIS, 3 December 1985, W1–4.

48. Emily Lau, "The Grey Paper: Policy on Political Reform Falls Short of Promises," *FEER*, 18 February 1988, 14.

49. Chapters 5 and 7 will discuss these matters.

50. "Zhong Ying Shuangfang Guanyu Xianggang Wentide Qige Wenjian" [Sino-British Seven Documents about the Hong Kong Question], *Renmin Ribao: Haiwai Ban* [People's Daily: Overseas Edition], 29 October 1992, 3. The secret documents were disclosed by both British and Chinese governments because they interpreted these diplomatic exchanges differently in October 1992, when the British Hong Kong governor Christopher Patten launched a large-scale democratic reform of Hong Kong's political system. The English version of these confidential documents was published by the Hong Kong colonial government. See "Britain, China Reveal 'Secret Deal' Letters," *South China Morning Post*, 30 October 1992, 1. For details of Patten's reform and Sino-British confrontation on it, see Chapter 7.

51. In July 1989, shocked by the Tiananmen incident in June of that year, Hong Kong's Executive and Legislative Councils urged the British government in London to introduce direct election to the colony's Legco in 1991. The two councils proposed that of fifty-seven seats in 1991, twenty directly elected seats be introduced, increasing to 50 percent of all seats in 1995 and 100 percent in 2003. See Emily Lau, "Fog and Drizzle: Britain Hesitates on Political Development," *FEER*, 25 January 1990, 17. Concerning the agreement between Britain and China on the introduction of direct election to Hong Kong's Legco from 1991 to 2007, see Table 3.1.

52. Catherine Sampson, "Britain Accepts Peking Formula on Hong Kong," *The Times*, 15 February 1990, 10; Jonathan Braude and Catherine Sampson, "Deal with Peking on Hong Kong Is Branded a Sell-Out," *The Times*, 16 February 1990, 8; "An Unacceptable Accord," *The Times*, 16 February 1990, 13; and "Hurd Accused of Cave-in On Hong Kong," *The Times*, 17 February 1990, 4.

53. Chapter 7 will discuss Wilson's view and his cooperation with China in more detail.

54. The Basic Law states that if the composition of the Legco and its members meet the requirements of the law, British Hong Kong's last Legco produced in 1995 will take the "through train" and become the first Legislative Council of the SAR.

55. Byron S. J. Weng argued, based on the draft Basic Law, that the chief executive resembles the powerful British colonial governor of Hong Kong. See Byron S. J. Weng, "The Hong Kong Model of 'One Country, Two Systems': Promises and Problems," in Wesley-Smith and Chen, eds., *The Basic Law and Hong Kong's Future*, 79.

56. Xiao Weiyun, *Yiguo Liangzhi Yu Xianggang Jiben Falu Zhidu* [One Country, Two Systems and Basic Legal System of Hong Kong] (Beijing: Beijing Daxue Chubanshe, 1990), 238.

57. Ibid., 227.

58. Wang Shuwen, *Xianggang Tebie Xingzhengqu Jibenfa Daolun* [A Guide to the Basic Law of Hong Kong Special Administrative Region] (Beijing: Zhonggong Zhongyang Dangxiao Chubanshe, 1990), 243.

59. See the Joint Declaration, Annex I, Part I.

60. See ibid.

4

Does the Hong Kong SAR Have a High Degree of Autonomy?

Besides the issue of Hong Kong's reform toward democracy, another controversial question during the Basic Law drafting process concerned the relationship between sovereign China and autonomous Hong Kong. Since the Chinese promise in the 1984 Joint Declaration was that the SAR would have "a high degree of autonomy," the Basic Law drafters from both the mainland and Hong Kong disputed how much autonomy the SAR should have. For instance, both the declaration and the Basic Law state that the SAR would be authorized with executive, legislative, and independent judicial power, including that of final adjudication. How will these powers be exercised? Will the chief executive be appointed by the Central People's Government based on local consultation and election, or will it be only the affair of the SAR? Which institution should have the power to interpret and amend the Basic Law? Unfortunately, there is no direct answer to these questions. This chapter focuses on the issue of the autonomy of the SAR and tries to answer a difficult question—does the Hong Kong SAR have a high degree of autonomy, as stated by the Basic Law? Or, to frame the issue another way, if it is to have a high degree of autonomy what powers should the SAR possess?[1]

One approach to the question is to compare the SAR under the Basic Law with other autonomous regions. Surprisingly, there are very few studies that concern regional autonomy under a sovereign state, and results of a comparison of the Hong Kong SAR with only one or two other cases of regional autonomy would not be very persuasive. In addition, each autonomous region is unique in terms of history, background, and the reasons for which jurisdiction was established, making comparison difficult. Fortunately, Hurst Hannum and Richard Lillich contributed a comprehensive study on regional autonomy,[2] which is very useful for the present analysis. Hannum and Lillich examined twenty-five cases with "a high degree of autonomy," the term used by the two authors. They also drew a theoretical picture of what a region with a high degree of autonomy would be like.

This chapter examines China's position that Hong Kong will be highly autonomous by comparing the Hong Kong SAR, as regulated in the Basic Law, with autonomous regions investigated by Hannum and Lillich. The comparison will determine whether Hong Kong's autonomy will be of a "high degree." Moreover, this chapter examines another relative issue—if the autonomy of the Hong Kong SAR is great, what were the major factors that facilitated creation on paper, in the Basic Law?

Before making any comparisons, it is necessary to define the term autonomy, and to distinguish an autonomous region from a sovereign state and from a political unit of a federation. This analysis will establish that the Hong Kong SAR itself is an autonomous region of unitary China.

An Autonomous Region

Autonomy means, in the legal political vocabulary, self-government.[3] Therefore, a regional autonomy is self-government of the entity under a sovereign government. The establishment of an autonomous region is an agreement between the national government and the autonomous region for the purposes of maintenance of the sovereignty of the national government over the local region and protection of local distinctiveness in such areas as religion, ethnicity, culture, and economy. However, within a state only the national government possesses sovereignty—the highest authority in foreign and domestic affairs. Therefore, the relationship between national and autonomous governments is not one of coordinate authorities; rather, the autonomous region is subordinate to the national government. Nevertheless, in a comparison between the autonomous region and other subdivisions within that state, the autonomous region possesses more power over local matters.

In terms of the authorities by which the autonomous regions are created, there are two kinds of autonomous regions in the world. One type is created by international organizations through treaties. Here, the autonomous entity is an international issue under international law—examples are Puerto Rico and the Saar (1945–1956). The other kind is the autonomous region that is created by its national government—examples are Greenland under Denmark and Catalonia under Spain. These autonomous cases involve only domestic matters, and no international organizations or foreign countries were involved in their creation. Because the Hong Kong SAR under the Basic Law is China's domestic issue rather than an international matter, this study will focus on the issue of autonomous politics as a domestic matter.

Autonomous Region and Sovereign State

Theoretically, the key difference between an autonomous region and a sovereign state is that the state possesses supreme authority while the autonomous region does not. Whatever independent powers the autonomous region has, its government is not the highest authority. The autonomous region is permitted to handle its internal affairs independently, but in external affairs, such as foreign relations and defense, the national government is responsible. The national government usually retains the authority to interpret the relationship between the national and autonomous governments. Moreover, an autonomous region is not recognized as a member of the world community. There are currently some 180 nation-states (including the independent former Soviet Republics), and generally, no autonomous regions are official members of world organizations such as the United Nations. (The Ukraine and Belorussia under the former Soviet Union were exceptions. However, though the two entities participated in the United Nations as official members—as part of a compromise to provide the Soviet Union with more than one vote—the two subdivisions of the Soviet Union were not independent in the United Nations but followed instructions from Moscow.) An autonomous region also does not have formal political relations with other sovereign states, such as establishment of its embassy on foreign soil. Although an autonomous region may participate in certain international organizations or conduct external cultural and economic relations, these activities must be approved by its national government. Cases such as that of Greenland under Denmark will be discussed later.

The relationship between a national government and an autonomous region is described well by Louis B. Sohn. He argued that the concepts of autonomy—self-rule of a region and independence—were entirely different from the complete self-determination of "a larger entity." Sohn said that while the larger entity grants autonomy to a region, allowing the people there to "exercise direct control over important affairs of special concern to them," it still retains certain powers over the autonomous region and exercises "those powers which are in the common interest of both entities."[4] Actually, Sohn could have indicated more clearly that his larger entity is the sovereign state, because only it possesses, at least in theory, the power of "independence or complete self-determination."[5] Nevertheless, Sohn is right when he indicates that the autonomous region is not separated from the larger entity, which exercises certain powers over the region for the interests of both entities.

Is China a Federal State Under the Basic law?

If China became a federal state under the Basic Law, it would be more reasonable to compare the Hong Kong SAR with constituent units of a federation, like New York State and Georgia in the United States, and not with the autonomous regions of unitary countries. Some scholars have argued that China became a "quasi-federation" under the Basic Law.[6]

There are two kinds of states that are distinguished by their national constitutional laws: federations (including confederation) and unitary systems. Surprisingly, though the terms *federation* and *unitary state* are used often there is limited research that directly and clearly distinguishes a federation from a unitary state. Scholars seem to favor studies on the theory and practice of federalism, but show little interest in distinguishing a federation from a unitary state.

It is necessary to distinguish further a federation from a unitary state. There are two ways to make this distinction. One way is the intergovernmental (central-local) power distribution approach, which examines the institutional structure under which the real powers that the local and central governments possess are actually used, not how constitutional law divides those powers. The other is to examine how constitutional law arranges the powers between national and local governments. Using the intergovernmental power distribution approach, several studies found that the differences between federations and unitary states are unclear. William H. Riker compared six pairs of federal and unitary states "with similar political culture" (Australia–New Zealand; Malaysia-Indonesia; Ghana-Nigeria; Chile-Argentina; Yugoslavia-Poland; United States–United Kingdom), and found that in no case "is the federal member of the pair significantly more permissive to local and regional interests than is the unitary member."[7] In other words, in practice local governmental powers are similar in these pairs of federal and unitary states. Douglas E. Ashford and Alberta May Sbragia found that strong autonomous powers existed in local governments in unitary United Kingdom, France, and Italy.[8] Steven R. Reed argued that in the intergovernmental approach, real policymaking is more important than constitutional regulation. For Reed, though the constitutional laws of federations and unitary states may differ significantly, in the real world the national-local "intergovernmental policymaking looks remarkably similar in both unitary and federal states."[9] However, if more cases were included in this intergovernmental policymaking approach, the conclusion might be different. Take China, Thailand, and Burma as examples; in these countries, both in constitution and in practice the local governments really have very limited power compared with the constituent units of federal states.

However, from the legal and constitutional perspective the difference between a federation and a unitary state is much clearer. To better understand the constitutional difference between the two kinds of states, it is first necessary to review the main feature of a federation. Ramesh Dutta Dikshit wrote:

> A federation is born when a number of usually separate or autonomous political units (or units with some pretensions to autonomy) mutually agree to merge together to create a State with a single sovereign central government, while retaining for themselves some degree of guaranteed regional autonomy.[10]

Dikshit further explained that under a federal constitution, each level of government is autonomous within its own sphere of competence and is free from any intervention from the others, unless in those exceptional circumstances provided by the constitution. Dikshit therefore concluded that the significant difference between federalism and a unitary government is the constitutional autonomy, as distinguished from formal division of powers, between the central and unit governments.[11]

This conclusion is acceptable where a unitary state without an autonomous region is concerned. In the case of a state with an autonomous region, further discussion is needed to differentiate a federation from a unitary government. The relationship between the national and local autonomous governments in a unitary state looks similar to the ties between federal and unit governments in a federation. When an autonomous region is established in a unitary governmental system, the constitutional statutes of the autonomous region are similar to the constitution of a federation—the national and autonomous governments agree to divide their powers clearly within the constitutional establishment. However, in essence, a federation and a unitary state are different.

Xiao Weiyun listed several differences between a federation and a unitary state in terms of constitutional law:

1. Constituent units in a federation possess inherent power. Inherent power is possessed by the constituent units before the establishment of the federal government. However, in a unitary state, subdivisions have no inherent power; and all powers the subdivisions have are authorized by the central government. (This standard is basic to distinguishing a federation from a unitary state.)

2. Under a federation, each constituent unit has its own constitution as well as the power to decide governmental form and structure. Yet, under a unitary state, constituent units do not.

3. Constituent units participate in the federal system, and the federal congress consists of representatives of the people and representatives of the constituent units. For example, the Senate of the United States consists of two representatives from each of the fifty states. Again, in a unitary state, the constituent units do not participate in the national system.

4. The power distribution between the federal government and the constituent units is regulated and protected by a federal constitution. In a unitary state, though the power distributions between the national and local government are also divided by the state constitution, local authorities have no legal basis for contesting laws that have been enacted by the national government alone.[12]

Rudolph Bernhardt, a German scholar, made a special contribution on the subject of the difference between federalism and regional autonomy. He said that federalism "means the distribution of powers between a central authority and subordinated units which have their own organs and competences." Bernhardt also argued that "autonomy means the autonomous self-determination of an individual or entity, the competence or power to handle one's own affairs without interference." Accordingly, the two concepts of federalism and autonomy are entirely different.[13] Bernhardt's view actually accords with the above discussion.

Both Xiao and Bernhardt described general differences between a federation and a unitary government and between federalism and autonomy. It is necessary to further distinguish a federation from a unitary state with an autonomous region. In a federal state, the federal system is created by the federal constitution. This means that the federal government does not exist before the enactment of the constitution. However, in a unitary state the constitutional statute of the autonomous region creates only the regional government, not the national government. The national government existed before the enactment of that statute. Moreover, the constitutional statute of the autonomous region does not change the existing relationships between central and local governments, and the nation's institutional structure as a whole is not changed. The establishment of the autonomous region is the national government's special policy toward the autonomous area only. Furthermore, in a federation all constituent units, as subdivisions of that federation, enjoy equal rights and powers in the federal system. In a unitary state, however, the autonomous region enjoys many more powers than other subdivisions of the state. That is the purpose for which an autonomous region is created.

If the above analysis is acceptable, China under the Basic Law is not a federation but a unitary state, and the Hong Kong SAR will be an autonomous region. First, China and Hong Kong are not coordinate or equal political units merging to create a new state. China as a sovereign state existed before the enactment of the Basic Law. Also, the Basic Law is not China's constitution, but only China's special statute that creates the Hong Kong SAR and regulates the relationship between the Central People's Government and the SAR. Moreover, the statute was enacted by China's NPC, though Hong Kong citizens participated in the drafting process.

Second, China's constitution clearly states that the NPC has the power to establish special administrative regions if necessary (art. 31; 62, sec. 13). The Basic Law also states clearly that all powers of the SAR are authorized by the NPC. Therefore, the SAR's powers are not inherent.

At this point, a constitutional and legal approach to assessing the Hong Kong SAR's status and power under the Basic Law is useful; but only after 1997 can the actual practice of China's and Hong Kong's powers be examined. However, an examination of experiences in other autonomous regions and a comparison of those autonomous experiences with the situation of the Hong Kong SAR under the Basic Law may help to predict what this actual practice may become.

The Autonomy of the Hong Kong SAR
and the Practice of Autonomy for the Chinese Nationalities

The theory of autonomy is not new in the PRC, which practices regional autonomy in the areas where minority nationalities live. Currently, China consists of fifty-six nationalities, among which the Han nationality comprises 93 percent of the whole population. Although the remaining fifty-five small nationalities make up only 7 percent of China's population, they live in huge areas that cover 60 percent of China's territory.[14] These minority nationalities live mainly in the inland and border areas of the country, and are undeveloped economically and culturally. The economic and cultural weakness of the nationalities in such fields as education, transportation, and communication stands in contrast to the relative modernization and prosperity in Han regions. Historically, the Han nationality subordinated these small nationalities when its government was stronger and lost that ascendancy when it was weaker. There were two primary exceptions. One occurred when the Mongols of the Yuan Dynasty ruled China from 1271 to 1368, and the other was the governance by the Qing Dynasty of the Manchurians from 1644 to 1911.

Historically, there were tensions between the Hans and the minority nationalities and tensions among the nationalities themselves. The PRC has tried to improve relationships among nationalities on the basis of equality, and since the 1950s the ethnic minority regions have been allowed to practice regional autonomy. Currently, China has five autonomous regions, thirty-one autonomous prefectures, and eighty autonomous counties (or banners).[15] However, in practice the nationality regions still have very limited autonomous powers. The grant of autonomy was nothing but the Central People's Government's limited favorable policy toward these regions. Such policy included respect for nationality culture, religion, and customs, and assistance in economic development and education. Some of these policies, such as assistance in the economy and education, were easily carried out. Special funds and personnel including engineers, doctors, and other specialists were sent to assist the local peoples.

Other policies were challenged by the reality of the nationality regions. For instance, in the 1950s Tibet was still a society in which serfdom existed; and the serf owners were also religious leaders. The political system and religion were integrated. Chinese Communist leaders saw it as their duty to liberate those poor serfs. From the Communist point of view, the "democratic reform" launched by the Communist government in Tibet in 1959 was progressive, because it destroyed the cruel system of serfdom and liberated the oppressed serfs. However, for the local religious elite the reform was a Communist violation of Tibetan autonomy in culture, religion, and customs. As a result, the Dalai Lama, the Tibetan political and religious leader in the 1950s, and his followers left Tibet for exile in foreign countries.

During the Cultural Revolution (1966–1976), regional autonomy was greatly violated, and the religions and cultures of minority nationalities were not well respected. In Tibet, some temples were destroyed and normal religious activities were forced to cease. After the Cultural Revolution, the Chinese government tried to correct its misconduct by reaffirming, in the 1982 Constitution and the 1984 Law on Regional Autonomy for Minority Nationalities, the autonomous status of nationality regions.[16] These new laws generally reasserted the Communists' former policies toward the minority regions. Although after the 1980s local religion, culture, and customs were restored and respected and standards of living of the nationality peoples were improved, under these new laws local autonomy in the executive, legislature, and judiciary were still limited.

Like other countries that have ethnic minority problems, the policy of ethnic regional autonomy was not as ideal in practice as the Beijing authorities had expected. Currently, tensions between the Hans and other nationalities have not ended. For instance, several conflicts between the Communist regimes and the Tibetans occurred in the 1980s, and the Beijing regime failed to persuade the Dalai Lama to abandon his effort to obtain Tibet's independence from China.

It is too simple to conclude from the experience of ethnic regional autonomy in China that the autonomy of Hong Kong will be doomed. It is true that both kinds of autonomy arrangements involve local governments under Chinese sovereignty. However, a comparison of the statutes on the nationality regions with the Basic Law of the Hong Kong SAR demonstrates that the two kinds of autonomies in China are fundamentally different.

First, and most importantly, the ethnic autonomous regions practice one country, one system while the Hong Kong SAR will be based upon the principle of one country, two systems. As Ngapoi Ngwang Jigme, a Tibetan who was then vice-chair of the NPC Standing Committee and chair of NPC Nationality Committee, pointed out:

> The fundamental guideline for the regional autonomy law is to uphold the four cardinal principles—to keep to the socialist road, to the people's democratic dictatorship, to the leadership of the Communist Party and to Marxism-Leninism and Mao Zedong Thought.[17]

In other words, China's political system is applied in all ethnic autonomous regions, which are thereby self-governed with socialism under Communist leadership. Politically, there is little difference between the ethnic regions and the rest of China. In contrast, China's political system will not be applied in the Hong Kong SAR and the social and economic systems and way of life of Hong Kong will remain as they are. The Hong Kong SAR will have autonomous powers exercised by its own executive, legislature, and judiciary.

The second related difference is the economic system. In nationality autonomous regions, the economic system is the same as in the rest of China—a socialist economy under a system planned by the state. According to the 1984 Law on Regional Autonomy, the regional governments may work out their own policies and plans on the economy and conduct their own construction projects, but these policies and plans must be approved by the Central People's Government. The financial and monetary systems of these autonomous regions are the same as in the rest of the nation. The economic, financial, and monetary systems of the Hong Kong SAR, on the other hand, will be independent of the systems of the Central People's Government.

The third difference between the ethnic autonomous regions and the Hong Kong SAR lies in the composition of their governments. In ethnic autonomous regions, prefectures, and counties, most leading government posts are filled by members of local nationalities who are members of the Communist Party and appointed by higher-level officials or by the Central People's Government. In some cases, leading government posts are taken by nonlocal officials sent by the central authorities. However, the Hong Kong SAR will not be governed by Communists appointed by the central authorities; all government officials will be selected by the Hong Kong people locally.

In conclusion, it is true that autonomous nationality regions have more powers in the local economy than nonautonomous regions of China, and can promote their own nationalities' education, culture, and language. But in the executive, legislative, and judicial branches, the autonomous nationality regions have a low degree of autonomy compared with autonomous regions of other countries (this point will be discussed later). The Hong Kong SAR, which is fundamentally different from China's nationality autonomous regions, has a much higher degree of autonomy.

Hannum and Lillich's Contribution to Understanding the Theory and Practice of Autonomy and the Autonomy of the Hong Kong SAR

Sponsored by the U.S. State Department, Hannum and Lillich contributed a general survey of twenty-five cases of nonsovereign autonomous entities that offers "a wide range of examples of different degrees of governmental autonomy and internal self-government."[18] The purpose of Hannum and Lillich's study was to help the State Department examine the question of possible autonomy for the West Bank and Gaza regions under Israeli sovereignty. The twenty-five cases that Hannum and Lillich surveyed are:

1. Federal states, including the Turkish Federated State of Cyprus (1975); Eritrea (Ethiopia) (1952–1962); Catalonia and other autonomous regions under the Second Spanish Republic (1931–1936); Euzkadi [the Basque country] (Spain) (1979); United Arab Emirates; Switzerland (1848–1874); Greenland under Denmark (1978); and Belgium (1971).

2. Internationalized territories and territories of particular international concern, including the Free City of Danzig (1919–1945); Free Territory of Trieste (1947); International Settlement of Shanghai (1845–1944); Memel Territory (1924–1939); the Saar (1920–1935 and 1945–1956); and the Aland Islands.

3. Associated states, including nonself-governing territories under the United Nations; states associated with New Zealand—the Cook Islands, Niue, and the territory of Tokelau; states associated with the United States—the Commonwealth of Puerto Rico, territories of Guam and the U.S. Virgin Islands, and

the Trust Territory of the Pacific Islands; and Netherlands Antilles, which is associated with the Netherlands.

4.   Other cases, including British proposals for provincial autonomy in Palestine (1946–1947); the millet system in the Ottoman Empire; and the Isle of Man.[19]

Only the cases in the first category in Hannum and Lillich's list, which is titled "federal states" but includes autonomous regions of unitary governments, will be compared with the Hong Kong SAR. To explain why the cases of federal states are selected and other categories excluded, the terms Hannum and Lillich used should be examined.

Hannum and Lillich defined the term "federal state" broadly, as referring to a state in which subdivisions enjoy some degree of local rule while a central government has full authority over foreign affairs. According to their standard, a unitary state with subdivisions enjoying autonomous powers is a federal state. Their concept of federal states is not equivalent to the concept of federations used in the foregoing discussion, but also includes unitary states with autonomous regions, such as Spain (with Catalonia and the Basque country) and Denmark (with Greenland). Of the eight cases in Hannum and Lillich's category of federal states, two are federations (the proposed Turkish Federated State of Cyprus, which still exists only on paper, and Switzerland); one is a confederation (United Arab Emirates); five are autonomous regions of unitary states (Eritrea under Ethiopia, Catalonia and other autonomous regions under the Second Spanish Republic, the Basque country under Spain, Greenland under Denmark, and Belgian linguistic communities under Belgium).

Also, as discussed above in theoretical terms, unit governments under a federation maintain inherent power that makes local autonomous powers strong. Indeed, as will be shown, both the proposed Turkish Federated State of Cyprus and cantons of Switzerland maintain strong independent powers under federal governments. As for United Arab Emirates, it is a confederation of sovereign entities. The remaining five autonomous cases under unitary governments were selected by Hannum and Lillich because these cases are considered to have a high degree of autonomy in terms of the central-local relationship. Therefore, the federal state in Hannum and Lillich's study is similar to the Hong Kong SAR under unitary China. In this study, comparison will be focused on the autonomous practice of the entities in this category only. The two federal cases (the Turkish federated state of Cyprus and the cantons of Switzerland) and a case of confederation (United Arab Emirates) will also be examined simply because they are in this same category of eight autonomous regions.

Cases in Hannum and Lillich's categories of "internationalized territories" and "associate states" will be excluded from comparison for several reasons. The two authors defined an internationalized territory as "somewhat analogous" to a guaranteed or protected state, which is an entity that has been created under international supervision. Although an internationalized territory generally retains full authority over local affairs and is restricted only by the international constituent document by which it was created, the entity is not a sovereign state.

According to the two authors, an associated state is a modern political arrangement by the United Nations for certain nonself-governing territories. Under this arrangement, an entity has delegated certain of its powers (particularly the powers of foreign affairs and defense) to a principal state, although its international status as a state is maintained. Hannum and Lillich's categories of internationalized territory and associated state refer to subjected entities, because they do not have full sovereignty and are dependent on the international organizations or on more powerful foreign sovereign states.

Thus, autonomous regions (as in the category of federal state) and subjected states (internationalized territories and associated states) are different in terms of their relationships with sovereign authorities. First, subjected entities are created by international organizations and retain a certain degree of international status that is recognized by the world community. However, the autonomous region of a sovereign state has no such international status. It is created by its national government and may participate in international negotiations in the area of commercial affairs, as in the case of Greenland, but only with the status of a nonsovereign entity. Usually local participation in international affairs requires permission by the region's central government.

Second, because the territory of the subjected entity is not a formal and permanent territory of the sovereign state to which it submitted, the subjected entity is not permitted to participate in the national government. For instance, there are no representatives of Puerto Rico, Guam, or the U.S. Virgin Islands in the United States Senate and House of Representatives. However, an autonomous region of a country is a permanent territory of that state, and the region is equal to other subdivisions of that state.

In conclusion, though the subjected entity and the autonomous region have common characteristics, they are not the same. The relationship between the subjected entity and its sovereign state is an international arrangement, while the relationship between the autonomous region and the sovereign state is a domestic matter. Hence, because the establishment of the Hong Kong SAR is a Chinese domestic issue under the Basic Law, only Hannum and Lillich's federal state category was chosen for comparison.

Why is Hannum and Lillich's study important? The two authors examined most autonomous regions under unitary states, if not all.[20] These cases involve not only the constitutional statutes of autonomous regions on paper, but also real autonomous arrangements in practice. A comparison of the Hong Kong SAR with these cases is meaningful because if regions with a high degree of autonomy can exist in other states, a Hong Kong SAR with a high degree of autonomy under Chinese sovereignty may be possible. Most importantly, Hannum and Lillich examined several key issues about the relationship between an autonomous region and sovereign government, and their comprehensive research presented a clear theoretical picture or standard of what a high degree of autonomy is. Other research on this topic has lacked such a general theoretical approach on regional autonomy. Therefore, this comparison is undertaken not to create theory but rather to test, against an existing typology, the case of the Hong Kong SAR. The comparison will follow Hannum and Lillich's pattern, including: (1) the general governmental structure, including executive, legislative, and judicial authority; (2) particular issues and powers, including foreign affairs, defense, land, national resources, social services, finance, and economy.

General Governmental Structure

Executive Authority

Hannum and Lillich's examination of characteristics of the executive branches of the autonomous regions included the selection of the chief executive and whether the chief executive represents the central or local governments; the authority of the executive in relation to the legislative process; local authority over foreign relations and defense; and local police powers. They found that:

1. Citizens of autonomous regions are responsible for the selection of their chief executive official. The national governments generally do not influence this selection. The Basque autonomous region of Spain is an exception, because the appointment of the region's president by the Basque parliament must be approved by the Spanish King. Since the chief executive is chosen locally, he or she is responsible to the local people and does not represent the central government.

2. The autonomous region is authorized to enforce certain national laws within its autonomous area, and the national government retains the right to supervise the implementation of these laws. In some cases, the national governments reserve power to enforce national laws in autonomous regions because of local distrust of or dislike for the national government. The autonomous regions of Eritrea, Catalonia, and the Basque country are examples of such cases.

3. The sovereign government retains power over the national defense of autonomous regions, and the autonomous regional government absolutely has no power over defense. Moreover, in most cases, national governments conduct foreign affairs on behalf of the autonomous regions. Some autonomous entities are granted special authority to sign international agreements on economic, cultural, and social affairs (as opposed to political and military agreements). The treaties between autonomous regions and foreign states must be approved by the national governments. This arrangement exists in the cases of Turkish Federal State of Cyprus, the Basque country, Swiss cantons, emirates of the United Arab Emirates, and Greenland.

4.   In most cases, local police forces are considered as merely exercising a local competence and are controlled by the autonomous government, while military forces are controlled by the national government. The only exception is the Belgian linguistic communities because they are more cultural autonomous communities than political autonomous regions.

The executive of the SAR.   According to the Basic Law, the chief executive of the Hong Kong SAR will be the head of the region and will represent the region (BL 43, sec. 1). The chief executive will be selected by the Hong Kong people through election and consultation and will be appointed by the Central People's Government (BL 45, sec. 1). This arrangement is similar to the case of the Basque country. Because the chief executive will be the most important post of the SAR government, the necessity of China's approval may limit the SAR's autonomy. Yet, this is the only provision in the Basic Law that makes the SAR's autonomous power weaker than that of other autonomous entities compared in this study.

The Hong Kong chief executive "shall be accountable to the Central People's Government and the Hong Kong Special Administrative Region in accordance with the provisions of this law" (BL 43, sec. 2). This seems an unclear and inconsistent stipulation: how can the chief executive be accountable to both the Hong Kong SAR and the Central People's Government? This provision will produce a serious question: To whom will the chief executive be accountable if the SAR and the Central People's Government come into conflict on an issue? Xiao Weiyun and Wang Shuwen tried to answer the question and may represent the Chinese official position.[21] Xiao explained that although the chief executive does not represent the Central People's Government, he or she can only exercise power when formally appointed by the central authorities. Therefore, the chief executive must be accountable to the people of Hong Kong who will select him or her and to the Central People's Government that will appoint him or her.[22] Wang Shuwen explained, however, the areas in which the chief executive will be accountable to the Central People's Government. These include his or her responsibility for the implementation of the Basic Law and other laws in force in the SAR; asking the Central People's Government to appoint or remove major local officials; implementing certain instructions of the central authorities about the Basic Law; and representing the SAR in dealing with foreign affairs of the SAR.[23] However, both Xiao and Wang failed to answer the key question: whether the chief executive will be accountable to the central authorities or to the people of the SAR if central and local interests conflict.

Another issue is the implementation of national laws in the SAR. Generally, the national laws will not be applied to the SAR except for the six national laws listed in the Basic Law.[24] These six laws, however, are only symbols of Chinese sovereignty over the SAR, so clearly the chief executive of the SAR will play a small role in administering the national law in the region.

The chief executive will have the power to return a bill passed by the Legco when he or she thinks that bill is not compatible with the overall interests of the region (BL 49). If the chief executive refuses to sign a bill passed the second time by the Legco, and the differences between the chief executive and the council cannot be settled, the chief executive has the power to dissolve the council. However, the veto power of the chief executive over the Legco is conditional: the chief executive can only dissolve the Legco once in each term of his or her office. If the chief executive again refuses to sign a bill over which he or she has dissolved the previous Legco but which the new Legco passes again, he or she must resign. He or she must also leave office after the Legco is dissolved because it has refused to pass a budget or any other important bill and the new council refuses to pass the original bill in dispute (BL 52, sec. 2 and 3). Here the principle of checks and balances is introduced. This regulation is helpful in restraining the chief executive from abuse of power. The introduction of checks and balances represents important progress in the development of Hong Kong's political system.

Not surprisingly, the SAR will have impressive powers in conducting its external affairs. The Central People's Government will be responsible for the foreign affairs of the SAR, but the SAR will also be authorized to conduct relevant foreign affairs on its own (BL 13). Representatives of the SAR will be part of the Chinese delegation in negotiations with foreign countries on affairs directly affecting the SAR (BL 150). The SAR will use the name of "Hong Kong, China" to maintain and develop relations and conclude agreements with foreign countries and regions and relevant international organizations in the economic, trade, financial and monetary, shipping, communications, tourism, cultural, and sports fields (BL 151). Moreover, the representatives of the SAR can participate, under the name of Hong Kong, China, in international organizations and conferences not limited to states. China will help Hong Kong retain its status in international organizations in which China is or is not a member (BL 152). In addition, the SAR is authorized to issue passports and other trade documents to all permanent residents of Hong Kong, valid for all countries and regions (BL 154). Generally, in foreign affairs, the SAR will have more powers than the other autonomous regions examined by Hannum and Lillich.

Why is Hong Kong granted so much power in the area of its external affairs? China promised that Hong Kong's social and economic system will remain unchanged after 1997, and the SAR's powers in foreign affairs are nothing but competences that the Hong Kong government currently has in this area. The Basic Law is only a confirmation that Hong Kong's powers in foreign affairs under British rule will remain unchanged in 1997.

The SAR's power in defense generally parallels that of other autonomous regions examined by Hannum and Lillich. The central authorities will be responsible for Hong Kong's defense. Chinese military forces stationed in Hong Kong will not interfere in local affairs, and soldiers in Hong Kong will abide by national laws and local laws. Military expenditures will be paid by the Central People's Government (BL 14).

Finally, the Basic Law states that Hong Kong's existing police force will be maintained, except that the commissioner of police must be a local Chinese citizen (art. 100, 101).

Table 4.1 summarizes the above comparison between the eight autonomous cases and the Hong Kong SAR with regard to executive authority. Table 4.1 shows that the SAR parallels the eight cases of high-degree autonomy, except that local selection of the chief executive of the SAR must be approved by the Central People's Government.

Legislative Authority

Hannum and Lillich focus on three points in evaluating local legislative power: (1) residual power[25] of the autonomous region, (2) veto powers of the sovereign government, and (3) the constitutional amendment process in the autonomous region.

The authors found that in seven of eight autonomous cases, there is a regional legislative body that is elected locally. The only exceptions are the sheikdoms of the United Arab Emirates (UAE), in which the ruling families have legislative power and an emirate may establish a legislature, elected locally,

Table 4.1   Executive Authority of Autonomous Regions

	Chief Executive Officer Selected by		Foreign Relations and Defense		Local Treatymaking Power		Police Powers	
	Local	Central	Local	Central	Yes	No	Local	Central
Turkish Federal State of Cyprus	✓		✓		✓		✓	
Eritrea	✓			✓		✓	✓	
Basque country	✓[a]			✓	✓		✓	
Catalonia	✓			✓		✓	✓	
UAE emirates	✓			✓	✓		✓	
Swiss cantons	✓			✓	✓		✓	
Greenland	✓			✓	✓		Unclear	Unclear
Belgian linguistic communities				✓		✓		✓
Hong Kong SAR	✓[a]			✓[b]	✓		✓	

Sources: Excerpted from PAIL Report, vol. 1, 11, except for the portion concerning the Hong Kong SAR, which is the author's own. The original figure includes twenty-five cases. Here only eight autonomous cases in Hannum and Lillich's "federal state" are copied. (Tables 4.2 and 4.3 are similar in this respect.)

Notes: a. Local selection of the chief executive must be approved by the national government.

b. The Central People's Government will be responsible for foreign affairs relating to the Hong Kong SAR, although the SAR is authorized to conduct relevant external affairs on its own.

only if the authorities permit. Concerning the above three points, Hannum and Lillich further found that:

1.   Surprisingly, all autonomous regions of unitary states, such as Eritrea, the Basque country, Catalonia, and Greenland, do not have the power to amend their constitutions; and even the Swiss cantons have no such power. The national governments of autonomous regions retain the power to amend the local autonomous statutes. Only in the proposed Turkish Federated State of Cyprus and in UAE emirates do local authorities retain the power to amend local constitutions. In the case of Belgian linguistic communities, the power of constitutional amendment is not clearly stated in Belgian constitutional law.

2.   Four of the five autonomous regions of unitary states have no residual power; Eritrea is an exception in this matter. But in federated and confederated cases (Turkish Federated State of Cyprus, UAE emirates, and Swiss cantons), it is the constituent units, not the central government, that enjoys residual power. Also, the ultimate power to amend the constitutions is somewhat linked with which government (central or local) enjoys residual power. The autonomous regions of unitary states (again, Eritrea is an exception) have no residual power, so that the autonomous entities have no power to amend their constitutional laws. In federal cases, Turkish Federated State of Cyprus and UAE emirates have both residual power and the power to amend their constitutional laws. The exception is the Swiss cantons, which have a residual power but no power to amend constitutional statute.

3.   Whether the central government retains a veto power over local legislation is key to knowing the real significance of local legislative power. In six of the eight cases in this study, the central governments cannot veto local legislation. The exceptional two cases are Eritrea and the Belgian linguistic communities, in which central governments have the power to veto laws passed by local legislatures. Yet, the Eritrean parliament has the power to override, by two-thirds majority of the local parliament, the central veto.

The legislative power of the SAR.   First, the SAR will have its own Legislative Council and all its members will be elected locally (BL 2, 3, 66, 68). The legislative power of the SAR will parallel that of autonomous regions examined by Hannum and Lillich. Residual power is not mentioned in the Basic Law, but some Basic Law drafters from Hong Kong argued that residual power should be given to the SAR and should be written clearly into the law. Nevertheless, two drafters from the mainland, Xiao Weiyun and Wang Shuwen, asserted that there was no residual power for the SAR because China will remain a unitary state, and that because the powers that the SAR will enjoy are not inherent, there could be no such thing as residual power in the case of Hong Kong.[26] Xiao and Wang also maintained that Article 20 of the Basic Law would solve the problem if the SAR needed new powers not included in the Basic Law.[27] Obviously, the NPC, the NPC Standing Committee, and the National People's Government will decide whether it is necessary to grant the SAR such additional rights.

Second, the central authorities will not veto laws enacted by the Legislative Council of the Hong Kong SAR (BL 17, sec. 2). However, the central authorities may veto the SAR's laws regarding affairs within the responsibility of the central authorities as well as within the relationship between the central authorities and the SAR (BL 17, sec. 3). This provision is understandable given that the SAR is only an autonomous region. The problem is to define what constitute affairs within the central authorities' competence and matters affecting the relationship between the central authorities and the SAR, because only the NPC Standing Committee has the power to interpret the Basic Law.

Third, the SAR will have no power to amend the Basic Law. The NPC retains this constitutional authority, although the SAR can propose amendments of the law (BL 159).

Table 4.2 concludes the above comparison between the SAR and the other eight autonomous cases on legislative authority. The table shows that the legislative power of the Hong Kong's SAR parallels that of other autonomous entities.

Judicial Authority

Hannum and Lillich found an independent judiciary in all autonomous regions, although this independence does not necessarily imply total separation from central judicial authority. Judicial powers of the autonomous regions differ on

Table 4.2 Legislative Authority of Autonomous Regions

	Locally Elected Legislature		Residual Powers		Central Veto Power		Constitutional Amendment Approval	
	Yes	No	Local	Central	Yes	No	Local	Central
Turkish Federal State of Cyprus	✓		✓			✓	✓	
Eritrea	✓		✓		✓			✓
Basque country	✓			✓		✓		✓
Catalonia	✓			✓		✓		✓
UAE emirates	N/A	N/A	✓			✓	✓	
Swiss cantons	✓		✓			✓		✓
Greenland	✓			✓		✓		✓
Belgian linguistic communities	✓			✓	✓		N/A	N/A
Hong Kong SAR	✓			✓		✓		✓

Sources: Excerpted from PAIL Report, vol. 1, 19, except for the portion concerning the Hong Kong SAR, which is the author's own.

two points: (1) the manner in which the local judges are selected, particularly the judges of the highest local court; and (2) whether local matters may be appealed to a central tribunal. Hannum and Lillich discovered that local judges are appointed in two ways. The first pattern is that the autonomous entities appoint local judges, and the central government does not intervene. This arrangement exists in Eritrea, Catalonia, the proposed Turkish Federal State of Cyprus, the UAE emirates, and the Swiss cantons. The second pattern is that the central government makes the appointment, based on recommendations of the autonomous government. For instance, the president of the Supreme Court of the Basque country is appointed by the Spanish central government. Another example is the Belgian linguistic communities, for which challenges to jurisdiction of a local decree are presented to a section of the Council of State.

However, even in autonomous regions where local judges are selected entirely within the area, local matters may be appealed to a central court. Such an arrangement exists in the Basque country. Furthermore, in most cases, the central governments retain final constitutional jurisdiction concerning local decisions and the relationship between the autonomous and principal governments.

The judicial power of the SAR.   The Hong Kong SAR will have a judiciary power and a Court of Final Appeal. The selection and appointment of judges of all courts of the SAR will be local matters, and the central authorities will not intervene. The SAR courts will be authorized to exercise judicial powers on all local matters, and the Court of Final Appeal will be the supreme court of the SAR. However, the central authorities will retain ultimate constitutional jurisdiction. On provisions of the Basic Law concerning the responsibility of the central authorities and the relationship between the central authorities and the SAR, the courts of the SAR must seek an interpretation from the national legislature (BL 88, 90, 19, 158). Generally, the rights of the SAR parallel those of the other eight autonomous cases. Table 4.3 summarizes the above discussion about the judicial authorities of the Hong Kong SAR and the eight autonomous cases.

Particular Issues and Powers

Land and Natural Resources

Hannum and Lillich found that in general, land ownership remains as before the establishment of the autonomous region, and that both the central and local governments have certain powers concerning land. Where ownership of public lands is mentioned in the constitutional law of the autonomous entities, lands and property formally owned by the sovereign government are a grant to the local government.

Table 4.3   Judicial Authority of Autonomous Regions

	Highest Local Court Selected by		Appeals to Central Government on Local Matters		Ultimate Constitutional Jurisdiction	
	Local	Central	Yes	No	Local	Central
Turkish Federal State of Cyprus	✓			✓	✓	
Eritrea	✓			✓	✓	
Basque country		✓	✓			✓
Catalonia	✓			✓		✓
UAE emirates	✓			✓		✓
Swiss cantons	✓		✓			✓
Greenland[a]						
Belgian linguistic communities		✓	✓			✓
Hong Kong SAR	✓			✓		✓

Sources: Excerpted from PAIL Report, vol. 1, 26, except for the portion concerning the Hong Kong SAR, which is the author's own.

Note: a. The Greenland home rule provisions make no reference to the establishment of a local judiciary.

Hannum and Lillich also discovered that the power of autonomous regions over natural resources varies greatly. Autonomous regions that enjoy more independent powers generally have more power to control national resources.

Hong Kong has very limited land and natural resources. The Basic Law states that the land and natural resources within the SAR will be state property but that the government of the SAR will be responsible for their management, use, and development. The SAR will get all revenues derived from land and natural resources (BL 7). Currently, public land in Hong Kong is owned by the British Crown, but the Hong Kong government has the power to release the land. Actually, the change of government in 1997 will transfer the British Hong Kong government's right of management of public lands to the government of the SAR.

Social Services

The term "social services" refers to such matters as health, education, and welfare. In the eight autonomous cases, the autonomous region rather than the sovereign government is responsible for social services.

The SAR parallels the eight autonomous cases in social services. The government of the Hong Kong SAR will be responsible for social services and will regulate, on its own, education, medical and health services, science and technology, and culture and sports. Generally, the SAR will maintain current British policies in these areas (Chapter VI of the Basic Law).

Finance and Economy

Hannum and Lillich found that the autonomous entities generally form part of an economic and Customs union with the central government. It is the central government rather than the autonomous government that maintains economic and financial powers. These include regulation of currency and the coinage of money, regulation of foreign and interstate commerce, and regulation of the banking system. However, the authority to impose local taxes generally has been within the jurisdiction of the autonomous region.

Unlike the other autonomous entities, which have very limited powers in economy and finance, the Hong Kong SAR will enjoy independent power in this area. Indeed, the Hong Kong SAR's tremendous power in these areas is an exception. Because Hong Kong is a major financial and trading center, maintaining its economic and financial systems is in China's best interest and is one of the major purposes for the establishment of the SAR. The way to maintain Hong Kong's prosperity is to keep its capitalist system and free market economy intact. Chapter V of the Basic Law, entitled "Economy," describes in detail the powers that the SAR will enjoy in the economy:

1.   The SAR will protect the right of private ownership of property (BL 6). The dominance of public ownership in the PRC and of private ownership in Hong Kong are key factors in the difference between the PRC's socialism and Hong Kong's capitalism. For both the Hong Kong government and its citizens, the success of Hong Kong's economy relies on the existence of private ownership and the free market. Therefore, maintaining private ownership is the most important economic power of the SAR.

2.   The SAR will have independent finances and will use its financial revenues exclusively for its own purpose. Revenues of the SAR will not be transferred to the Central People's Government and the Central People's Government will not levy taxes in the SAR. The government of the SAR will draw up its own budget and make its own financial policy (BL 106, 107). The finances of the SAR will not be directed by China's Financial Ministry.

3.   The SAR will be a separate Customs territory from that of China, and it will maintain the status of a free port and will not impose any tariff (BL 116, 114). Hong Kong's status as a free port was a key factor in the city's success as an international trading center, and the maintenance of Hong Kong's free port is essential to Hong Kong's economy.

4.   The government of the Hong Kong SAR will provide an economic and legal environment for the maintenance of the status of Hong Kong as an international financial center (BL 109). The government of the SAR will, on its own, formulate monetary and financial policies (BL 110, sec. 2). There will be no foreign exchange control policies in the SAR and the Hong Kong dollar will be freely convertible (BL 112). These powers granted to the SAR are compatible with Hong Kong's current reality as one of the monetary and financial

centers of the world. The majority of the big banks of all countries have established branches in Hong Kong, where the currencies of all countries can be freely converted. The Hong Kong dollar itself is convertible in the market, in contrast with the inconvertible renminbi, the currency of the PRC.

5.   The SAR will "pursue the policy of free trade and safeguard the free movement of goods, intangible assets and capital" (BL 115).

6.   Hong Kong is one of the primary shipping centers in the world. Its current shipping management and regulations will be maintained, and the government of the SAR will have the power to make policy on shipping (BL 124).

According to Hannum and Lillich, the local/central power distribution in finance and the economy can be seen most clearly in such areas as customs and taxation, currency and the coinage of money, foreign and interstate commerce, and the banking system. Sovereign governments generally control all the powers in these fields, but the case of Hong Kong will be an exception. The government of the SAR will hold these powers, and the SAR will be a completely independent economic entity.

Conclusion

This chapter examined whether the SAR will in fact have "a high degree of autonomy," as the Chinese government announced in the Sino-British Declaration of 1984 and in the Basic Law of the SAR. Without an acceptable standard, it is difficult to determine whether the SAR will have a high degree of autonomy. Hannum and Lillich's investigation offered such a standard.

Hannum and Lillich concluded that five principles are the keys with which to assess "a fully autonomous territory": (1) There should be a locally elected legislative body, which should have authority over local matters and should be independent. (2) The chief executive of the autonomous region should be chosen locally, and may be approved by the national government. The chief executive is responsible for the administration and execution of local laws, and he or she may also be authorized to implement national laws. (3) There should be an independent local judiciary. Some members of the local judiciary may also be subject to the approval of the national government. Nonlocal matters or questions involving the relationship between the autonomous region and the national government may be appealed to a national court or a joint commission for final settlement. (4) The national government generally controls foreign relations, national defense, customs, and monetary and financial matters. (5) The central and autonomous governments may share powers in such areas as control over ports and other transportation facilities, police, and natural resources. For Hannum and Lillich, the above-mentioned principles are the main features of full autonomy. Though the specific characteristics of autonomous regions are different, their constitutional statutes generally deal with the five issues enumerated.

The governmental power the Hong Kong SAR will possess generally meets Hannum and Lillich's standard for a high degree of autonomy. However, in one important point—the selection of the chief executive of the SAR, in which the local selection must be approved by the Central People's Government—the SAR's autonomy seems to be less than most of the autonomous regions compared. (The SAR will parallel the Basque country in this arrangement.) But with regard to foreign affairs and the economy, the SAR will enjoy much more power than other autonomous regions. The powers that the SAR will enjoy are compatible with the Chinese policy of one country, two systems.

Further examination of the SAR's autonomy demonstrates that the Basic Law actually reconfirms the autonomy of current Hong Kong government under British colonial rule, particularly in economy and foreign affairs. Currently, in practice (as distinguished from the provisions of the Letters Patent and Royal Instructions), though London maintains the power of final appeal for Hong Kong, the colony's judiciary is generally independent concerning local matters. London is responsible for Hong Kong's defense and foreign relations, but Hong Kong has the power to further conduct external affairs in commercial areas; and Hong Kong also participates in international economic organizations such as GATT. The Crown colony is independent in finance, the taxation system, the customs system, and monetary affairs. Finally, the Hong Kong government also has the power to lease and grant land, to regulate the port and shipping, and to control the police. Only in two areas will there be a change in 1997 in terms of sovereign-local relationships: London will no longer appoint the governor of Hong Kong and the leading officials of the Hong Kong government; and the people of the Hong Kong SAR will select their chief executive with a final approval by the Chinese authorities in Beijing. The executive must be a Chinese national and a Hong Kong citizen. Also, London will no longer house the final appeals court for Hong Kong; nor will Beijing have such authority. The Hong Kong SAR will have its own Court of Final Appeal.

The foregoing analyses indicate that a highly autonomous Hong Kong SAR may indeed be possible. The Basic Law does not create a wholly new autonomous system that is not grounded in experience; on the contrary, the Chinese government pledges, through the Basic Law, to continue autonomous practices in Hong Kong—a workable arrangement. Therefore, as long as the Basic Law is implemented the autonomy of Hong Kong will be protected. It is too simplistic to argue that China's record of constitutional practice under Communist rule indicates that the Hong Kong SAR's autonomy is doomed. Chapter 6 will discuss the possibilities for China in the way it undertakes to implement the Basic Law. The autonomy of the SAR is only one side of the central-local relationship. Several aspects of the Basic Law also protect Chinese sovereignty over the SAR. These relationships will be considered next.

Notes

1. See Jibenfa Zixun Weiyuanhui, ed., *Zixun Baogao*; Ming K. Chan and David J. Clark, eds., *The Hong Kong Basic Law: Blueprint for "Stability and Prosperity Under Chinese Sovereignty"?* (Armonk, N. Y.: M. E. Sharpe, 1991), 92–144; Wesley-Smith and Chan, eds., *The Basic Law and Hong Kong's Future*; and McGurn, *The Basic Law, Basic Questions*, 37–52.

2. See PAIL Institute, *The Theory and Practice of Governmental Autonomy*, 2 vols., (Washington, D. C.: The Libraries of the American Society of International Law and the PAIL Institute), hereafter cited as PAIL Report, as shortened by Hannum and Lillich. PAIL Report is a comprehensive study of regional governmental autonomy, prepared by the Procedural Aspect of International Law Institute under a contract with the U.S. State Department, as a reference for discussion concerning the status of the West Bank and Gaza. Hurst Hannum and Richard B. Lillich published the outline of the PAIL Report, entitled "The Concept of Autonomy in International Law," in *The American Journal of International Law* 74, no. 4 (1980): 858–889. Hereafter, the substantial citations from Hannum and Lillich are, if not noted, from this published paper. Also, because Hannum and Lillich's entire report is cited in this chapter, no separate footnotes will be made for the various findings of the two authors.

3. Yoram Dinstein, "Autonomy," in Yoram Dinstein, ed., *Models of Autonomy* (New Brunswick, N. J.: Transaction Books, 1981), 291.

4. Louis B. Sohn, "Models of Autonomy Within the United Nations Framework," in Dinstein, *Models of Autonomy*, 5.

5. Ibid.

6. See Xiao Weiyun, *Yiguo Liangzhi Yu Xianggang Jiben Falu Zhidu* ["One Country, Two Systems" and Hong Kong's Basic Legal System] (Beijing: Beijing Daxue Chubanshe, 1990), 125–126.

7. William H. Riker, "Six Books in Search of a Subject or Does Federalism Exist and Does It Matter?" *Comparative Politics* 2, no. 1 (October 1969): 135–146.

8. Douglas E. Ashford, "Are Britain and France 'Unitary'?" *Comparative Politics* 9, no. 4 (July 1977): 483–499; Alberta May Sbragia, "Urban Autonomy within the Unitary State: A Case Study of Public Housing Policies in Milan, Italy," (Ph.D. Diss., University of Wisconsin, Madison, 1974).

9. Steven R. Reed, *Japanese Prefectures and Policymaking* (Pittsburgh, Penn.: The University of Pittsburgh Press, 1986), 6–7.

10. Ramesh Dutta Dikshit, *The Political Geography of Federalism: An Inquiry into Origins and Stability* (New York: John Wiley & Sons, 1975), 1; about the issue, also see K. C. Wheare, *Federal Government*, 4th ed. (New York: Oxford University Press, 1964), 35; and William H. Riker, *Federalism: Origin, Operation, Significance* (Boston: Little, Brown, 1964), 11.

11. Dikshit, *The Political Geography of Federalism*, 3–4.

12. Xiao, *Yiguo Liangzhi Yu Xianggang Jiben Falu Zhidu*, 125–126.

13. Rudolph Bernhardt, "Federalism and Autonomy," in Dinstein, *Models of Autonomy*, 23–28.

14. Ngapoi Ngawang Jigme, "Explaining Regional Autonomy Law," *Beijing Review* 27, no. 26 (25 June 1984): 17.

15. Ibid. The five major autonomous regions are Mongolia, Xingjing, Xizang [Tibet], Guangxi, and Ninxia, where primarily the Mongols, the Uygurs, the Tibetans, the Zhuangs, and the Huis respectively live.

16. Regarding Chinese regulations on regional autonomy, see *Constitution of the People's Republic of China of 1982*. Also see Zhou Enlai, "Some Questions on Policy Towards Nationalities," *Beijing Review* 23, no. 9 (3 March 1980): 14–23 and no. 10 (10

March 1980): 18–25; An Zhiguo, "Regional Autonomy for Minorities," *Beijing Review* 27, no. 24 (11 June 1984): 4–5; and Ngawang Jigme, "Explaining Regional Autonomy Law," 17–19.

17. Ibid., 17.

18. PAIL Report, vol. 1.

19. According to Hannum and Lillich, two elements were considered when they selected the twenty-five cases for their special purpose. One element was that the cases of autonomous arrangements "have to some extent been recognized or discussed in international law." The second element was that the historical and legal context of the cases "was not so different or unique as to lessen their value." Under these restrictions, cases such as Monaco, San Marino, Andorra, and Liechtenstein were omitted.

20. Omitted, for example, is the case of autonomous South Tyrol under Italy. See Christoph Schreuer, "Autonomy in South Tyrol," in Dinstein, *Models of Autonomy*, 53–66. In his other study of sovereignty and autonomy, Hurst Hannum also examined, besides most of the cases already mentioned, the cases of Hong Kong; India and the Punjab; the Kurds; the Atlantic Coast of Nicaragua; Northern Ireland; the Saami (Lapp) People of Norway, Sweden, and Finland; Sri Lanka; and Sudan. However, he surveyed these cases individually without making comparisons among them.

21. See Xiao, *Yiguo Liangzhi Yu Xianggang Jiben Falu Zhidu*; and Wang Shuwen, *Xianggang Tebie Xingzhengqu Jibenfa Daolun* [A Guide to the Basic Law of the Hong Kong Special Administrative Region] (Beijing: Zhonggong Zhongyang Chubanshe, 1990). Both Xiao Weiyun and Wang Shuwen were leading Chinese scholars of constitutional law and also Basic Law drafters. Their works were the products of two groups of scholars organized by the Chinese government and were key research projects in China's Eighth Five-Year Plan. Therefore, certain of Wang's and Xiao's views may also be, in a sense, the Chinese government's interpretations of the Basic Law.

22. Xiao, *Yiguo Liangzhi Yu Xianggang Jiben Falu Zhidu*, 238.

23. Wang, *Xianggang Tebie Xingzhengqu Jibenfa Daolun*, 181–182.

24. The six national laws that shall be applied in the Hong Kong SAR are as follows: (1) Resolution on the capital, calendar, national anthem, and national flag of the PRC; (2) Resolution on the national day of the PRC; (3) Order on the central emblem of the PRC proclaimed by the Central People's Government; (4) Declaration of the government of the PRC on the Territorial Sea; (5) Nationality Law of the PRC; (6) Regulations of the PRC concerning diplomatic privileges and immunities.

25. Residual power is the power that is not written into the autonomous statute of the autonomous region and therefore it is not clear which governments—national or local authorities—will exercise it.

26. Xiao, *Yiguo Liangzhi Yu Xianggang Jiben Falu Zhidu*, 100–101; and Wang, *Xianggang Tebie Xingzhengqu Jibenfa Daolun*, 116–117.

27. Ibid., Xiao, 100–101; Article 20 states, "The Hong Kong Special Administrative Region may enjoy other powers granted to it by the National People's Congress, the Standing Committee of the National People's Congress or the Central People's Government."

5

China's Sovereignty over the Hong Kong SAR

The previous chapter demonstrated that the Hong Kong SAR will have a high degree of autonomy. However, local autonomy is only one side of the relationship between Beijing and Hong Kong. For a better understanding of the relationship between China and Hong Kong as set forth in the Basic Law, it is also necessary to look at China's sovereignty. The tension between China's sovereignty and Hong Kong's autonomy was the most controversial issue in the drafting of the Basic Law, and this issue will continue to be the key problem after 1997. In a sense, how China handles sovereignty over the SAR will determine the success of the SAR's autonomy.

The Chinese government was sensitive to the issue of sovereignty in the settlement of the Hong Kong question. During the Sino-British negotiations before 1984, China insisted that the settlement would not be a "treaty," but a "declaration." For the Chinese, signing a Sino-British treaty would mean that China recognized the legitimacy of the three former unequal treaties and British colonial rule over Hong Kong.[1] The British government finally agreed that the conclusion of the negotiations would be a declaration, not a treaty. In the 1984 Joint Declaration, Beijing also carefully chose the words "recover the Hong Kong area" and "resume the exercise of sovereignty over Hong Kong," to indicate that Hong Kong had been Chinese territory. Beijing and London declared that "the government of the United Kingdom will be responsible for the administration of Hong Kong with the object of maintaining and preserving its economic prosperity and social stability" during the transition period,[2] not mentioning which country was then sovereign. In this way, the declaration actually avoids the sensitive issue of the legitimacy of the unequal treaties and British colonial rule over Hong Kong.

During the Basic Law drafting process, several participants from Hong Kong argued that the issue of sovereignty had been settled by the 1984 agreement, so that the Basic Law should not stress sovereignty, but emphasize the autonomy of the SAR and its powers.[3] Wang Shuwen, a mainland legal expert who participated in the drafting of the Basic Law and may represent the Chinese authorities' view on the relationship between sovereignty and autonomy, argued that the 1984 agreement only clarified which country had sovereignty. Wang maintained that sovereignty of the Central People's Government over Hong Kong must be assured in the Basic Law.[4]

How did China assure its sovereignty in the Basic Law; or in other words, how does the Basic Law demonstrate that China, not Britain, is sovereign over Hong Kong? In what ways is Beijing sovereign over the SAR? Moreover, what were the differences between Beijing and Hong Kong on sovereignty?

As Chapter 1 discussed, sovereignty is the supreme and absolute power of the state, which usually exercises sovereignty over the territories it claims. However, during the period when the modern concept of sovereignty was developing, there was a theoretical dispute over the concept of state sovereignty versus sovereign people. This dispute also occurred between the Chinese central authorities and some Hong Kong citizens and between mainland and Hong Kong drafters of the Basic Law Drafting Committee. The process of drafting the Basic Law demonstrated that the concept of sovereignty has important consequences for Chinese thought about constitutional practice and laws, as well as for discussion of public policy aims. The Basic Law made clear two positions of the Chinese policymakers on Hong Kong after 1997: first, that China has sovereignty over Hong Kong, the British colonial rule having ended, and second, that the central authorities are sovereign over the Hong Kong SAR.

The Basic Law States that China, Not Britain, Possesses Sovereignty

The Inalienability of Hong Kong from China

The Basic Law states that "The Hong Kong Special Administrative Region is an inalienable part of the People's Republic of China" (BL 1). This provision simply expresses an important principle of the Beijing authorities' basic position on Hong Kong in terms of territorial sovereignty; it can also be explained as a reiteration of the 1984 Joint Declaration. In its preamble, the Basic Law states that China's recovery of sovereignty over Hong Kong is "for upholding national unity and territorial integrity."

For Chinese authorities and mainland drafters, the assertion of the inalienability of Hong Kong also describes the status of Hong Kong after 1997—a local region of unitary China. According to this Chinese thinking, China first recovers sovereignty over Hong Kong from the British, and then grants Hong Kong autonomy. In other words, Hong Kong's autonomy can only be granted after the PRC resumes Chinese rule. In this way, Hong Kong's autonomous powers exercised after 1997 derive from the Central People's Government rather than being inherited directly from the British rule. However, Hong Kong citizens may view the transfer of government in 1997 differently. As a Hong Kong scholar argued, under the Chinese concept of sovereignty, "it is not surprising the will or wishes of the people of Hong Kong are not recognized. . . . It is the state, not the people of Hong Kong" that decided to resume the exercise of sovereignty over Hong Kong.[5] A major source of dispute between Beijing and Hong Kong during the Basic Law drafting process involved these contending theories of state sovereignty versus the sovereign people.

Another related issue was inherent power. The Beijing authorities insisted that Hong Kong has no inherent power. Because China would continue to be a unitary state under the Basic Law, the SAR's autonomous powers by definition are granted by the central authorities. Under the Chinese concept of state sovereignty and unitary government, the Basic Law is, in a sense, a formal explanation of how much autonomous power is granted to the Hong Kong SAR. The dispute on sovereignty and autonomy was predictable because Basic Law drafters from Hong Kong wanted as many autonomous powers as possible, while Beijing authorities emphasized their sovereignty and seemed not to expect Hong Kong to be too independent of the central government.

Chinese Citizens Will Govern Hong Kong

The Basic Law rules out the possibility that Hong Kong residents who have received British or other foreign passports will govern Hong Kong after 1997. This deliberate elaboration in the Basic Law is a direct response to London's program of "the right of abode in Great Britain." On December 20, 1989, six months after the Tiananmen incident, the Thatcher administration announced that Britain would grant 50,000 heads of households in Hong Kong and their dependents (about 225,000 people altogether) full British citizenship with right of abode in Britain.[6] The British government asserted that Britain had a duty to people employed in Hong Kong and to those essential to maintaining its prosperity, and that the purpose of offering passports was to maintain the confidence of the Hong Kong people so that they would stay after 1997.[7] Later, the 50,000-person citizenship quota was allocated among four sections. The biggest section (70 percent of the total) was "business and professions." This category included persons in business and management (managers and administrators), accounting, engineering, information services, medicine and science, law, and education. The "disciplined service section" would offer 7,000 places for those people working in the colony's prisons department, customs and excise services, fire services, immigration, police, armed service, and the Independent Commission Against Corruption. The "sensitive service section" would allocate 6,300 places for people such as senior police officers, senior civil servants, and journalists. Finally, the "key entrepreneurs section" would provide 500 places for people who were "well-known and respected entrepreneurs."[8] The Hong Kong government welcomed London's program. Governor David Wilson, who was one of the major contributors to the policy of right of abode in

Britain, said the program would give a "psychological boost" to the colony. Most of the executive and legislative councillors also expressed their support of the program. The ordinary Hong Kong citizens demonstrated much less interest, however, because they were ignored.[9] Within Great Britain, serious debates occurred in Parliament over the program of the right of abode in Britain, officially "the British Nationality (Hong Kong) Bill." Some conservatives, headed by Norman Tebbit, the former chair of the party, rebelled against the Thatcher government. These conservatives argued that the 50,000 figure was too high and that the government broke election commitments on immigration. The opponents also asserted that the bill was unacceptable because it would anger the Chinese government and undermine the agreement with China. A large number of MPs from the Labour Party attacked the bill on the grounds that it granted citizenship based only on wealth, power, and influence.[10] However, the bill was finally adopted by Parliament on July 23, 1990.

Beijing objected to the British policy of the right of abode in Great Britain, asserting that London violated its promise in the Sino-British Joint Declaration. Beijing also suspected that the right of abode in Britain was intended to arrange for some key individuals loyal to London to stay in Hong Kong for the purpose of administering the government of the SAR after 1997. Beijing's formal response to the British program involved several points: (1) China would not recognize Britain's transfer of Chinese citizenship into British citizenship under the program of right of abode in Britain, (2) those who received British passports would not have British consular protection in the SAR and other parts of the PRC, (3) Hong Kong Chinese citizens accepted as British citizens would not be allowed to use their British citizenship to enter and depart from Hong Kong and other parts of the PRC.[11]

The program of the right of abode in Britain was announced when the drafting of the Basic Law was about to come to an end. To prevent Hong Kong residents who would become British citizens and remain in the SAR from taking key government positions, Beijing immediately revised the draft. The revised Basic Law added the provision that only Chinese citizens are qualified to assume the main public posts of the SAR, including those of the chief executive, principal officials of the government,[12] over 80 percent of members of the Legco, and judges in the highest court (BL 44, 55, 61, 101, 71, 67, 90).

Obviously, China's response to Britain's right of abode in Britain program produced contradictory information. On the one hand, China announced that all Hong Kong citizens would be Chinese citizens and China would not recognize Britain's transfer of the status of Chinese citizens into British citizens. In other words, China would continue to treat Hong Kong citizens who obtained full British citizenship under the right of abode in Britain as Chinese citizens. On the other hand, the revision of the Basic Law indicated that China would treat those Hong Kong citizens who had full British citizenship as having British nationality. The major purpose of that revision was to prevent those British from taking major government posts of the SAR.

In conclusion, China has been consistently sensitive on the issue of sovereignty. During the Sino-British negotiations over Hong Kong in the early 1980s, China rejected the British proposal of divided sovereignty. In 1990, fearing that the British would continue their influence through the right of abode in Britain, the Chinese again revised the draft Basic Law. As will be shown in Chapter 7, from 1992 to 1994 China seriously attacked Governor Christopher Patten's political reforms, again fearing that Britain was trying to continue its influence over Hong Kong after 1997.

Besides making clear that it is China, not Britain, that is sovereign over Hong Kong, the Basic Law also declares that the central authorities are sovereign over the Hong Kong SAR. In fact, essential parts of the Basic Law formulate the relationship between the central authorities' sovereignty and the SAR's autonomy.

The Basic Law States that
Beijing Is Sovereign over the SAR

China's sovereignty over the Hong Kong SAR is stressed by the Basic Law in several ways, although the Beijing regime and the Hong Kong drafters disagreed during the drafting process.

China's Constitution and the Basic Law

The Basic Law declares that its legal base is the Chinese Constitution. The preamble of the law states:

> the People's Republic of China has decided that upon China's resumption of the exercise of sovereignty over Hong Kong, a Hong Kong Special Administrative Region will be established in accordance with the provisions of Article 31 of the Constitution of the People's Republic of China . . . the National People's Congress hereby enacts the Basic Law of Hong Kong Special Administrative Region of the People's Republic of China, prescribing the systems to be practised in the Hong Kong Special Administrative Region, in order to ensure the implementation of the basic policies of the People's Republic of China regarding Hong Kong.

Wang Shuwen explained that the Basic Law's legal base is the entire Chinese Constitution, not just Article 31, and that the constitution as a whole will be applied to Hong Kong in 1997. For instance, Wang said that the constitution states that China is a unitary socialist country; the highest legislature of the country is the NPC; the highest government of China is the Central People's Government; and China has only one constitution (the Constitution of the People's Republic of China). All of these aspects of the constitution should be applied to the SAR. Wang further stated that many provisions of the Basic Law were based on China's constitution and that there are four principles for the application of the constitution in the SAR: (1) the constitution as a whole will be applied to Hong Kong; (2) the application must follow the principle of one country, two systems; (3) all of the constitution's provisions about safeguarding national sovereignty, unity, and territorial integrity would apply to Hong Kong; and (4) provisions in the constitution about socialist policies would not apply.[13] However, Wang also recognized that it is difficult to explain which particular articles of the constitution would apply to Hong Kong and which would not, and that the enumerated four points provided only a general basis for the application.[14]

Nevertheless, Article 31 and Wang's explanation clearly indicated that China's constitution is above the Basic Law—in other words, the Basic Law is the highest law only within the Hong Kong SAR, not in the whole of China.

During the Basic Law drafting process, some Hong Kong residents were dissatisfied with the provisions about the relationship between China's constitution and the Basic Law. These citizens suggested that China's constitution should make clear the principle of one country, two systems and the legitimacy of capitalism in the SAR. They argued that the Basic Law should be independent of China's constitution and they said that it was necessary to state clearly that even if the Basic Law contravened China's constitution, the Basic Law would be effective.[15] In the end, however, these views did not prevail.

The Special Administrative Region

The Basic Law states that the Hong Kong SAR will be a local administrative region of the PRC, and will have a high degree of autonomy but come directly under the Central People's Government (BL 12). This declaration rejects Hong Kong's proposal that Beijing and Hong Kong be coordinated after 1997. According to that proposal, Beijing's sovereignty is specified as only pertaining to the central government's responsibilities in foreign affairs and defense for the SAR. In other matters, Beijing and Hong Kong should be equal; and Beijing should have no power to intervene in the SAR's internal affairs. Any disputes between the Central People's Government and the SAR should be settled by an independent judicial committee or by a constitutional court that should consist of an equal number of judges from both sides.[16]

Mainland scholars argued that this proposal distorted the relationship between the Central People's Government and the SAR. They maintained that according to the Chinese Constitution, the Central People's Government was the "executive body of the highest organ of state power" and the "highest organ of state administration."[17] Therefore, the scholars continued, the Central People's Government should have the power to exercise leadership over all local governments of China, and there should be no exception for the government of the SAR. The autonomy of the SAR should be supervised by the Central People's Government. Otherwise, it would not be autonomous but completely independent from Beijing. The relationship between the Central People's Government and the SAR must be between a leader and the led, a supervisor and the supervised, and there could be no other relationship.[18] Both the Basic Law itself and the mainland scholars made it clear that the central authorities were sovereign over the SAR. This explanation may be another example of Wang Shuwen's argument that the Chinese Constitution as a whole would apply to Hong Kong. In this argument, Wang asserted that the Central People's Government as the highest executive body of the state should lead all local governments, including the government of the SAR.

The Central People's Government Is Responsible for Foreign Affairs and Defense

As defined in Chapter 1, sovereignty means supreme power to conduct domestic and international affairs. Also, as is discussed in Chapter 4, there is a general phenomenon that in all states with autonomous regions the national government has the power to conduct foreign affairs and defense.

In this matter, the Hong Kong SAR follows the pattern. The 1984 Joint Declaration makes it clear that the Chinese central government will be responsible for the defense and foreign affairs of the Hong Kong SAR. However, during the Basic Law drafting process and particularly after the 1989 Tiananmen incident, China's position on defense of the SAR became controversial. The dispute focused on the Basic Law's provision about stationing the People's Liberation Army (PLA) in the SAR.[19] Some people of Hong Kong objected to stationing the PLA in the SAR and wanted to amend the provision authorizing it. Their major arguments were: First, no foreign forces would invade Hong Kong, so therefore it was not necessary for the PLA to defend it. Hong Kong's police forces were strong enough to play the role of the PLA in the defense of the SAR. Second, the Sino-British Declaration only provided that China "may" send military forces to be stationed in Hong Kong; the declaration did not require that the PLA "must" be there.[20] Therefore, the absence of a PLA garrison in the SAR would be in accord with the joint declaration. Third, since China's sovereignty over Hong Kong is clearly recognized by the joint declaration, it would not be necessary to station troops to symbolize Chinese sovereignty. Finally, if the PLA must be present in Hong Kong, it should be stationed in Shenzhen or Luohu, China's border areas which are close to Hong Kong.[21]

The final version of the Basic Law retains the original policy of stationing the PLA in Hong Kong. In fact, as Chapter 2 discussed, China had no plan to station troops in Hong Kong after 1997. Deng Xiaoping's insistence later that the stationing of the PLA was part of the symbol of China's recovery of sovereignty over Hong Kong left little room for concession.[22] Wang Shuwen argued that the stationing of the PLA in Hong Kong was necessary for national defense and as an embodiment of China's sovereignty over the region, and that the arguments against the PLA in Hong Kong were intended to restrict China's recovery of sovereignty.[23]

Beijing's Authority

The Basic Law states that although the SAR will have a high degree of autonomy, those autonomous powers are authorized by the NPC of the People's Republic. The word *authorize,* used in the Basic Law many times,[24] is the key to understanding China's sovereignty as it prevails over the SAR's autonomy. The Basic Law determines Beijing's authority in stating that "the Central People's Government shall appoint the Chief Executive and the principal officials of the executive authorities of the Hong Kong Special Administrative Region" (BL 15). There is a question as to whether Beijing's appointment of the SAR's officials is a real power or a symbolic one. Can the Central People's Government reject local selection of the chief executive and the "principal officials"? Some Hong Kong residents asked: Is the word *renming* [appoint] equal to the English word "endorse"?[25]

Wang Shuwen, whose works seem to express the Beijing authorities' opinion on the Basic Law, maintained that the power of the Central People's Government to appoint the chief executive and principal officials reflects the PRC's sovereignty over the SAR. Therefore, the power of appointment must be a real power, which gives the Central People's Government authority to approve or veto the local selection of the chief executive and other government officials. If the Central People's Government vetoes the local selection, a new election and consultation or a new nomination should be held in the SAR, and the new candidates should be reported again to the Central People's Government for appointment.[26] However, if the Central People's Government vetoes candidates selected locally for the SAR's major offices, there will be tensions between Beijing and the SAR. As Joseph Y. S. Cheng suggested, "There will be a constitutional crisis with a serious adverse impact on the stability and prosperity of the territory."[27] How can the central authorities avoid such a possible crisis? Wang Shuwen suggested that if the names of candidates were sent to Beijing before a final decision was made in the SAR, the Central People's Government would say whether or not the candidates would be approved. If the Central People's Government confirmed that all candidates would be approved, any potential constitutional crisis would be avoided.[28]

For the Beijing authorities, the power to appoint local officials is not only a symbol of China's sovereignty, like the British Crown's appointing the governor of Hong Kong, but also a mechanism of supervision over the government of the SAR. Also, the chief executive will be the most important position in the SAR, and the Central People's Government's retention of the power to appoint him or her will assure that the SAR will not be too independent. In this case, the practice of Hong Kong people ruling Hong Kong will be on Beijing's terms.

Interpretation and Amendment of the Basic Law

The Basic Law stipulates that Hong Kong's legal system, including all British laws applied in Hong Kong, will remain unchanged except in the area of sovereignty after 1997 and that the Basic Law will be the highest law of the SAR. However, serious disputes occurred over the question of which authority would have the power to interpret the Basic Law. In China, the constitution makes it clear that it is the NPC, the Chinese legislature, that interprets the Chinese Constitution and laws. But in Hong Kong and other territories where common law systems apply, it is the courts that interpret laws. Albert H. Y. Chen, a constitutional law expert of Hong Kong, explained that the different procedures for the interpretation of laws may result from different political ideologies. The common law system stresses the importance of separation of the executive, legislative, and judicial authorities. However, in socialist China the NPC is not only the only legislative authority but also the supreme "organ of state power," which exercises unified political power on behalf of the people. All other authorities, such as the executive, judiciary, and procuratorial organs, are derived from and accountable to the NPC system.[29] The Basic Law states that the power to interpret the Basic Law will be vested in the NPC Standing Committee, and power to amend the Basic Law will be vested in the NPC (BL 158, 159). Also, although courts of the SAR are authorized to interpret the Basic Law, they cannot interpret provisions concerning the responsibility of the central authorities or the relationship between Beijing and the SAR. On cases involving these provisions, the court of the SAR must seek interpretation by the NPC Standing Committee (BL 158).

During the drafting process, the regulations about interpretation and amendment of the Basic Law aroused serious debate among the Basic Law drafters and the Hong Kong people.[30] Some Hong Kong residents opposed vesting the power to interpret the Basic Law in the NPC Standing Committee. They argued: (1) This regulation contravenes the Sino-British Joint Declaration. In Annex I of the declaration, it was clearly written that "the Hong Kong Special Administrative Region will be vested with executive, legislative and independent judicial power, including that of the final adjudication." The declaration does not clarify that Beijing will interpret the Basic Law. (2) If Beijing alone were vested with the power to interpret, the entire Basic Law would be meaningless. If the power of interpretation were to be vested in the NPC Standing Committee, the interpretation would be likely to follow the will of the leaders of the Communist Party. (3) The interpretation of the Basic Law should be the power of the judiciary, but the NPC Standing Committee is not a judiciary institution. Therefore, this regulation would weaken the SAR's independent judicial power.[31] Martin Lee, a Basic Law drafter from Hong Kong and a leading prodemocracy liberal, indicated that he fought with the mainland drafters on interpretation of the Basic Law for four years during the drafting process. Lee insisted that the power of interpretation of the Basic Law may be vested in the NPC Standing Committee; but the courts of the Hong Kong SAR should be allowed to interpret all the provisions of this law. Otherwise, Lee asserted, the SAR's power of final adjudication would be diminished.[32]

Even those Hong Kong residents who were not against the regulations about interpretation and amendment of the Basic Law had their reservations. These individuals believed that the scope of "the affairs which were the responsibility of the Central authorities" and of those matters "concerning the relationship between the Central People's Government and the local authorities" should be defined. They also complained that Article 158 failed to indicate who had the power to define the matters concerning the relationship between the central and local authorities.[33] Some argued that the SAR should have more power to amend the Basic Law.[34]

Wang Shuwen argued that Hong Kong had already gotten enough powers in the interpretation and amendment of the Basic Law. He explained that China's constitution stipulates that only the NPC Standing Committee has the power to interpret laws. However, in the application of this function, the Standing Committee also authorizes the Supreme Court, the Supreme Procuratorate, and the State Council to interpret laws in certain areas. In contrast, no local governments have power to interpret laws, with the exception of the courts of the SAR, which were authorized with such power because of Hong Kong's different judicial system. Moreover, the courts of the SAR would interpret all the provisions of the Basic Law except those relating to the central authorities. Wang concluded that the power of interpretation vested in the NPC Standing Committee is limited only to matters concerning the responsibility of the central authorities or the relationship between the central authorities and the SAR. In addition, the NPC Standing Committee would consult a Committee for the Basic Law of the Hong Kong SAR[35] before the Standing Committee made its interpretation. In this way, the power of interpretation vested in the NPC Standing Committee would not interfere with the judicial independence and power of final adjudication of the SAR.[36]

According to Wang, the procedures of interpretation of laws by the European Community (EC) were consulted when Article 158 of the Basic Law was enacted by the BLDC. The EC has its own laws, which are applied to all of its member states that are sovereign. According to the treaty of the EC, the power of interpretation of laws of the EC is vested in the EC Court located in Luxembourg, not in the EC's member states. In addition, the courts of the EC member states may request the EC Court to interpret certain EC laws when the national judicial bodies try cases. If a trial involves the interpretation of EC laws and if that will result in a final adjudication in a member state, the courts of member states must ask the EC Court to interpret before making their final judgment. Wang further argued that the nature of the relationship between the SAR and the Central People's Government, on the one hand, and the relationship between EC member states and the EC itself, on the other, are fundamentally different. All of the EC's member states are sovereign states, but Hong Kong will be only a Special Administrative Region. However, since even the courts of EC member states must seek interpretations of EC laws by the EC Court, why cannot the courts of the SAR, as local courts, seek the interpretation of the NPC Standing Committee?[37]

In conclusion, the NPC and its Standing Committee's power of interpretation and amendment of the Basic Law stresses the central authorities over the

SAR. For the policymakers in Beijing, the sovereignty of the central authorities cannot be encroached upon in any way whatsoever. Also, the legal and judicial system will not be completely independent of the supervision of the central authorities.

The Power to Decide a State of Emergency in the SAR

The Basic Law establishes that a state of emergency in the SAR will be declared by the NPC on one of the following two conditions: (1) the country is in a state of war with a foreign state; (2) a turmoil has occurred within the SAR, and that turmoil endangers the national unity or security and is beyond the control of the government of the Hong Kong SAR (art. 18, sec. 4).

Some Hong Kong residents worried that this regulation meant that the central government could at any moment abandon the Basic Law and replace it with other national laws. These people hoped that the government of the SAR, not the Central People's Government, would decide whether the SAR was "in turmoil beyond control" and whether Hong Kong should be under a state of emergency. They argued that the central government and the Hong Kong citizens might see things differently, and gave as an example the demonstration in 1989 of a million Hong Kong inhabitants in support of the Beijing students. Was this activity "a turmoil beyond control?"[38]

Wang Shuwen defended the provision and argued that it was "reasonable," because the law specified the two conditions under which the state of emergency would be announced. In the first condition, if the whole country were in a state of war against a foreign country and the central government issued wartime policy, it would be impossible for the SAR, as a part of China, to be out of a state of war. In the second condition, if the turmoil in the SAR were endangering the life and property of the people and the national integrity, and also could not be controlled by the local government, it would be necessary for the Central People's Government to intervene.[39]

Conclusion

Both China's sovereignty and Hong Kong's autonomy were specified in the Basic Law. It is clear that the central authorities not only conceded the government of the SAR tremendous power but that the central authorities also are sovereign. Beijing's sovereignty over Hong Kong can be perceived in two aspects. First, the Basic Law specifies that China is sovereign over Hong Kong, that Hong Kong is "an inalienable part" of the PRC, and that only Hong Kong's Chinese citizens will be qualified to govern the SAR. Second, the central authorities in Beijing are sovereign over the local authorities of the SAR. The sovereignty of the central government is stressed in several provisions of the Basic Law, such as its responsibility for the foreign affairs and defense of the

SAR, its power to appoint major local governmental officials, and the NPC's power to interpret and amend the Basic Law.

China's stress on sovereignty in these two areas may result from Chinese perceptions of history. Historically, Hong Kong was ruled by Britain for over 150 years, and the region is more British than Chinese in terms of political and legal systems. The provisions discussed above can be seen as efforts to end British political influence in Hong Kong. Also, the Chinese government officials perceived that their sovereignty over the SAR was an assurance of the fundamental interests of both Beijing and the SAR. In his speech in 1987, Deng Xiaoping said that no one could assure that "Hong Kong would be entirely free from disturbance and destructive force." Deng continued:

> If the central government gives up all its rights and powers, there would be chaos and Hong Kong's interests would be adversely affected. Thus the central government's reservation of certain powers could only be beneficial to Hong Kong. We should soberly consider this: will Hong Kong encounter problems that cannot be solved without Peking acting on its behalf? In the past, whenever Hong Kong has encountered such problems it has always had Britain to count on. There will be problems that you cannot solve without the central government acting on your behalf.[40]

Clearly, Deng perceived those powers reserved by the central government to be more a benefit to the SAR than a restriction of the local autonomy. In his argument he revealed the Chinese concept of sovereignty and the guiding principle in Beijing's sovereignty over the SAR. In addition, as Chapter 4 shows, the central government's reservation of sovereign powers over local autonomous governments in certain areas is normal practice. The differences between the central government and the local entity are only a matter of how the relationship between sovereignty and autonomy is to be established in that case. Differences between the central authorities and Hong Kong are understandable. The real issue is how the central authorities will exercise their powers after 1997.

It should be noted that concerning the relationship between the central authorities' sovereignty and the SAR's autonomy, disputes occurred not only between Beijing and Hong Kong, but also between the Hong Kong citizens themselves. *Zixun Baogao* [Consultative Report], collections of Hong Kong citizens' opinions solicited by the BLCC, demonstrated that there was also substantial support for the provisions for central sovereignty. Since most of these opinions are similar to those of Wang Shuwen's, this chapter does not introduce these views.

As for the local dissatisfaction with the provisions about China's sovereignty in the Basic Law, obviously, distrust of the government in Beijing was a major cause. Another source for the central-local unease can be traced to different legal and political systems, which resulted in different ways of thinking. As David J. Clark, who obviously disagreed with the Chinese view of sovereignty, wrote:

> The Chinese view of sovereignty is, by modern standards, rather primitive. . . .
> In the Chinese view sovereignty is absolute and indivisible and may not be
> infringed upon by either citizens or foreign states. . . . The modern view is that
> the sovereignty of the state may be divided, as in federal states, and may be
> limited by appropriate international or domestic arrangements.[41]

No matter how one explains the causes of disagreement between the central
government and Hong Kong, these differences were not eliminated by the final
enactment of the Basic Law. As will be shown in Chapter 7, even during the
transition period disputes that involved China's sovereignty and Hong Kong's
autonomy occurred over the establishment of the Hong Kong Court of Final
Appeal. After 1997, those differences will appear again when the Basic Law is
carried out. Only when mutual trust and mutually acceptable forms for relationships between the central authorities and the SAR are established will the disputes over sovereignty be diminished. The Basic Law only outlines a simple
structure for the exercise of sovereignty and autonomy. The implementation of
the law in the real politics after 1997 will be much tougher than the drafting of
the law on paper. However, the SAR's autonomy will be easily infringed upon
if the central authorities strictly stress their sovereignty in a central-local conflict, because the central authorities are much more powerful than the local
government, and because the mainland's socialism will be dominant under the
one country, two systems formula.

Notes

1. Lane, *Sovereignty and the Status Quo*, 102. What is the difference between a
treaty and a declaration in terms of interpretation in international law? According to J. L.
Brierly, an expert on international law at Oxford University, "Contractual engagements
between states are called by various names—treaties, conventions, pacts, declarations,
protocols. None of these terms has an absolutely fixed meaning; but a treaty suggests the
most formal kind of agreement; . . . a declaration is generally used of a law-declaring or
law-making agreement." See J. L. Brierly, *The Law of Nations: An Introduction to the
International Law and Peace*, 6th ed. (New York: Oxford University Press, 1963), 317.
Because of this difference, the Chinese refused to use the word "treaty" as the term for
the 1984 Sino-British agreement.
2. See the 1984 Sino-British Joint Declaration.
3. Wang, *Xianggang Tebie Xingzhengqu Jibenfa Daolun*, 90.
4. Ibid.
5. Albert H. K. Chen, "The Relationship Between the Central Government and
the SAR," in Peter Wesley-Smith and Albert H. Y. Chen, eds., *The Basic Law and Hong
Kong's Future* (Hong Kong: Butterworths, 1988), 117.
6. Robin Oakley, "Passports Scheme Is a Delicate Balancing Act," *The Times*, 21
December 1989, 6. After Hong Kong and Kowloon were ceded to Great Britain, the
Chinese inhabitants in the two regions became British subjects. Since the New Territories were leased in 1898, all inhabitants in the region were also naturalized and became
British subjects. Before 1962, all Chinese inhabitants in Hong Kong were entitled to be
full British citizens and had the right to live permanently in Britain. However, this right

of abode in Britain for the citizens of Hong Kong was abolished that year. In 1982, Parliament passed a new nationality law under which British Dependent Territories citizens (BDTCs) were created. The new nationality law clarifies that the BDTCs can continue to get assistance from British consular staff when traveling in foreign countries, but have no right of abode in Britain. This new nationality law was seen in Hong Kong as a sign of London's desire to distance itself from Hong Kong because under the same law the inhabitants in Gibraltar and Falkland were granted full British citizenship with the right of abode in Britain. In the memorandums Britain and China exchanged as an annex of the 1984 Joint Declaration, the two countries stated their positions on the nationality of Hong Kong citizens. Britain declared, "All persons who on 30 June 1997 are, by virtue of a connection with Hong Kong, British Dependent Territories citizens (BDTCs) under the law in force in the United Kingdom will cease to be BDTCs with effect from 1 July 1997, but will be eligible to retain an appropriate status which, without conferring the right of abode in the United Kingdom, will entitle them to continue to use passports issued by the Government of the United Kingdom." China declared: "Under the Nationality Law of the People's Republic of China, all Hong Kong Chinese compatriots, whether they are holders of the 'British Department Territories citizens' passports or not, are Chinese nationals." Nevertheless, the Chinese government would "permit Chinese nationals in Hong Kong who were previously called 'British Dependent Territories citizens' to use travel documents . . . for the purpose of travelling to other states and regions." In addition, China stated that the BDTCs would not be entitled to British consular protection in the Hong Kong SAR and other parts of the PRC. See Miners, *The Government of Politics of Hong Kong*, 4th ed., 16, 27; and the "Exchange of Memoranda" annexed to the 1984 Sino-British Joint Declaration. Therefore, London's 1990 grant of "right of abode in Great Britain" changed the status of 225,000 Hong Kong citizens from BDTCs to full British citizens.

7. Robin Oakley, "Passports Scheme Is a Delicate Balancing Act," *The Times*, 21 December 1989, 6; and Philip Webster, "Tory and Labor Attack Bill: Points to Win Passports in Hong Kong," *The Times*, 15 April 1990, 1.

8. Philip Webster, "Hong Kong Told of Citizenship by Points," *The Times*, 5 April 1990, 2.

9. Jonathan Braude, "Campaigners Give Hurd's Plan a Guarded Welcome," *The Times*, 21 December 1991, 6; Emily Lau, "Skimming the Cream," *FEER*, 4 January 1990, 9.

10. Philip Webster, "Tory and Labor Attack Bill: Points to Win Passports in Hong Kong," *The Times*, 15 April 1990, 1.

11. "China Regrets HK Decision by London," *China Daily*, 30 July 1990, 1.

12. The principal officials of the SAR include secretaries and deputy secretaries of departments, directors of bureaus, the Commissioner Against Corruption, the Director of Audit, the Commissioner of Police, the Director of Immigration, and the Commissioner of Customs and Excise. See BL. 48.

13. Wang, *Xianggang Tebie Xingzhengqu Jibenfa Daolun*, 68–69.

14. Ibid.

15. Jibenfa Zixun Weiyuanhui, ed., *Zixun Baogao*, 3:7. In the following part of this chapter, Hong Kong citizens' views are cited from this valuable *Zixun Baogao*, which includes collections of opinions of the Hong Kong people on the draft Basic Law. These opinions were solicited by the BLCC for the further improvement of the draft Basic Law. However, the opinions collected in the *Zixun Baogao* are not polls on certain particular questions but a record of all opinions solicited. Therefore, arguments in the *Zixun Baogao* may be only one person's opinion, or they may be opinions of large numbers of Hong Kong citizens.

16. Jibenfa Zixun Weiyuanhui, ed., *Zixun Baogao*, 2:29.

17. See *Constitution of the People's Republic of China* (1982), Article 85.

18. Wang, *Xianggang Tebie Xingzhengqu Jibenfa Daolun*, 89.
19. Article 14, Section 3 states: "Military forces stationed by the Central People's Government in the Hong Kong Special Administrative Region for defence shall not interfere in the local affairs of the region. The Government of the Hong Kong Special Administrative Region may, when necessary, ask the Central People's Government for assistance from the garrison in the maintenance of public order and in disaster relief."
20. Actually, this is not true. Article 12 of "Annex I" of the Sino-British Joint Declaration states that "military forces sent by the Central People's Government to be stationed in the Hong Kong Special Administrative Region for the purpose of defence shall not interfere in the internal affairs of the Hong Kong Special Administrative Region." The declaration uses neither the word *ke* [may] nor *yiding* [must].
21. Jibenfa Zixun Weiyuanhui, ed., *Zixun Baogao*, 3:33–39, 5:48–54, and vol. 2, the whole chapter "About the Stationing of the Military Forces."
22. David Bonavia, "Get Back in Step: Deng Blasts Two Colleagues Who Said PLA Troops Will Not Be Stationed in Hong Kong," *FEER*, 7 June 1984, 13–14.
23. Wang, *Xianggang Tebie Xingzhengqu Jibenfa Daolun*, 95–97.
24. See BL 1, sec.2; BL 125; BL 153, sec.2; BL 154, 155, 158.
25. Jibenfa Zixun Weiyuanhui, ed., *Zixun Baogao*, 3:40.
26. Wang, *Xianggang Tebie Xingzhengqu Jibenfa Daolun*, 98.
27. Joseph Y. S. Cheng, "Political System," in Wesley-Smith and Chen, eds., *The Basic Law and Hong Kong's Future*, 147.
28. Wang, *Xianggang Tebie Xingzhengqu Jibenfa Daolun*, 98. Joseph Y. S. Cheng offered a similar suggestion. He said: "It will obviously be politically prudent for the Chinese authorities to indicate their preferences and objections before the selection process so as to influence the outcome and thus to avoid the actual use of their veto power. It appears that the community is willing to concede that the CE [the Chief Executive] has to be someone acceptable to Beijing." Cheng, "Political System," in Wesley-Smith and Chen, eds., *The Basic Law and Hong Kong's Future*, 147.
29. Albert H. Y. Chen, "The Relationship Between the Central Government and the SAR," in Wesley-Smith and Chen, eds., *The Basic Law and Hong Kong's Future*, 130.
30. Concerning the debates among the Basic Law drafters, see Martin C. M. Lee, "A Tale of Two Articles," in Wesley-Smith and Chen, eds., *The Basic Law and Hong Kong's Future*, 309–325.
31. Jibenfa Zixun Weiyuanhui, ed., *Zixun Baogao*, 2:263–269.
32. Martin C. M. Lee, "A Tale of Two Articles," in Wesley-Smith and Chen, eds., *The Basic Law and Hong Kong's Future*, 309–325.
33. Jibenfa Zixun Weiyuanhui, ed., *Zixun Baogao*, 2:263–269.
34. Ibid., 2:268–270.
35. The proposed Committee for the Basic Law of the Hong Kong Special Administrative Region is to be a working body under the NPC Standing Committee. The function of the Committee for the Basic Law is "to study questions arising from the implementation of Articles 17, 18, 158, and 159 of the Basic Law" and submit its views to the NPC Standing Committee. There will be twelve members in the Committee for the Basic Law, six from the mainland and six from Hong Kong, including persons from the legal profession, appointed by NPC Standing Committee. See the Basic Law, Appendix: "Proposal by the Drafting Committee for the Basic Law of the Hong Kong Special Administrative Region on the Establishment of the Committee for the Basic Law of the Hong Kong Special Administrative Region Under the Standing Committee of the National People's Congress."
36. Wang, *Xianggang Tebie Xingzhengqu Jibenfa Daolun*, 101–105; concerning the Chinese view on this provision, also see Yang Yi, "'Controversy' Over Hong Kong's Draft Basic Law," *China Daily*, 18 June 1988, 4, in FBIS, 22 June 1988, 30.

37. Wang, *Xianggang Tebie Xingzhengqu Jibenfa Daolun*, 104.
38. Jibenfa Zixun Weiyuanhui, ed., *Zixun Baogao*, 3:46–52.
39. Wang, *Xianggang Tebie Xingzhengqu Jibenfa Daolun*, 98–99.
40. Rafferty, *City on the Rocks*, 451.
41. David J. Clark, "The Basic Law, One Document, Two Systems," in Ming K. Chan and David J. Clark, eds., *The Hong Kong Basic Law: Blueprint for "Stability and Prosperity" under Chinese Sovereignty?* (Armonk, N. Y.: An East Gate Book, 1991), 38.

6

China's Modernization
and the Hong Kong Question

This chapter addresses two questions: Will the government in Beijing honor the 1984 Sino-British Declaration and the Basic Law? Is China preparing well for the recovery of Hong Kong?

Though no one knows the future, the direction government actions are taking can be analyzed by examining their roots and tracing their developments while taking into account external conditions that may affect trends. The 1984 Hong Kong agreement, the initiative of one country, two systems, and the enactment of the Basic Law were compatible with China's modernization drive and economic reform since 1978. In other words, China's flexible policy toward Hong Kong and the enactment of the Basic Law were products of China's modernization. Deng Xiaoping made it clear that peaceful settlement of the Hong Kong, Macao, and Taiwan questions under the principle of one country, two systems was an important aspect of socialism with Chinese characteristics.[1] In examining Beijing's policy toward Hong Kong and tracing its developments, this chapter focuses on how China's modernization drive is related to policy toward Hong Kong, and how China's economic reform is favorable to Hong Kong's return under one country, two systems. The discussion will show that Deng's reforms in the last sixteen years assure Hong Kong's capitalism and that Beijing will implement its one country, two systems policy after 1997.

Deng Xiaoping's Economic Reform and Open Door Policy

As described in Chapter 2, China's policy toward Hong Kong was formulated in the 1970s and early 1980s when Deng Xiaoping initiated his new modernization programs. The word "new" is used here because China's modernization was first proposed by Mao Zedong in 1957, when the Chinese socialist order was formally established. Mao called for "uniting the people of all nationalities in our country for the new battle, the battle against nature" and inspired the people to "make China a socialist country with modern industry, modern agriculture, and modern science and culture."[2] This article is the Communists' earliest appeal for modernization. In his report on government work to the Third NPC in 1964, Premier Zhou Enlai, on behalf of the party and Chairman Mao, proposed for the first time to realize "four modernizations"—industry, agriculture, national defense, and science and technology—by the end of the century.[3]

Mao did not fully put his modernization programs into practice. Instead, he launched several political movements, such as the Anti-Rightist Movement in 1957, the class struggle movement in the early 1960s, and, particularly, the Great Cultural Revolution of 1966 to 1976, which delayed China's modernization. In addition, Mao's target dates for modernization were often unrealistic. In the 1950s, Mao initiated the Great Leap Forward, wanting to modernize in a short period. The slogans of "overtaking Great Britain in fifteen years and catching up with the United States in thirty years" show that Mao underestimated the effort needed to modernize his backward country. The Great Leap Forward resulted in economic chaos and disaster. Deng Xiaoping and his followers learned from Mao's lessons.

Deng regained power in 1978, and gradually defeated Mao's faction within the party. Deng persuaded the party to abandon Mao's slogan of "class struggle" and concentrate on the four modernizations. In the early period of the new modernization drive, Deng and his followers thought that the four modernizations could be realized by the end of the century.[4] However, a more realistic strategy for modernization was adopted in the early 1980s. At the Twelfth National Congress of the Communist Party of 1982, Hu Yaobang—general secretary of the party and a strong supporter of Deng—proposed that China would quadruple its 1980 GNP by the year 2000, at which time the country's GNP would reach 2.8 trillion yuan.[5] Later, China developed a more mature modernization blueprint. In his speech in the Soviet Union on May 17, 1991, Jiang Zemin, general secretary of the party, asserted that China's three-step strategy for modernization was:

> First, to take ten years to double the 1980 gross national product in terms of constant prices and solve the problem of inadequate food and clothing. We have accomplished this task ahead of schedule.
> Secondly, to quadruple the 1980 GNP in terms of constant prices by the end of the century so that the people nationwide could live a relatively comfortable life. We are now working hard towards this end.
> Thirdly, to make China's per capita GNP reach in general the level of moderately industrialized nations by the middle of 21st century, basically realizing socialist modernization.[6]

Yet it is more important to know what China achieved under Deng's new modernization drive than what the Chinese leaders planned to do. Revolutionary changes have taken place in China since 1978 that will significantly affect China's policy toward Hong Kong.

Shifting from a Planned Economy to a Market Economy

Before Deng's reforms, the Chinese were fettered by the Stalinist model of a state-planned economy. Influenced by Marxist ideology, Mao's Communists perceived the capitalist economy, based on private ownership and the free market, as erroneous because capitalism existed on the basis of the exploitation of the working class and hindered the development of productive forces. The Communists believed that only the Soviet model of a planned economy, as a correction of the anarchy of capitalism, reflected the superiority of the socialist order. A large number of Chinese Communist leaders had studied in the 1920s and 1930s in the Soviet Union, and these officials were impressed by the achievements of Soviet industrialization. Chinese Communists believed that China had to follow the Soviet socialist road. They had a saying that the "Soviet Union's today would be China's tomorrow."

How was the Soviet model of socialism applied in China? In 1954, when the People's Republic had been in existence for five years, the Stalinist planned economic system was formally established. According to a Chinese official reference, the new economic system operated as follows: Each year, the State Planning Commission made a complete plan for agriculture, industry, transport, and the postal and telecommunications services. These plans were passed down to the various enterprises by the ministries of the Central People's Government. The plans were so concrete that they involved each key link in the chain of national economy, including production targets, the amount of investment, the distribution of materials, the budget, workers and staff, wages, and the purchase and marketing of main commodities, foreign trade, and prices.[7] At the beginning, because materials and resources were limited as a result of the decades-long civil war, the planned economy played a positive role in the recovery of the economy and national industrialization. However, in the following decades the centralized system disclosed its weaknesses. Because the State Planning Commission determined each link of the production process, the production of the enterprise was not for profit, but for fulfilling the volume of the output that was required. The quality of that output (except in the military-industrial sector) was often not an issue. Therefore, the enterprise lost its initiative for increasing output of production and development of new products and techniques. As a result, the central planning system produced low efficiency, low quality, and bureaucrats.

In the rural areas, Mao established the People's Commune system, under which private lands were banned and the village became a production unit. After paying the state taxes in kind, the village, which was called a production team, distributed a portion of the harvest to each household according to its labor and size. The peasants could not sell their products in the market. Because incomes of the peasants were so low, they lost enthusiasm for production under the system. Liu Shaoqi, then President of China, and Deng Xiaoping tried to reform this system in the 1960s but failed because of Mao's opposition.

Until Deng appealed for his new modernization drive in the late 1970s, the unprofitable planned system and People's Commune organization had not been changed at all. When Deng called for reforms, Chinese economists debated whether it was necessary to reform the planning system and introduce the market mechanism. Xue Muqiao, a noted Chinese economist, argued in 1980 that reforms should focus on the economic management system: "Better management requires that our enterprises have certain rights over their own personnel, finances and materials, over supply, production and marketing."[8] In 1980, the concepts of market economy and competition were new to the People's Republic. Wu Tongguang, a Chinese scholar, argued that the traditional theory that competition meant capitalism was wrong and that "competition itself does not indicate the characteristics of the relations of production. It is correlated with the law of movement in a commodity economy, that is, the role of law of value." Wu further pointed out that since there were still commodities production and exchange in a socialist economy, and production and circulation were still regulated by the law of value, there should be competition among commodity producers. He argued:

> If the consumers may freely select what they want on the market, the factories which are in a favorable position in competition by supplying cheap but good commodity will have a better future.[9]

Wu's article may be the earliest appeal for a market economy after Deng launched his reforms.

At that time, not all economists accepted the market economy theory. For example, Jin Mingjun argued that competition was a commodity producer's fight against other producers and that "the essence of competition is exclusiveness." Jin concluded that competition protected "sacred private ownership" of a capitalist society:

> I think that there will be three harmful developments if competition is practised in a socialist economy: (1) Competition will bring along anarchism in production and major imbalances in the national economy. (2) Competition will corrupt the ideology of the party organization and that of the workers and staff. (3) Competition will undermine, in a fundamental way, the socialist relationship between the state and the enterprise and between enterprises themselves.[10]

Jin's argument represented Communism's traditional attitude toward market economy. Deng's first imperative was to break the orthodox thinking of Mao's era and allow scholars to introduce the new theory for his reforms. The mechanism of the market began to be introduced at that period of time. Zhu Jiaming, an economist, argued that "competition helped capitalism create a great mass of wealth and high productive forces in the short span of several hundred years. We must acknowledge the positive role that competition played in history." Zhu suggested that the market economy should be expanded and more goods should be allowed to enter the market, that the enterprise collective should have more power of decision and should be allowed to sell its products directly in the market, and that the practice of setting prices by the state in a unified way should be reformed.[11]

In fact, at the end of the 1970s the key disputes concerned whether the planning system would be continued. These disputes contrast with the overwhelming support of a free market economy by 1992. However, the disputes marked a beginning for the introduction of the market economy. Policymakers in Beijing partially accepted the argument for the introduction of market mechanism and applied it, on a trial basis, in Deng's reform programs. However, for a decade the party did not solve the theoretical issue of the relationship between a planned and a market economy. Traditionally, the party held that the planned economy was socialist while a market economy was capitalist. The party's dilemma can be perceived in party general secretary Jiang Zemin's speech in 1991. Jiang said:

> The excessively centralized system of [the] planned economy of the past was gradually transformed into a system and an operational mechanism that combine a planned economy with market regulation and are suited to the development of a planned commodity economy based on public ownership.[12]

Jiang's speech indicated the difficult situation of China's economic reforms by 1991—the Communist Party lacked a new theory to justify Deng's reforms. On one hand, the party had not been bold enough to abandon the theory of a planned economy, which was considered the foundation of socialism. On the other hand, the application of market economics was really workable; and the nonstate economic sectors became the major source of China's rapid economic growth. China came to a crossroads.

The turning point occurred in the spring of 1992, when the party finally announced that the planned economy and the market economy should not be the standard by which to distinguish socialism from capitalism, and that the economy could be managed through both planning and the market. This theoretical breakthrough was again a contribution of Deng Xiaoping. During his tour of Southern China in the spring of 1992, Deng challenged the traditional theory that only a planned economy is the foundation of socialism. He argued:

> one does not essentially distinguish between socialism and capitalism by the amount of planning and the number of markets. The planned economy is not equal to socialism for capitalism also has planning; the market economy is not equal to capitalism for socialism also has markets. Both planning and the market are economic means.[13]

The Chinese government finally decided to reform its economic system toward a free market. The introduction of market economics is one of the most important achievements and major characteristics of Deng's reforms. In fact, Deng's talk and the party's new policy favoring a market economy represented the conclusion of China's reform efforts in the last sixteen years, because various economic systems, based on the market, had emerged in socialist China. Components of these systems include:

1.   The peasant-household-responsibility system: In rural areas, where 800 million peasants live, the People's Commune system was dismantled and replaced with the peasant-household-responsibility system. Under the new system, land was distributed to peasant households, which become the basic units of production. Peasants have the right to decide what, when, and how they will cultivate their land and are free to sell products in the market after paying taxes in kind.

2.   Private business in both urban and rural areas: By September 1992 there were fourteen million private businesses with twenty million employees, which were involved in areas such as commerce, industry, construction, and transportation.[14] Another source indicated that by the end of 1992, there were 15.3 million private industrial and commercial units, with 24.6 million employees.[15] The private sector continued to grow rapidly in 1993. According to an official source, by the end of June 1993, individual businesses and privately owned enterprises reached 15.48 million and 184,000, respectively, 9.8 percent and 31.8 percent increases over the end of the last year. The economic strength of private enterprises also increased dramatically in the first half of 1993. Their average capital increased from 159,000 yuan (about US$26,140) in 1992 to 246,000 yuan (about US$43,175), an increase of 54.7 percent. By the end of June 1993, individual businesspeople accumulated a total capital of 67.66 billion yuan (about US$10.24 billion), up 34.7 percent over the same period of the previous year. Also, in the first half of 1993, the output value created by private business in the areas of industry, construction, and transport topped 58.41 billion yuan (about US$10.24 billion), up 35.9 percent over the same period in 1992.[16] Among the private-business owners emerged the first group of millionaires in socialist China. According to one Chinese report, there were 500 private enterprises whose assets were more than one million yuan. In Southern China, hundreds of millionaires appeared one after another.[17]

3.   Price reform: The transition from a state-controlled price system to a market price system was one of the major achievements in Deng's reform. In 1978, prices of 97 percent of retail commodities were fixed by the state, while prices of 94 percent of agriculture commodities and of 100 percent of capital goods were fixed by the state. Fifteen years later, the percentage of state-fixed prices in the three categories—retail commodities, agriculture goods, and capital goods—were dramatically reduced. In 1992, only 10 percent of retail commodities were priced by the government, while 15 percent of agriculture goods and 20 percent of capital goods were priced by the government. By the end of 1993, the number of prices of goods in the three categories that were fixed by the state further dwindled to 5 percent, 10 percent, and 15 percent respectively.[18]

4.   Rural industry: Medium- and small-scale enterprises, run by rural authorities and based on market regulation instead of planning management, were established. These rural industries demonstrated high efficiency in production. By the end of 1992, rural enterprise production topped 1,000 billion yuan, accounting for 39 percent of China's gross national product.[19]

5.   The introduction of Western management skills into state-run enterprises: The mechanism of competition was also introduced into state-owned enterprises. Consequently, salaries, bonuses, and promotions were decided by the quality and quantity of one's work. The enterprise-contract system was one of the reforms in state-run enterprises. Under the new system, the enterprise contracted with the state for certain production quotas. Apart from tax payments and a proportion of profits submitted to the state, the contracted enterprise was free to distribute the remaining profits as reinvestment funds, collective welfare, and bonuses for managers and employees. The more profit the enterprise made, the more funds it would reserve for itself and the more income the employers and managers would get. However, if an enterprise failed to fulfill its quotas in the contract, managers and employees would lose their bonuses. In addition, the enterprise was authorized to fire unqualified workers and employ new workers. Moreover, the Bankruptcy Bill authorized the government to announce the bankruptcy of a state enterprise when it incurred losses over several years. These new policies destroyed the traditional "iron rice bowl"[20] in the Chinese socialist system, encouraged the initiative of enterprises, and improved the living standards of a majority of the workers.

After Deng's tour of Southern China in the spring of 1992, the Chinese further abandoned the unprofitable planned sectors in their economic system and launched market-oriented reforms. From one perspective, the breaking away from the Stalinist planned economy and the introduction of the market economy are the most significant characteristics of Deng's reforms—more important even than doubling the GNP in the 1980s[21] and improving the living standard of the people, because an economic boom resulted from this policy change. Though the party continued to emphasize the "four cardinal principles" as the guiding ideological foundation of the country, Marx, Lenin, and Mao were no longer as respected as before. During Mao's era, quotations from Marx, Lenin and Mao were the highest instructions of the party and the country; but this phenomenon does not exist any more. One clear difference between Mao's era and Deng's era is that current Chinese policymakers tend to favor a more pragmatic theory—"socialism with Chinese characteristics."

Opening to the Outside World

Another characteristic of Deng's reform was the "open door" policy [Kaifang Zhengce].[22] From 1949 to the 1970s, China's economic contact with foreign countries, especially Western capitalist countries, was narrow and limited, partly because of the Western countries' economic blockade against China, beginning with the Korean War. Deng's open door policy was announced when China's relations with the West improved in the 1970s. The open door policy was aimed at expanding economic contacts with foreign countries, particularly economically advanced capitalist countries, and importing foreign capital, technology, and advanced managerial expertise to promote modernization. For these purposes, the Chinese government established the Special Economic Zones (SEZs) and opened coastal regions to the outside world.

China set up five SEZs in the 1980s. SEZs were not new. Before the emergence of China's SEZs, there were about 300 special economic zones established by seventy-five countries and regions. These entities were also called free trading zones, processing-exporting zones, or tax-free trading zones. The purpose of these zones is to provide favorable conditions to attract foreign investors who manufacture export-oriented products.[23] The economic motivation behind China's SEZs was similar to that of other countries and regions. Nevertheless, China was the first socialist country to establish SEZs. Moreover, China's zones also were expected to link mainland China and Hong Kong, Macao, and Taiwan and to help underpin China's reunification. China's SEZs were Shenzhen, Zhuhai, and Shantou, located in Guangdong Province; Xiamen in Fujian Province; and Hainan, which covered the whole Hainan Province. Table 6.1 shows the location, size, population, and date of establishment for these zones.

After the first four SEZs were established, Xu Dixin, a well-known Chinese economist, said the functions of the SEZs were several. They included introducing advanced technology and equipment; regulating production according to market demands and improving efficiency of production; absorbing a considerable amount of foreign exchange; serving as experimental units in economic reform; and providing jobs.[24] Therefore, China's SEZs were part of a larger plan for economic reform.

The five zones are all located near Hong Kong, Macao, and Taiwan. Shenzhen is adjacent to Hong Kong, and the two regions are separated by the small Shenzhen River. The locations of the SEZs are prudent politically and economically. Politically, the SEZs are expected to serve as a bridge for the integration of Hong Kong, Macao, and Taiwan.[25] As the Beijing regime planned,

Table 6.1   China's Special Economic Zones (SEZs)

SEZ	Location	Area (sq. km.)	Population	Time of Establishment
Shenzhen	Guangdong	328	1,020,000	August 1980
Zhuhai	Guangdong	121	190,000	August 1980
Shantou	Guangdong	53	60,000	August 1980
Xiamen	Fujian	131	370,000	August 1980
Hainan	Hainan	34,000	6,540,000	April 1988

Source: Based on Huang Taihe, "Development of China's SEZ," *Beijing Review* 32, no. 12 (8 April 1989): 21.

the economic systems in the zones are similar to those operated in Hong Kong, Macao, and Taiwan, thereby reducing the differences between the mainland and the three regions (Hong Kong, Macao, and Taiwan). Early in 1982, visitors to the SEZs noted that if China could persuade capitalists around the world to invest in the SEZs, there should be no problems to worry Hong Kong capitalists after 1997.[26] In a sense, the establishment of SEZs was an important step for the application of the one country, two systems principle to Hong Kong, Macao, and Taiwan. Also, the SEZs were established to attract economic investments from Hong Kong, Macao, and Taiwan. As expected, a large portion of foreign investment in Shenzhen came from Hong Kong, because of geographical proximity and the same Chinese dialect used by the two cities.

To encourage foreign investment, special policies were formulated for the SEZs. First, the zones were given certain powers to manage their own economies. For example, zone governments enjoyed the same authority as provincial governments to examine and approve new projects. Therefore, the zones enjoyed the power to sanction most of the intended investments. Corporations in the zones were given the power to manage themselves according to market regulation, while corporations in nonzone areas were restricted by regulated prices, planned supplies of raw materials and other links of planned economy. Second, both foreign and domestic enterprises in the zones were given favorable tax policies. Tax rates for enterprises were set at 15 percent, much lower than the rate of more than 30 percent in nonzone areas. Also, preferential treatment was granted to export-oriented and high-technology enterprises in terms of taxation.[27]

As a result of these preferential policies, China attracted many foreign investments to the SEZs. By 1990, some 6,489 projects involving foreign investment were approved, accounting for 26 percent of foreign-funded projects in the country. About US$4.5 billion in foreign capital was invested in the SEZs, accounting for 27 percent of foreign investment in China. Large corporations from about thirty countries and regions—including Hong Kong, Japan, the United States, and Western Europe—invested in the SEZs.[28] Most of the foreign investments in the SEZs came from Hong Kong. For instance, by the end of 1991 Hong Kong accounted for 80 percent of the 4,000 foreign-funded factories in Shenzhen and 65 percent of the foreign capital of US$3.7 billion.[29]

Not only foreign-funded enterprises but also domestic cooperations were set up in the SEZs. In Shenzhen, for instance, there were three types of enterprises: foreign-funded, which produced about 70 percent of total industrial output of the zone; province and municipality-owned; and state-owned. Furthermore, private ownership also existed in Shenzhen.[30]

The SEZs also serve as trial laboratories for China's economic reforms. Varieties of reforms were first tested in Shenzhen. These trials included entering a bid on construction projects; selecting managers by election, public competition, or contract; lifting price restrictions; renting and leasing land; and establishing a foreign currency exchange center and stock market.[31]

Generally, Shenzhen's economic system operated on a market mechanism rather than by state planning. Therefore, establishment of the SEZs narrowed the economic gap between the zones and Hong Kong, and between China and the outside world. In addition, the zones maintained the fastest economic growth in China, and the disparity in living standards between the zones and Hong Kong also was reduced. According to Liang Xiang, the Mayor of Shenzhen, his zone's GNP per capita will be $4,000 by the end of this century,[32] a target to be reached in other areas of the country in forty years. However, according to some leading Chinese economists, not only the SEZs but also the entire Guangdong Province may catch up with the "four Asian dragons"—Hong Kong, Taiwan, Korea, and Singapore—in twenty years.[33]

Because of differences between Shenzhen's economic system and that of other parts of the country, as well as the SEZ's rapid economic growth, Shenzhen was granted legislative power in 1992, giving the Shenzhen Municipal People's Congress and its Standing Committee the right to make and implement rules and regulations reflecting local practical needs. The Shenzhen Municipal People's Government was also granted similar rights.[34] Shenzhen was the first local government to be granted legislative power. The Hainan SEZ was authorized to make its own laws in 1993 and the Xiamen zone was granted that power in 1994. This new legislative progress revealed the dramatic decentralization of power in China.

The second aspect of the open door policy was that fourteen coastal port cities and three coastal regions were opened to the outside world. In 1984, at the suggestion of Deng Xiaoping, China opened the cities of Dalian, Qinhuangdao, Tianjin, Yantai, Qindao, Lianyungang, Nantong, Shanghai, Ningbo, Wenzhou, Fuzhou, Guangzhou, Zhanjiang, and Beihai. At the same time, China opened three larger regions, including the Changjiang (Yangtze) Delta, the Zhujiang (Pearl River) Delta, and Southern Fujian Province. In fact, the east coast of China from the port of Dalian in the north to the Pearl River Delta in the south became an open belt to the outside world, including 291 cities and counties and covering an area of 320,000 square kilometers.[35] In some of the coastal cities, fourteen Economic and Technological Development Zones (ETDZs) were gradually established to attract foreign investors. The ETDZs enjoyed more privileges than the coastal cities but less than the SEZs as regarded foreign economic relations.

According to a Chinese State Statistical Bureau report issued in 1986, two years after the announcement of the opening of the fourteen coastal cities, 2,741 contracts between the cities and foreign investors were signed. These contracts accounted for $1.26 billion, of which the actually invested foreign capital amounted to $320 million, or 13.3 percent more than in 1985. The focus for investments also was changed. Before 1985, foreign capital was mainly invested in service projects such as hotels and recreational facilities. In 1986, foreign investors targeted projects involving high technology and exports. In Shanghai ETDZ, most foreign-funded projects were industrial and technological, manufacturing commodities such as laser products, electronics, and chemicals.[36] According to the Chinese State Land Administration, from 1987 to June of 1990 eighty tracts of land in the SEZs and the ETDZs were leased to foreign developers. Most of the tracts—fifty out of eighty—were awarded to Hong Kong firms, followed by Taiwan companies with fourteen parcels. Five were awarded to Japan; five to Singapore; three to the Philippines; two to the United States; and one to Thailand.[37] In the coastal cities, foreign investors also established their own special investment districts, including the Korean Industrial Park, the Singapore Industrial Park, and the Taiwanese Investment Districts.

In conclusion, the development of the fourteen ETDZs in the open coastal regions was successful. Take the Tianjin ETDZ as an example. By the end of 1993, 1,709 foreign firms from forty-six countries and regions had established their businesses in the zone. Contracted investment volume reached US$2.53 billion, and US$1.66 billion of foreign capital had been employed. Among the foreign investors in the Tianjin zone, the Motorola Company of the United States, which produces half the world's mobile telephones, invested US$120 million. From April 1993, when Motorola began to manufacture goods, to the end of the year, the sales income reached 1 billion yuan and export volume US$10 million. As a result of this success, Motorola decided to increase its investment in the Tianjin zone to US$400 million within three to five years. Kodak, another investor from the United States, signed a contract intended to put in US$140 million in investment in Tianjin zone. Besides foreign-funded firms, there were also many joint ventures in the Tianjin zone, such as Tianjin Yamaha Electronic Musical Instruments (a Sino-Japan joint venture), Tianjin Merlin Gerin (a Sino-France joint venture), and Tianjin De Pu (DPC) Biotechnological and Medical Products (a high-tech Sino-U.S. joint venture).[38]

China's economic reforms and open door policy did not proceed smoothly, and they were challenged by the 1989 Tiananmen incident and the major changes in Eastern Europe and the Soviet Union. Within the Communist Party, conservatives argued that the economic reforms might result in the loss of power for the organization. However, Deng and his followers rejected such an argument and renewed their commitment to reform. Deng stressed that only successful economic development could ensure the power of the Chinese socialist regime. In April 1990, China announced the opening of Pudong, Shanghai City, as a new development area. The planned Pudong Development District was to be different from the five established SEZs. Pudong would be a zone with high-technology industry, a commercial zone with a free port like Hong Kong, and a financial center with foreign banks.

The Pudong Development District covers 350 square kilometers and it is located at an estuary of the Changjiang River. Because of its geographical location, Pudong is ideal for establishing a commercial and transportation center. At the beginning of this century, Dr. Sun Yet-sen proposed, in *Jianguo Fanglue* [Program of National Construction], to develop Pudong and build a large port there. In 1980, Lin Tongyuan, a Chinese-American architect, again suggested developing Pudong. However, for years Chinese leaders disagreed on the role of Pudong in the entire Chinese economic development scheme and on the relationship between development of Pudong and other reform programs as well as between the district and the five SEZs.[39] Finally, it was decided that Pudong would be an industrial, financial, and commercial center. According to Beijing authorities, the development of Pudong will be completed in three periods. The first period (1990–1995) will include infrastructure construction, including the development of transportation, a port, and a power station. The second period (1995–2000) will focus on setting up industrial projects. The entire Pudong development plan will be completed in the third stage (2000–2030), when Pudong will be an industrial, commercial, and financial center.[40]

Shanghai's local economists proposed that Shanghai and Pudong would be prosperous only if Shanghai became a trade center under market mechanisms. The economists maintained that the trade should include not only imports and exports but also exchanges of capital, investment, commodities, real estate, transportation, technology, and information. For Shanghai to become a successful economic center, these economists also believed that the city should borrow the experience of successful capitalist economies, including early industrial Britain, postwar Japan, Hong Kong, Taiwan, South Korea, and Singapore.[41] Though the economists did not tell how and what capitalist experiences should be emulated, their proposal demonstrated that they wanted to establish a market system in Pudong.

Within five months after the opening of Pudong, 1,350 foreign business delegations visited. About 4,000 foreign businessmen—including potential investors from Japan, the United States, Hong Kong, Taiwan, France, Britain, Italy, the Netherlands, Canada, and Germany—and over 2,000 domestic businesspeople discussed possible investment with the Pudong Development District authorities. By late 1992, 15,000 overseas businesspeople had visited Pudong and 704 foreign-funded projects involving more than US$3 billion had been approved and established. Most of the foreign-funded projects were in the high-tech sector and involved microelectronics, chemicals, medicines, telecommunications, aviation, microbiology, and automobile parts. World-famous international corporations such as the Du Pont Company from the United States and C. Itoh and Company from Japan had established divisions in Pudong. In addition, forty foreign banks had applied to set up branches at Pudong. By late 1992, the Chinese government had approved the applications of eleven foreign banks—including the First National City Bank of the United States, the Industrial Bank of Japan, and Credit Lyonnais of France—to open branches. At the same time, a dozen Chinese banks also set up branches in Pudong.[42]

Strategically, the development of Pudong was significant for the Chinese economy. Sociologist Fei Xiaotong suggested that the Pudong Development District was likely to "turn Shanghai into a mainland Hong Kong." According to his analysis, Hong Kong handled 60 percent of mainland China's exports in 1990. As China's economy and international trade expanded, the mainland would need its own Hong Kong. Shanghai, according to Fei, was the best choice for a mainland Hong Kong. Fei believed that Shanghai should be developed into a center of trade, finance, information, transportation, and science and technology. The city would become a "general control room" that would manage the industrial and agricultural commodities produced in nearby provinces and cities along the Changjiang River. By supervising and coordinating the economic activities of those areas, "Shanghai will be a second 'Hong Kong' with broad hinterlands."[43] Fei's suggestion was accepted by policymakers in Beijing. Pudong will become a free trading and financial center of China. By 1993, Waigaoqiao Free Trade Zone[44] was established in Pudong and about 200 state trade companies had entered the Zone. Also, by the same time, a number of Chinese and foreign banks and financial organizations began their businesses in Pudong's Lujiazui financial center.[45]

Another promising economic development zone is Yangpu, a 150-square kilometer peninsula located in Danxian County in Northwestern Hainan Province. Yangpu was selected as an economic zone for its geographical advantages. Yangpu has a natural harbor and a coastline of 110 kilometers. The whole Yangpu peninsula is able to accommodate twenty-six deep-water docks for 10,000-ton-class ships. In terms of international trade, Yangpu is located in the center of the Asian-Pacific economic sphere and is also in the center of international shipping lanes. In addition, Yangpu and its surrounding areas are rich in natural resources, such as oil, gas, salt, titanium, brown coal, and limestone ore, for the development of petrochemical and material industries. A modern harbor at Yangpu was a desire of several generations of Chinese, including Dr. Sun Yat-sen and Zhou Enlai.

In 1988, Hainan Province and the Kumagaya-gumi (Hong Kong) Company signed a contract under which the Hong Kong company obtained a seventy-year lease of thirty square kilometers of land at Yangpu for its development. However, the lease of Yangpu aroused serious disputes among Chinese leaders. Opponents argued that the lease of so large a territory for seventy years was equivalent to signing another unequal treaty, and that the lease of Yangpu to a foreign developer would infringe upon Chinese sovereignty. Under the support of Deng Xiaoping and Wang Zhen, vice-president of the PRC and a close confident of Deng, the State Council finally approved the lease contract. During his inspection tour of Hainan, Jiang Zemin, the party's general secretary, talked about Yangpu; and his remarks might represent Deng's view on the matter. Jiang said: "The introduction of foreign capital to develop land is a purely commercial action. We exercise control over administration of justice and public security there; it will not infringe upon China's sovereignty."[46] Consequently, the State Council finally approved the contract between the Hainan and Hong Kong's Kumagaya-gumi company on March 9, 1992. According to the agreement, the company would invest a total of HK$136.4 billion (US$17.5 billion) in infrastructure construction and import projects in Yangpu over a fifteen-year period. In the preliminary plan, the Yangpu zone would include light, heavy, and tertiary industries (service, banking, and tourism); and the zone would have an urban center with a population of 250,000.[47]

The third aspect of Deng's open door was emergence of the Free Trade Zones (FTZ) in China since 1990. China's FTZs are virtually special economic zones which enjoy low-tax and tariff-free privileges. The FTZs primarily handle international entrepôt trade, bonded warehouse storage and distribution, the processing of export products, and international financing. From 1990 to 1993, thirteen FTZs were established in coastal opened cities or the SEZs. These FTZs are, from north to south: Dalian, Tianjin, Qingdao, Zhangjiagang, Waigaoqiao in Shanghai, Ningbo, Fuzhou, Xiamen, Shantou, Shenzhen (Shatoujiao and Futian), Guangzhou, and Haikou. Currently, these FTZs cover a small bonded area each. The largest FTZ in terms of area is the Shanghai Waigaoqiao zone, which covers ten square kilometers. The smallest FTZ in China is the Shenzhen Shatoujiao zone, which covers an area of only 0.2 square kilometers.

The development of the FTZs seemed to be successful. In less than three years since their establishment, total investment in the thirteen FTZs has reached US$3 billion. The Shanghai Weigaoqiao Free Trade Zone, the first and biggest FTZ, has attracted US$1.6 billion in foreign capital.[48] The growth of the Tianjin FTZ was even faster. From October 1991, when the zone was officially established, to May 1993, 1,483 firms with a total investment of US$1.2 billion were approved, of which foreign-owned firms accounted for 70.1 percent. Foreign businesspeople came from forty-one countries and regions, including mainly Hong Kong, Taiwan, Japan, Singapore, and Republic of Korea.[49] It is expected that the thirteen FTZs will become new hot spots for foreign investments in China, and more FTZs will be announced in the future. According to Chinese officials, the FTZs will be expanded into free ports like Hong Kong. Therefore, Hong Kong's successful operation as a free port and international trading center is a valuable model for the Chinese in building their free ports.[50]

Yangpu, Pudong, the five earlier-established SEZs, and the thirteen newly emerged FTZs may become examples of Deng Xiaoping's plan to "build a few Hong Kongs" on the mainland. In June 1988, Deng had articulated such a goal.[51] His endorsement for the establishment of those SEZs and his support for establishing stock markets in Shenzhen and Shanghai were important steps toward attaining his ends.

Deng's Call for Further Reforms Toward Market Economy

As is noted above, during his tour of Southern China in the spring of 1992, Deng encouraged local leaders to be bolder in launching new market-oriented reforms and speeding up economic growth. He also encouraged Guangdong Province to catch up with Hong Kong, Taiwan, Singapore, and South Korea as soon as possible.[52] As a result of Deng's call, large-scale market-oriented reforms were launched in all parts of China. The goal of the new reforms was to abolish the unprofitable planned sectors of the economy and to establish a mar-

ket economy. In fact, the state-planned sector of the economy has been dwin-
dling since the 1980s. According to the Chinese National Information Center,
in 1981 the state sector accounted for 78 percent of the total industrial output,
while collective and private sectors accounted for 21 percent and 1 percent,
respectively. In 1991, the state sector's share of the total production dwindled
to only 53 percent, while output from the collective and private sectors increased
to 36 percent and 11 percent, respectively. By 2000, the state sector is projected
to account for 27 percent of all products, while collective and private sectors
will account for 48 percent and 25 percent, respectively.[53]

Deng's speeches were made before the Fourteenth Party Congress held in
October 1992. These talks actually set a basic line of that congress—to continue the reforms toward market economy and opening of the country to the
outside world. The Fourteenth Congress formally accepted the theory of establishing a socialist market economy. In his report to the congress, General Secretary Jiang Zemin said:

> Practice in China has proved that where market forces have been given full
> play, the economy has been vigorous and has developed in a sound way. . . .
> Now that we have gained a deeper understanding in practice, we should ex-
> plicitly state that the objective of the reform of the economic structure will be
> to establish a socialist market economy that will further liberate and expand
> the productive forces.[54]

The general secretary also suggested ways to establish a socialist market
economy. The key point is to reform the state-owned enterprises and "push
them into market." Other methods include establishing the market system, reforming the distribution and social insurance systems, and changing the functions of the government.[55] On the endorsement of Deng, the Fourteenth Party
Congress elected younger reformists such as Zhu Rongji and Hu Jintao as members of the Politburo Standing Committee to replace the Long March generation. It is likely that these new leaders will continue Deng's reforms as China
enters the twenty-first century.

In order to consolidate the reform policies and achievements of the past
sixteen years as well as to further promote reforms and economic growth, the
Eighth NPC amended the Chinese Constitution in March 1993. The amendment was designed to continue Deng's policies of economic reform and opening to the outside world. The new constitution incorporated new theories and
experiences developed under Deng's reform program, which included building
socialism with Chinese characteristics and the replacement of the centrally
planned economy with a socialist market economy. In the amended constitution, the "state-run" economy was changed to a "state-owned" economy. Since
a state-owned enterprise is not necessarily run by the state, the purpose of this
amendment was to separate the ownership from the management of state-owned
enterprises—the most difficult work for transferring a planned economy to a
market economy. In addition, the amended constitution stressed the autonomy

of the state-owned enterprises.[56] This amendment indicated that the Chinese intended to continue Deng's reforms in the following decades.

Retrospectively, Deng's reforms did not proceed smoothly. They experienced setbacks and disasters, which included the fall of reform leaders such as Party Secretaries Hu Yaobang and Zhao Ziyang and, particularly, the 1989 Tiananmen incident. However, these setbacks did not change the direction of reform, and China continues its modernization drive. A comparison of China's reforms with the revolutionary changes in Eastern Europe and the former Soviet Union demonstrates that China's reforms only involve the economic system and are not political. However, comparing Deng's China with Mao's, it is clear that the country has indeed made revolutionary economic changes. If the Western political system is applied as a measure, the changes in East European Communist countries and the Soviet Union are more successful than China's. However, if economic growth and improvement in people's living standards are the criteria, China's is more successful. In the last decade, China's economy was one of the fastest growing in the world, and 1.1 billion Chinese people enjoyed the results of Deng's economic reforms. A new study showed that the Chinese economy was the third largest economy in the world by 1992.[57] As planned, China will quadruple its 1980 GNP by the year 2000 if the GNP of the country grows 6 percent each year. However, China's GNP increased 9 percent annually in the 1980s. In the 1990s, China maintained the fastest economic growth in the world—the country's GDP increased 12 percent in 1992, 13 percent in 1993, and 11.8 percent in 1994.[58] Moreover, the Chinese government planned to maintain an annual economic growth rate of 8 to 9 percent in the following decade. Therefore, it is likely that China will quadruple its GNP of 1980 before the year 2000.

In conclusion, China still has many socialist characteristics. Politically, the Communist Party holds power; and the "four cardinal principles" (Communist leadership, dictatorship of the proletariat, the socialist way, and Marxist-Leninist-Mao Zedong thought) are still the core ideology, at least in the Chinese Constitution and the party's main documents. In reality, however, the Chinese Communist regime is in transition—a process from traditional Communist rule to a less ideological and more pragmatic authoritarian government. Economically and socially, revolutionary changes have taken place. Capitalistic elements such as private ownership and the free market have become important factors in China's economic system. Those factors have been encouraged, and they may form the mainstream of the economic system in the following decades. In the rural areas where 80 percent of the population lives, Mao's People's Commune system has been dismantled and replaced by the peasant-household-responsibility system. In both urban and rural areas, private ownership emerged in a variety of economic sectors. Even in state-run sectors, the traditional Stalinist planning system was reformed. Furthermore, while China reformed its economic system at home, it opened doors to the outside world.

Deng's reforms and open door have dramatically changed China and will continue to influence China's development in the next century. As a Taiwanese political scientist commented:

> mainland China has been experiencing a second revolution—the sweeping political and economic reforms undertaken by Teng Hsiao-ping [Deng Xiaoping] and his followers. These reforms, which started in 1978, have become so complex and immense in scope that the entire society has been reshaped.[59]

Deng's reforms make it unlikely that China will return to the system of Mao's time. One reason is that over 800 million peasants would not like returning to their former life under the People's Commune. Moreover, the market mechanism and open door policy are major sources of China's economic boom. The change of these policy directions and the cancellation of the market forces would result in economic decline, because economic initiative and competition are the real impetus for the Chinese economic expansion. Also, Deng's reforms have redistributed power from the Central People's Government to local (provincial) governments and enterprises, and there would be resistance from them if the central government tried to recover its former power.

Deng's Reforms and Hong Kong

Deng's modernization programs will facilitate Hong Kong's return to China in 1997. The gap between the mainland and Hong Kong in economic systems and ways of life has been narrowed. Furthermore, the mainlanders have changed their attitude toward capitalism, as described above. They no longer think that capitalism is something horrible; on the contrary, the Chinese elite has recognized that a market economy is more efficient than a planned economy. This conceptual change will have an important effect on policy toward Hong Kong. Moreover, the Fourteenth Party Congress officially approved economic reforms toward a market mechanism, an action that indicated that China's development in the following decades will proceed in a direction significant to Hong Kong. If the Chinese Communist Party and government have tacitly approved the development of capitalism in the SEZs and if China itself has a market economy, the Central People's Government is certain to maintain Hong Kong's capitalism.

In addition, economic exchange and cooperation between the mainland and Hong Kong built a bridge between the two regions. Before the Great Cultural Revolution was ended in 1976, economic exchange between China and Hong Kong was limited, though Hong Kong was an important source of Chinese hard currency. After 1978, China's open door offered an opportunity for economic cooperation. The SEZs around Hong Kong, as well as kinship and geographical connections, linked the mainland and Hong Kong for economic exchange.

Hong Kong's Direct Investment in the Mainland

Hong Kong individuals and corporations were major foreign investors in the mainland and accounted for about two-thirds of total foreign investment there. Most of Hong Kong's investments were in joint-venture manufacturing projects. According to China's State Statistical Bureau, direct investment in China from Hong Kong and Macao together (primarily from Hong Kong) accounted for US$7.9 billion from 1979 to 1988, about 70 percent of all foreign investment. It was estimated that about US$5 billion was concentrated in the SEZs and the coastal cities of Guangdong Province, amounting to 60 percent of Hong Kong's investment in China.[60] By June 1991, of the 15,000 foreign-funded projects approved in Guangdong, which were worth US$20 billion, 80 percent came from Hong Kong. Taiwanese-funded projects followed second. Hong Kong companies employed two million mainland workers in Guangdong, and only 700,000 workers in Hong Kong itself. Hong Kong businesspeople also invested in Fujian. Of the 4,000 foreign-funded projects, worth US$3.5 billion, Hong Kong's investment accounted for 30 percent, while Taiwanese accounted for one-third.[61]

Hong Kong businesspeople not only invested in the processing industry and the tertiary sector, but also in infrastructure projects. For example, Hong Kong Hopewell Holdings invested in the Guangzhou-Shenzhen-Zhuhai Expressway and the Shajiao Power Plant; Hong Kong Nuclear Power Investment Company participated in the Daya Bay Nuclear Power Station, and Hong Kong New World Development Company invested in Guangzhou's round-the-city expressway.[62] Since 1991, Hong Kong businesspeople have turned their attention to other parts of China while continuing their investments in Southern China. Thus, in addition to the Pudong Development Zone of Shanghai, the chemical industry and real estate development in North and Northeast China began to attract Hong Kong businesspeople's investment. Some investors from Hong Kong even turned their eyes to the oil development in Northwest China.[63] After Deng Xiaoping called for further reforms toward a market economy during his South China tour in the spring of 1992, a new upsurge of foreign investment spread throughout the whole of China. Hong Kong businesspeople and Chinese nationals in other countries were major investors. For instance, in February 1992 Hong Kong's Li Ka-sheng and a Chinese Malaysian businessman signed contracts to develop a commercial area in Shanghai and two commercial areas in Beijing.[64] In September 1992, Li Ka-shing's Hutchison Whampoa and Shanghai's Port Authority signed an agreement to establish Shanghai Container Terminal as a joint venture. According to the agreement, the two sides would jointly spend 6 billion yuan (about US$1.09 billion) for the venture.[65] In April 1993, Cheng Yu-tung's New World Development Company contracted for a

US$1.2 billion project that would develop 80 hectares (0.8 square kilometers) of real estate in Beijing's Chongwen district. In addition, the New World Development Company has also agreed to build residential and commercial buildings in Guangzhou, Wuhan, Shanghai, and Tianjin.[66]

Hong Kong became China's reliable and most important foreign investor. According to a United Nations report, from 1979 to 1990, of the $43.8 billion total foreign investments in China, Hong Kong and Macao (mainly Hong Kong) alone accounted for $27 billion, or 62 percent, of total foreign investment.[67] Another source indicated that by mid-1991, actual foreign investment in China totaled $23.9 billion, of which Hong Kong and Macao accounted for 69.4 percent, a much larger sector than Japan's 13.2 percent.[68] According to a report of the Hong Kong government, by June 1994 the value of Hong Kong's realized investment in China totaled US$50 billion, accounting for about two-thirds of China's foreign investment. Also, by that time the cumulative value of Hong Kong's investment in Guangdong was estimated at US$24 billion, representing 70 percent of total foreign investment in the province. Hong Kong capital was involved in business with over 16,000 companies registered in Guangdong, representing about 90 percent of the total number of foreign-funded companies in the province.[69]

Trade

In the 1980s, China became Hong Kong's biggest trading partner and a large market for Hong Kong's consumer goods. In 1988, Hong Kong's direct exports to China were 17.5 percent of Hong Kong's total domestic exports. China absorbed 34 percent of Hong Kong's re-exports while supplying 31 percent of Hong Kong's imports.[70] In 1990, bilateral trade between Hong Kong and China further increased; forty-four percent of China's exports went to Hong Kong, while 60 percent of Hong Kong's imports came from China. Hong Kong and China became each other's biggest trading partners.[71] As China's entrepôt, Hong Kong benefited greatly from the re-export of Chinese goods, with benefits from this "switch trade" reaching about US$2.7 billion annually.[72] According to a report of the Hong Kong Government Industry Department, from January to November 1993 the value of Hong Kong's domestic export to China was US$7.4 billion and the value of Hong Kong's re-export to China was US$31.8 billion, compared with Hong Kong's export to the United States of US$7.0 billion and US$21.3 billion respectively. During the same period, Hong Kong's import from China was worth US$46.9, compared with Hong Kong's import from the United States that valued only US$9.4 billion.[73]

China's Investment in Hong Kong

Since 1978, China also has invested heavily in Hong Kong. In 1986, China became Hong Kong's third largest foreign investor, behind only the United

States and Japan. By the end of 1988, total Chinese investment in that region was over US$7 billion. China had interests in about 3,000 Hong Kong firms. The central government and also provincial governments established their business offices in Hong Kong. China's largest firms stationed in Hong Kong were China Resources; the China International Trust and Investment Corporation (Citic); the Bank of China; and the China Travel Service. Chinese investments were in fields such as manufacturing, transportation, travel, construction, and finance. By 1991, China became Hong Kong's biggest foreign investor; and total Chinese investment was HK$78 billion (about US$10 billion), while both the Japanese and the U.S. investments were about US$9 billion each.[74] By the end of 1992, China's investment in Hong Kong and Macao was more than US$20 billion.[75]

China's banks played an active role in Hong Kong. By mid-1986, the Bank of China had become Hong Kong's second largest bank, behind the Hong Kong and Shanghai Banking Corporation. The Bank of China erected a seventy-story, US$260 million headquarters. The structure was designed by I. M. Pei, a well-known Chinese-American architect. This building became the symbol of Chinese investment in Hong Kong. By the end of 1986, a group of Chinese banks, headed by the Bank of China, held 18.1 percent of all customer deposits and 7.2 percent of all bank assets. In customer deposits, the Chinese banks ranked second (behind the Hong Kong and Shanghai Banking Corporation). The Chinese banks played a significant role in combatting financial difficulties in Hong Kong. In 1985, the Bank of China helped the troubled Ka Wah Bank, thereby avoiding a more general banking crisis. In the 1987 stock market crisis, the Bank of China contributed HK$333 million to the Hong Kong government rescue package of HK$4 billion for the market's future. After the 1989 Tiananmen incident, when there was a massive withdrawal of Hong Kong dollars from China-owned banks, the Bank of China contributed a substantial amount of Hong Kong dollars (about US$2 billion) to silence the shocks.[76] In 1994, the Bank of China began to issue Hong Kong note and it became the third note-issuing bank in Hong Kong.

Chinese investment in Hong Kong itself showed China's determination to maintain Hong Kong's prosperity. Also, Chinese investment was helpful in maintaining the confidence of the Hong Kong people during the transition period and in encouraging other foreign investors to stay in Hong Kong. For instance, Japan rapidly increased its investment in the Hong Kong manufacturing sector, from $500 million in 1986 to 1.1 billion in 1989. Japan's investment in Hong Kong real estate also increased dramatically from $210 million in 1986 to about $1.4 billion in 1989. In 1988, Japan overtook the United States and became the second biggest foreign investor in Hong Kong.[77] According to the Industry Department of the Hong Kong government, foreign investment in the manufacturing industry in Hong Kong totaled US$4.8 billion by the end of 1992, which was more than three times the US$1.5 billion level of investment in 1984. Japan continued to be the biggest foreign investor in Hong Kong's manufacturing industry, accounting for 33 percent of the total, with US$1.6 billion. The United States was the second largest, accounting for 27 percent, with an investment value of US$1.3 billion. China came third, with investment totaling US$0.5 billion, 11 percent of the total.[78]

The Appeal for a "Greater China Economy"

The PRC's economic reform not only accelerated economic cooperation between the mainland and Hong Kong, but also encouraged mainland-Taiwan economic exchange. Because the Taiwan authorities prohibited Taiwanese businesspeople from trading with the mainland directly, the Taiwan-mainland trade was mainly conducted indirectly, through Hong Kong as a bridge. In the 1980s, particularly since 1986, indirect trade between the mainland and Taiwan has increased rapidly. From 1979 to 1983, two-way transit trade totaled US$1.47 billion, averaging only US$240 million per year. In the next three years, transit trade reached US$870 million per year, 3.5 times more than in previous years. From 1987 to 1989, mainland-Taiwan trade totaled US$7.72 billion, or US$2.54 billion annually. The 1989 Tiananmen incident had little effect on trade across the Taiwan Strait, which exceeded US$4 billion by 1990, US$5.8 billion by 1991, and US$8 billion by 1992.[79] By 1991, the mainland's imports from Taiwan accounted for 13 percent of total mainland imports. Thus, Taiwan became the mainland's second largest supplier after Japan, and the mainland became Taiwan's third largest market after the United States and Japan.[80] By the end of 1993, two-way trade between China and Taiwan reached US$21.2 billion. Another issue of the mainland-Taiwan trade is that Taiwan increasingly depended on the China market and gained a huge surplus in its trade with the mainland. Taiwan's export growth in the 1990s slowed compared to its double-digit expansion in the 1980s, and its trade surplus fell steadily from its peak of US$18.7 billion of 1987 until it reached US$7.8 billion in 1993. During the same period, however, Taiwan's trade surplus with China increased from US$3.4 billion in 1987 to US$16.7 billion in 1993. Without China trade, Taiwan would have faced trade deficit in international trade after 1991. It was projected that in 1994 Taiwan's total trade surplus would further decrease to US$4 billion, while another report in 1994 stated that its trade surplus gained from trade with China and Hong Kong reached US$19.7 billion, a record high.[81]

Taiwan, after Hong Kong, became a major "foreign" investor in the mainland. Because of a common dialect and kinship as well as geographical closeness, Taiwanese businesspeople primarily invested in the Xiamen SEZ. The Taiwanese immigrated from the Fujian area and speak the same dialect, and only the Taiwan Strait separates them. In addition, Taiwanese businesspeople invested in coastal cities in Guangdong and in other provinces.

The government in Taipei disliked Taiwanese businesspeople's large-scale investment in the mainland and held that Beijing was politically motivated when it encouraged investment. The Nationalist government asserted that Beijing's new Taiwan policy was closely related to the Communists' reunification strategy. Under Nationalist law, investment in the mainland had been illegal. Yet hundreds of Taiwan businesspeople ignored Taipei's restrictions and rapidly increased their business in the mainland. Several factors explain why Taiwanese businesspeople suddenly increased their search for economic opportunity in the still politically hostile mainland. In 1986, Taiwan's president Chiang Ching-kuo lifted the ban that prohibited Taiwan residents from visiting their relatives on the mainland, though direct commercial trade with and business investment in the mainland were still prohibited. Economically, as Taiwan became industrialized in the late 1980s, labor and land became expensive; but Taiwanese businesspeople could find cheap labor and land as well as rich natural resources on the mainland. Also, the Beijing regime encouraged economic exchange and cooperation with Taiwan.

The rate of increase of Taiwanese investments on the mainland was surprising. In 1988, Taiwanese investment on the mainland amounted to US$420 million, and one year later it increased another US$400 million in Xiamen alone, accounting for more than one-half of total foreign investment in Xiamen. In 1989, Taiwanese investment on the mainland exceeded US$1 billion.[82] By June 1990, the amount totaled US$1.56 billion,[83] and by 1991, US$4 billion.[84]

Since Taiwanese investments on the mainland could not be hindered, in October 1990 Taiwan's Ministry of Economic Affairs issued a policy, the "Methods of Control over Investment in and Technological Cooperation with the Mainland." The purpose of the Methods was to direct and control the Taiwanese investment on the mainland.[85] Though the Methods listed the products Taiwanese can manufacture on the mainland, the announcement of the new policy de facto recognized that investments were legal. For the first time, the Taiwan authorities formally recognized the facts that the Taiwanese invested on the mainland and that business activities should be permissible under certain conditions. As a result of this policy, Taiwanese investment in the mainland totaled US$10–15 billion from 12,000 companies. Beijing was also flexible in responding to the requests of the Taiwanese investors for protection of their interests. In December 1993, Beijing drafted "special domestic investment" rules for "Taiwanese compatriots." The draft's fifteen articles included stipulations that Taiwanese investment and private property would be protected by the law and, in a regulation that the Taiwanese requested the most strongly, that Taiwanese businesspeople would be allowed to send their profits to Taiwan after payment of taxes.[86]

The mutually beneficial cooperations and exchanges between the mainland, Taiwan, and Hong Kong encouraged a proposal for a "Greater China" economic alliance. The "Greater China Economy" was proposed by a Taiwanese professor and businessman in the spring of 1988. According to this initiative, direct trade between Taiwan and the mainland would result in the emergence of "a Great China Common Market." The formal common market would be established by the year 2000 and a "democratic United States of China" would be realized by 2050.[87] Although the structure of the Greater China Economy is not clear, the idea expressed is that Taiwanese businesspeople wanted to cooperate economically with the mainlanders. Politically, the Taiwanese perceived that economic exchanges between Taiwan and the mainland would ultimately result in China's reunification.

Though the Beijing authorities responded to the idea of a Greater China Economy cautiously, mainland scholars were enthusiastic. Fang Sheng, a professor of economics at the People's University, Beijing, and an executive councillor of the National Taiwan Studies Society, asserted that "it is possible to set up a body called the 'China Economic Conglomerate,'" a joint economic organization of the mainland, Hong Kong, and Taiwan that would help to "deal with external pressures and challenges" and "promote balance and stability in the Asia-Pacific region." He continued, "such an economic union can help members to learn from each other's economic might and offset each other's weakness, to promote each other, make common progress and enhance strength."[88] In addition, early in January 1989 a Beijing broadcast to Taiwan expressed the point that the establishment of a Greater China economic alliance was possible: "Interaction of the mainland's scientific research results, raw materials, and cheap labor with Taiwan's and Hong Kong's financial and communication facilities is certain to create an Asian economic power—a great Chinese economic entity."[89]

According to Edward K. Y. Chen, director of the Center for Asian Studies at the University of Hong Kong, the formation of Greater China "was already under way." Chen noted that Greater China was forming at the time of the emergence of regional economic cooperation worldwide. Such regional economic blocs include the United States and Canada, Australia and New Zealand, and most importantly, the European Community. Chen argued that the Greater China Economy has already come into existence de facto because of the rapidly increasing interactions in trade and investment among the mainland, Hong Kong, and Taiwan. Chen continued,

> Mainland China has very rich natural resources, a plentiful supply of trainable and cheap labor, and a huge potential in conducting basic research. Hong Kong has an ample supply of capital and professionals, the ability to commercialize invention, and all the infrastructures for being a service centre in finance, trade, telecommunication, and technology. Taiwan has built up a high level of technological capability to specialize in relatively sophisticated industrial manufacturing. On the demand side, the combined market of Hong Kong, Taiwan, and Mainland China is huge.[90]

The proposal for the Greater China Economy is in accord with the mainland's reunification policy under the principle of one country, two systems. Once the Hong Kong and Macao questions have been settled by agreements, the Taiwan issue will be high on Beijing's agenda. Economic cooperation between the mainland and Taiwan would be helpful for their mutual contact and understanding. Lang Kao, a Taiwanese scholar, pointed out that proposals from the mainland, Hong Kong, and Taiwan about a Greater China Economy indicated that cooperation among the three economies would be beneficial to all parties, and that such cooperation might help Taipei and Beijing to settle their political differences.[91]

No matter how and when the Greater China Economy is to be established, economic exchange and cooperation among mainland China, Hong Kong, and Taiwan are likely to increase. Beijing authorities as well as the mainland's local governments try to attract more economic investment from Taiwan while Taiwanese businesspeople are enthusiastically taking the opportunity to profit from their investments in the mainland. In addition, as the foregoing review has indicated, the mainland and Hong Kong, particularly Southern China and Hong Kong, are now economically interdependent. Chinese officials have appealed for further economic cooperation between China and Hong Kong. At a symposium on economic development in the Zhu Jiang [Pearl River] Delta, Guangdong Province, Wu Mingyu, deputy director of the State Council Economic Research Center, proposed to establish a Zhu Jiang Delta and Hong Kong economic alliance under the idea of one country, two systems. Wu said that Zhu Jiang Delta and Hong Kong had been closely linked economically, and the relationship between the two regions was like a "mutual dependence between lips and teeth." On the one hand, the economic miracle achieved by Zhu Jiang Delta in the last decade was because of Hong Kong's involvement in the region. On the other hand, Zhu Jiang Delta's rapid development helped Hong Kong to maintain continuous economic growth and to change its industrial structure during that period. According to Wu, the Zhu Jiang Delta and Hong Kong had already become "a regional community or a common market," and if the two regions were to form a new economic alliance, it would produce significant achievement in terms of long-term objectives.[92]

Gao Shangquan, a leading economist of the PRC and former vice-minister of the State Commission for Restructuring the Economy, described the China–Hong Kong economic interdependence as follows:

> There is no denying the fact that the coastal areas in south and east China and Hong Kong have combined to form the core of the Asia-Pacific region's economic growth. The engine-room of the economic growth of the Asia-Pacific region is China, especially the Guangdong–Hong Kong economic zone established between south China and Hong Kong. About 3 million Chinese workers are employed by Hong Kong businessmen in the zone, mass producing, assembling and manufacturing export products. The number of workers employed in the manufacturing industry now exceeds that of native Hong Kong workers and amounts to more than half the Hong Kong population. To date, 90 percent of Hong Kong's manufacturing industry has moved to south China.
>
> Everyday, processed foreign trade products are transported by about 80,000 trucks to Hong Kong and, through it, forwarded to destinations across the world. South China has become Hong Kong's manufacturing base and an interdependent relationship has taken shape in which Hong Kong serves as the sales outlet with south China as its backyard factory. Adjacent to Hong

Kong, the economy of south China, with a population of 100 million, is grow-ing at an astonishing rate of over 30 percent a year. Many foreign visitors to the region are convinced that the economic zone of Hong Kong and south China will be the most impressive zone in the Asia-Pacific region and, thus, in the global economy in the 21st century.[93]

As the mainland and Hong Kong economies become more interdependent, the likelihood diminishes that the mainland would change its one country, two systems policy. Such a change of policy would result in a decline of Hong Kong that would be costly to the mainland itself. Robert O. Keohane and Joseph S. Nye have suggested that interdependence carries with it benefit and cost, and restricts the related actors. These authors stated that interdependence has two dimensions: sensibility and vulnerability. "Sensibility involves degrees of re-sponsiveness within a policy framework—how quickly do changes in one coun-try bring costly changes in another, how great are the costly effects?" The two scholars said further that "vulnerability can be defined as an actor's liability to suffer costs imposed by external events even after policies have been altered."[94] As the foregoing review of the Hong Kong–China economic interactions indi-cated, Hong Kong has accounted for about 70 percent of China's foreign in-vestment and 30 percent of China's international trade, and also Hong Kong links China with the outside world. Hong Kong clearly plays a key role in Deng Xiaoping's modernization programs. In the near future, Hong Kong will con-tinue to be the major foreign investor on the mainland and a "window" for the PRC as it conducts business with the outside world. It is unlikely that there could be a substitute for Hong Kong in terms of its role in China's moderniza-tion drive. Obviously, China would be sensitive and vulnerable if Hong Kong could not continue its economic exchanges with China. The loss of this rela-tionship would be a cost that China could not bear. Because Hong Kong's eco-nomic function might be weakened if the one country, two systems policy were not observed, the Chinese government is likely to continue that policy in order to maintain Hong Kong's prosperity and underpin the modernization of the mainland.

Hong Kong is even more sensitive and vulnerable in terms of the China factor. Any change of China's policy toward the Hong Kong region would re-sult in its economic decline. China's one country, two systems and open door policies were and will be important reasons for Hong Kong businesspeople to invest in Hong Kong and the mainland. Under the Chinese policies, Hong Kong's economic systems and commercial environments will remain unchanged after 1997. A change in these Chinese policies would result in the loss of Hong Kong investors' confidence in Hong Kong and the mainland. Hong Kong will there-fore continue to make an effort to maintain its important role in China's mod-ernization drive. On the one hand, Hong Kong will maintain its status as an international trading and financial center and a link between the mainland and the outside world. On the other hand, Hong Kong will continue to be a major contributor to the mainland in capital, technology, and management science.

Conclusion

After sixteen years of Deng Xiaoping's reforms, China's economic system has been greatly changed—the unitary planned economy has been reformed toward a market economy, in which varieties of ownership have emerged. As a result of Deng's reforms, the Chinese government has welcomed investments from capitalist nations and tried to learn how to use market mechanisms. Internationally, China applied to regain its membership in GATT; and GATT has already considered China's application. GATT authorities encouraged China to further reform its economic and international trading systems, and since 1992 China has quickened its steps toward a free market system and the international trading system provided by GATT. It is true that China's reforms are only beginning. The country is far from having established a new economic model that transfers the system to a free market economy or combines a free market with a planned economy. However, China's Stalinist model of a planned economy and the political ideology of Mao's time were changed in the last decade. The modernization drive has been successful and can be expected to continue. This judgment results from a simple fact: Deng's reforms brought about the fastest economic growth in modern Chinese history, and the people's standard of living has greatly improved. China, under pragmatic leadership, concentrated on modernization rather than theoretical disputes. As Deng said, it doesn't matter whether the cat is black or white as long it catches mice.[95]

This chapter makes the point, ignored by other studies of China's policy toward Hong Kong, that Deng's new modernization drive has created favorable conditions for Hong Kong's return to China. The introduction of market mechanisms narrowed the economic gap between the socialist mainland and capitalist Hong Kong. The politics of "bourgeois spiritual pollution" and "bourgeois liberalization" were criticized in the 1980s and 1990s; but Western capital, technology, joint ventures, and market systems were encouraged. For Deng and his followers, China had only one priority—modernization. Foreign investments and market forces were useful tools in China's modernization drive; and for Deng and his associates, only a successful economy and modernization will demonstrate the superiority of socialism and strengthen the Communist regime.

China's "ladder development" strategy is another experiment that is obviously helpful in the integration of Hong Kong with the mainland. The term "ladder" refers to different speeds of economic growth in different regions of China. Three economic ladders have been formed in China in the last decade. The highest step of the ladder is represented by the SEZs, particularly Shenzhen and Zhuhai, which were organized first and which have enjoyed the fastest economic growth. The second step comprises the coastal areas, including Southern China and the eastern coastal regions, covering territory with a population of 200 million. In the last decade, Shenzhen's GNP increased 50 percent annually and Guangdong Province's GNP increased 12.8 percent each year, while the whole of China's GNP increased 9 percent annually.[96] On the third step of the ladder are the inland areas, where economic growth is much slower.

Actually, the term "economic ladder" is another description of the "coastal priority strategy" proposed by Zhao Ziyang, former general secretary of the Communist Party. Although Zhao was ousted during the 1989 Tiananmen incident, his economic policy was continued. Deng's speeches in the spring of 1992 as well as the Fourteenth Party Congress held in October 1992 further confirmed that Southern China and the coastal regions would continue to be the engine of China's economic growth.

The establishment of the SEZs around the Hong Kong and Macao areas and the economic boom in Southern China, particularly in Guangdong Province, created an economic bridge that connected Hong Kong to the mainland. Three of the five SEZs are located in Guangdong, and Guangdong absorbed over 70 percent of Hong Kong's investment on the mainland of China. Guangdong also led other provinces in international trade. As a result of its economic exchanges with Hong Kong, Guangdong's economic system is much closer to Hong Kong's than to the rest of China. In a sense, Guangdong Province, including Shenzhen and Zhuhai, functions as a buffer zone, because of which the gap between the mainland and Hong Kong is much narrowed. Though the two systems will coexist after 1997, Hong Kong and its mainland neighbor will be similar in terms of their capitalistic economic systems. Also, if Guangdong Province continues its current speed of economic growth it is expected to catch up with Hong Kong in fifteen years. Differences in living standards and ways of life between Hong Kong and Guangdong are likely to be quickly narrowed. As a result of this development, the economic interdependence between Hong Kong and China and their increasing economic similarities will lead to the maintenance of many of the existing characteristics of Hong Kong. In conclusion, China's modernization and open door reforms in the last sixteen years succeeded in creating a foundation that further assure that Hong Kong will remain capitalist after 1997.

Notes

1. Xianggang Tebie Xingzhengqu Jibenfa Qicao Weiyuanhui Mishuchu [Secretariat of Basic Law Drafting Committee of the Hong Kong Special Administrative Region], ed., *Guanyu Zhonghua Renmin Gongheguo Xianggang Tebie Xingzhengqu Jibenfa de Zhongyao Wenjian* [Important Documents about the Basic Law of the Hong Kong Special Administrative Region of the People's Republic of China] (Beijing: Renmin Chubanshe, 1990), 15.

2. Mao Zedong, "On the Correct Handling of Contradictions Among the People," *Selected Works*, vol. 5, 387, 397.

3. Regarding Mao's and Zhou's modernization programs, see Ren Tao and Zheng Jingsheng, "Why a Change in Emphasis?" *Beijing Review* 26, no. 1 (3 January 1983): 14.

4. "Tasks in the 80s," *Beijing Review* 23, no. 2 (14 January 1980): 5.

5. "Can China Reach Its Economic Targets by 2000?" *Beijing Review* 25, no. 40 (4 October 1982): 16.

6. Jiang Zemin, "China on Its March Toward the 21st Century," *Beijing Review* 34, no. 21 (27 May 1991): 13.

7. Ren Luosun, "Changes in China's Economic Management," *Beijing Review* 23, no. 5 (4 February 1980): 21.

8. Xue Muqiao, "On Reforming the Economic Management System (II)," *Beijing Review* 23, no. 12 (24 March 1980): 21.

9. Wu Tongguang, "Yes, There Is Competition," (excerpt from "Socialist Economy and Competition," *Guangming Ribao*, 24 March 1979) *Beijing Review* 23, no. 22 (2 June 1980): 19–20.

10. Jin Mingjun: "Competition No, Emulation Yes," (excerpt from "Competition Is No Good for the Socialist Economy," *Xueshu Yuekan*, no. 7, 1979) *Beijing Review* 23, no. 22 (2 June 1980): 20–21.

11. Zhu Jiaming, "Competition Means Progress," (excerpt from "Does the Economic System of Socialism Exclude Competition Absolutely?" *Xueshu Yuekan*, no. 7, 1979) *Beijing Review* 23, no. 22 (2 June 1980): 21–22.

12. Jiang Zemin, "China on Its March Toward the 21st Century," *Beijing Review* 34, no. 21 (27 May 1991): 13–14.

13. See Zhong Shiyou, "Fresh Impetus from Deng's Message," *Beijing Review* 35, no. 15 (13 April 1992): 5. Concerning the whole text of Deng's southern tour talk, see Deng Xiaoping, "Gift of Speeches Made in Wuchang, Shenzhen, Zhuhai and Shanghai," *Beijing Review* 37, no. 7 (7 February 1994): 9–20.

14. Che Shuming, "Zhongguo Geti Gongshanghu Shuliang Chuang Jilu" [Number of Private Business in China Set a Record], *Renmin Ribao: Haiwai Ban*, 30 October 1992, 1.

15. "Private Economy to Continue Booming," *Beijing Review* 36, no. 7 (15 February 1993): 4.

16. "Private Economy Maintains Growth Momentum," *Xinhua*, 21 August 1993, in FBIS, 23 August 1993, 50.

17. "Zhongguo Dalu de Baiwan Fuweng" [Mainland China's Millionaires], *Shijie Ribao*, 17 June 1992, 11. Concerning China's private business, see Willy Kraus, *Private Business in China: Revival between Ideology and Pragmatism*, Erich Holz, trans. (Honolulu: University of Hawaii Press, 1991).

18. Nicholas R. Lardy, *China in the World Economy* (Washington, D.C.: Institute for International Economics, 1994), 8–11.

19. Wang Yanbin, "Zhongguo Xiangzhen Qiye Honghong Huohuo, Qunian Chanzhi Tupo Yiwan Yi Yuan" [China's Rural Industry Is Prosperous and Its Output Topped 1000 Billion Yuan Last Year], *Renmin Ribao: Haiwai Ban*, 5 January 1993, 1.

20. The term "iron rice bowl" means that a state employee would not lose his job all his life until he retired. A rice bowl refers to the source of income on which one lives; an iron bowl, which is harder than a mud bowl or a china bowl, is not easily broken. The term means that the state employee's job is insured.

21. Jiang Zemin, "China on Its March Toward the 21st Century," *Beijing Review* 34, no. 21 (27 May 1991): 13.

22. Jude Howell translated the term as "open policy." He argued that "not only is this a direct translation from the Chinese (*Kaifang Zhengce*) but it also harbours fewer historico-political connotations, in particular concerning the gunboat diplomacy of the nineteenth century." See Jude Howell, *China Opens Its Doors: The Politics of Economic Transition* (Boulder, Colo.: Lynne Rienner Publishers, 1993), 3.

23. Xu Dinxin, "China's Special Economic Zone," *Beijing Review* 23, no. 50 (14 December 1981): 14.

24. Xu Dixin, "China's Special Economic Zone," *Beijing Review* 24, no. 50 (4 December 1981): 15–16.

25. Yun-wing Sung, *The China-Hong Kong Connection: The Key to China's Open-Door Policy* (New York: Cambridge University Press, 1991), 11.

26. See Robert Delfs, "Hongkong: 1997 and All That," *FEER*, 16 July 1982, 16.

27. Sung, *The China-Hong Kong Connection*, 22–23.

28. Huang Taihe, "Development of China's SEZs," *Beijing Review* 34, no. 26 (18 April, 1991): 24.

29. Elizabeth Cheng and Stacy Mosher, "Free for All: Economic Strategy Inspired by Hongkong," *FEER*, 14 May 1992, 29.

30. He Guanghuai, "Shenzhen: Chongman Huolide Jingji Yunxing Jizhi" [Shenzhen: Economic Mechanism Runs with Full Vitality], *Liaowang* [Outlook], no. 34 (20 August 1990): 9–10.

31. Li Shuzhong and He Guanghuai, "Shenzhen, Zhanqi Laile" [Shenzhen Has Stood Up], *Liaowang*, no. 34 (20 August 1990): 6–8. Also see He Chunlin, "Jingji Tequ: Tansuo he Fazhan de Shi Nian" [Special Economic Zone: Ten Years of Exploration and Development], *Liaowang*, no. 35 (27 August 1990): 4–6; Wei Jing, "Notes on a Trip to Shenzhen (1): Fruit of the Open Policy," *Beijing Review* 32, no. 33 (21 August 1989): 11–13; id., "Notes on a Trip to Shenzhen (2): Progress and Problem in Attracting Foreign Capital," *Beijing Review* 32, no. 34 (28 August 1989): 27–31; id., "Notes on a Trip to Shenzhen (3): Establishing an Export-oriented Economy," *Beijing Review* 32, no. 35 (4 September 1989): 29–31; and id., "Notes on a Trip to Shenzhen: a Glimpse of the Science and Technology Industrial Park," *Beijing Review* 32, no. 36 (11 September 1990): 27–31. Also, "Shantou SEZ (I): Establishment, Progress and Planning," *Beijing Review* 34, no. 42 (21 October 1991): 16–20; Zhang Zeyu and Weng Xiaoqing, "Shantou SEZ (II): Why More Foreign Investment?" *Beijing Review* 34, no. 42 (21 October 1991): 21–24; and Zhang Zeyu and Huang Yuxin, "Shantou SEZ (III): A Report on State-Run Corporations," *Beijing Review* 34, no. 42 (21 October 1991): 24–27. Additionally, see Han Guojian, "Stock Exchange Adds Wings to SEZ," *Beijing Review* 34, no. 25 (24 June 1991): 11; Elizabeth Cheng, "Small Leap Forward: Shenzhen Bourse Opens with a Whimper," *FEER*, 18 July 1991, 69–70; and id., "Through the Roof: Shenzhen to Curb Property Speculation," *FEER*, 24 October 1991, 75–76.

32. See Li Xian, "Tequ Shi Shehuizhuyide," [The Special Economic Zone is Socialist], *Liaowang*, no. 35 (27 August 1990): 7.

33. Chen Qiuping, "Guangdong, A Latent Dragon," *Beijing Review* 35, no. 21 (25 May 1992): 7.

34. "Shenzhen to Be Given Legislative Right," *Beijing Review* 35, no. 27 (6 July 1992): 13.

35. Huang Taihe, "Development of China's SEZs," *Beijing Review* 34, no. 15 (8 April 1991): 21; and Norman Y. T. Ng, "From Special Economic Zones to the Coastal Open Cities: A Strategy for Modernization of China," in Joseph Y. S. Cheng, *China: Modernization in the 1980s* (Hong Kong: The Chinese University Press, 1989), 447.

36. State Statistical Bureau, "Economic Progress in 14 Coastal Cities," *Beijing Review* 30, no. 13 (30 March 1987): 32–33; also see Elizabeth Cheng, "China's Changing Tide: Coastal Cities Rush to Offer Land after Peking Policy Shift," *FEER*, 28 June 1990, 68.

37. Ibid.

38. Li Rongxia, "Tianjin Zone Lures Foreign Investors," *Beijing Review* 37, no. 10 (7 March 1994): 11–15.

39. Elizabeth Cheng, "China Unveils New Development Direction: The East Is Ready," *FEER*, 31 May 1990, 57.

40. Jing Bian, "Pudong: An Open Policy Showcase," *Beijing Review* 33, no. 29 (16 July 1990): 29.

41. "Turn Shanghai into a Trade Centre," *Beijing Review* 33, no. 35 (27 August 1990): 9.

42. Tai Ming Cheng, "Clogged Arteries: Shanghai's Revival Hinges on Better Transport," *FEER*, 4 October 1990, 68–69; Li Zhai, "Shanghai Takes a Big Step Forward," *Beijing Review* 34, no. 24 (17 June 1991): 27; and Yao Jiaoguo, "Yangtze River Valley: A Soaring Dragon," *Beijing Review* 36, no. 7 (15 February 1993): 14–15.

43. Fei Xiaotong, "Turning Shanghai into a 'Mainland Hong Kong,'" *Beijing Review* 33, no. 43 (22 October 1990): 25–27.

44. This chapter will discuss Free Trade Zones later.

45. "Development in Shanghai's Pudong Area Viewed," *Xinhua*, 9 July 1993, in FBIS, 9 July 1993, 47.

46. Dai Yannian, "Yangpu: China's Largest Development Zone," *Beijing Review* 35, 23 (1 June 1992): 20.

47. Ibid., 19.

48. Li Rongxia, "Free Trade Zones in China," *Beijing Review* 36, no. 31 (2 August 1993): 14–19.

49. Li Rongxia, "Fledgling Free Trade Zone in Tianjin," *Beijing Review* 36, no. 31 (2 August 1993): 19–21.

50. Concerning other informations about the FTZs, see "Number of Free Trade Zones Increasing," *Xinhua*, 10 July 1993, in FBIS, 13 July 1993, 42; "Free Trade Zone Opened in Tianjin," *Beijing Review* 34, no. 43 (28 October 1991): 37–38; "Free Trade Zones Multiplying," *Beijing Review* 36, no. 30 (26 July 1993): 5; "Fuzhou Free Trade Zone Set Up," *Beijing Review* 35, no. 50 (12 December 1992): 38; and Li Ping, "Tianjin Profile (I): A Future Free Port in North China," *Beijing Review* 34, no. 33 (19 August 1991): 14–15.

51. Sung, *The China-Hong Kong Connection*, 13.

52. Zhong Shiyou, "Fresh Impetus from Deng's Message," *Beijing Review* 35, no. 15 (13 April 1992): 4–6; Lincoln Kaye, "Reformists' Attempted Comeback Is Reflected in Media," *FEER*, 13 February 1992, 10–11.

53. Nicholas D. Kristof, "Chinese Communism's Secret Aim: Capitalism," *The New York Times*, 19 October 1992, A4.

54. Li Haibo, "Party Congress Introduces Market Economy," *Beijing Review* 35, no. 42 (19 October 1992): 9–10.

55. Ibid.

56. "China's Constitution to Be Amended," *Beijing Review* 36, no. 9 (1 March 1993): 4.

57. According to a report issued by the International Monetary Fund (IMF), China's economy is four times as large as previously measured. That estimate makes Chinese economy the third largest economy in the world, behind the United States and Japan. Traditionally, a country's output was measured by valuing its goods and services in dollars, using international exchange rates. Under a previous method, by 1992, China's output was $430 billion and GNP per capita income was only $370; and China's economy was rated the tenth in the world. In the new method used by the IMF, national output is calculated by what goods and services a country's currency will buy, compared with the purchasing power of other countries' currencies. Using the IMF's new measure, by 1992, GNP per capita income in China was about $1,600, and China's output was 1.7 trillion. See Steven Greenhouse, "New Tally of World's Economies Catapults China Into Third Place," *The New York Times*, 20 May 1993, A1, A6.

58. Li Peng, "Report on the Outline of the Ten-Year Programme and of the Eighth Five-Year Plan for National Economic and Social Development," *Beijing Review* 34, no. 23 (15 April 1991): II; "China's 1992 GDP Increases by 12%," *Beijing Review* 36, no. 2 (11 January 1993): 5; and "'94 Economy Vigorous Despite Inflation," Beijing Review 38, no. 3 (16 January 1995): 5–6.

59. Lang Kao, "A New Relationship Across the Taiwan Strait," *Issues and Studies* 27, no. 4 (April 1991): 49.

60. Davies, *Hong Kong to 1994*, 51; also see Rafferty, *City on the Rocks*, 323–330.

61. "The South China Miracle: A Great Leap Forward," *The Economist*, 5 October 1991, 20.

62. Pamela Baldinger, "Guangdong's Rockefeller," *The China Business Review* 20, no. 1 (January–February 1993): 38–41; Shih Chuan, "New Trend in Investment in Mainland by Hong Kong Businessmen," *Zhongguo Tongxun She*, 14 February 1992, in FBIS, 28 February 1992, 83.

63. Ibid.

64. Zhao Jian, "Haiwai Hua Shang Touzi Zhongguo Xin Qushi" [New Trend in Investment in China by Overseas Chinese Businessmen], *Renmin Ribao: Haiwai Ban*, 12 January 1993, 5.

65. Cao Yong, "Billion-dollar Deal for Shanghai Port," *China Daily*, 4 September 1992, 1; or Carl Goldstein, "Stranglehold Loosens: Hongkong's Li Ka-shing Boosts Shanghai Port," FEER, 15 October 1993, 60–61.

66. Henry Sender, "Companies China Savvy," *FEER*, 22 April 1993, 64–67.

67. The figure is adapted from "Annex Table A-11. Source of foreign investment in China, 1979–1990," in United Nations Industrial Development Organization, *China: Towards Sustainable Industrial Growth* (Cambridge, Mass.: Blackwell Publishers, 1992), 156.

68. "Hong Kong and Foreign Businesses Increase Investment in Mainland China," *Zhongguo Tongxun She*, 17 February 1992, in FBIS, 28 February 1992, 83–84.

69. Chief Secretary's Office, "Hong Kong Information Note," September 1994.

70. Davies, *Hong Kong to 1994*, 52.

71. Zhou Nan, "Zhongguo Yu Xianggang de Hudong Jingji Guanxi" [The Economic Interdependence Between China and Hong Kong], *Renmin Ribao: Haiwai Ban*, 26 March 1992, 5.

72. Davies, *Hong Kong to 1994*, 52.

73. Hong Kong Government Industry Department, "Hong Kong Works," Spring 1994.

74. "Zhonggong Chengwei Xianggang Zuida Touzi Guo" [China Has Become Hong Kong's Biggest Foreign Investor], *Shijie Ribao*, 18 July 1991, 6. However, according to Kevin Rafferty, China's investment in Hong Kong had already reached US $10 billion by 1989. See Rafferty, *City on the Rocks*, 333. For other information about Chinese investment in Hong Kong, see Lane, *Sovereignty and the Status Quo*, 133–134; and Davies, *Hong Kong to 1994*, 53–54.

75. "Neidi Daju Touzi Xianggang Aomen, Qunian Zijin Yu Erbai Yi Meiyuan" [The Mainland Has Invested Hong Kong and Macao Dramatically, and Total Investment Exceeded US$20 Billion Last Year], *Renmin Ribao: Haiwai Ban*, 10 February 1993, 1.

76. Lane, *Sovereignty and the Status Quo*, 134–134; Davies, *Hong Kong to 1994*, 53–54.

77. Robert Broadfoot, "Wither Hong Kong Investment: All Eyes on the Japanese," *The China Business Review* 18, no. 1 (January–February 1991): 26–29.

78. Hong Kong Government Industry Department, "Hong Kong Works," Spring 1994.

79. Li Jiaquan, "Mainland-Taiwan Trade: Look Back and into Future," *Beijing Review* 34, no. 4 (28 January 1991): 26–27; and "Haixia Liang'an Zhuankou Maoyi Qunian Tupo 80 Yi Meiyuan" [Indirect Trade Across the Taiwan Strait Topped US$8 Billion Last Year], *Renmin Ribao: Haiwai Ban*, 8 January 1993, 5.

80. Sung Yun-wing, "Trade and Industry," in Joseph Y. S. Cheng and Paul C. K. Kwong, eds., *The Other Hong Kong Report 1991* (Hong Kong: The Chinese University Press, 1992), 190.

81. Julian Baum, "A Difficult Age: Taiwan Struggles to Engineer Sustainable Growth," *FEER*, 30 June 1994, 56; Louise do Rosario, "Port of Convenience: Taipei to

Keep Using Hong Kong as China Gateway," *FEER*, 1 September 1994, 22; Julian Baum, "Ready When You Are," *FEER*, 15 September 1994, 62; and *Zhong Yang Ribao,* 17 March 1995, 3.

82. Chu-yuan Chen, "Peking's Economic Reform and Open Door Policy after the Tiananmen Incident," *Issues and Studies* 26, no. 10 (October 1990), 59.

83. Li Jiaquan, "Mainland-Taiwan Trade: Look Back and into Future," *Beijing Review* 34, no. 4 (28 January 1991): 26–27.

84. "Taishang Zai Dalu Touzi Qunian Zengjia" [Taiwanese Businessmen's Investment in the Mainland Increased Last Year], *Renmin Ribao: Haiwai Ban*, 27 March 1992, 5.

85. See Yen Tzung-ta, "Taiwan Investment in Mainland China and Its Impact on Taiwan's Industries," *Issues and Studies* 27, no. 5 (May, 1991): 22–23.

86. Julian Baum, "Chinese Gambit," *FEER*, 30 December 1993, 14–15.

87. Hartland-Thurberg, *China, Hong Kong, Taiwan and the World Trading System,* 97.

88. Fang Sheng, "Economic Co-operation between Mainland, Taiwan and Hong Kong," *Beijing Review* 34, no. 46 (25 November 1991): 28.

89. "An Example of Mainland–Hong Kong–Taiwan Economic Cooperation," *GMT*, 5 January 1988, in FBIS, 9 January 1989, 71.

90. Edward K. Y. Chen, "The Hong Kong Economy in a Changing International Economic Environment," in Manfred Kulessa, ed., *The Newly Industrializing Economies of Asia* (Berlin, 1990), 105.

91. Lang Kao, "A New Relationship Across the Taiwan Strait," *Issues and Studies* 27, no. 4 (April 1991): 65.

92. He Sui-i, "Allied Economic Relations between Guangdong and Hong Kong—an Interview with Wu Mingyu, Deputy Director of the State Council Economic Development Research Center," *Ta Kung Pao*, 15 May 1992, 2, in FBIS, 27 May 1992, 41. Concerning the future development of the "Greater China Economy," see Zhiling Lin and Thomas W. Robinson, eds., *The Chinese and Their Future: Beijing, Taipei, and Hong Kong* (Washington, D.C.: The American Enterprise Institute Press, 1993); David Shambaugh, ed., *Greater China* (New York: Oxford University Press, 1994); and the entire issue of *China Quarterly,* no. 136 (December 1993).

93. Gao Shangquan, "China's Economy Vital for Asia-Pacific," *Beijing Review* 38, no. 3 (16 January 1995): 18–19.

94. Robert O. Keohane and Joseph S. Nye, *Power and Interdependence: World Politics in Transition* (Boston: Little, Brown, 1977), 12–13.

95. This aphorism was coined by Deng Xiaoping, who stresses the result of work, not the method of work.

96. "South China Miracle: A Great Leap Forward," *The Economist*, 5 October 1991, 19. Concerning the rapid change of Southern China, especially Guangdong Province, also see Ford S. Worthy, "Where Capitalism Thrives in China," *Fortune*, 9 March 1992, 71–74; Andrew Tanzer, "Cantonese Conquistadores," *Forbes*, 2 March 1992, 56–57; Frank Gibney, Jr., "China's Renegade Province: Guangdong Does Fine Without Either Marx or Mao," *Newsweek*, 17 February 1992, 35–36; Andrew Tanzer, "The Mountains Are High, the Emperor Is Far Away," *Forbes*, 5 August 1991, 70–76; and Elizabeth Cheng and Michael Taylor, "Delta Force: Pearl River Cities in a Partnership with Hong Kong," *FEER*, 16 May 1991, 64–68.

7

China's Policy Toward Hong Kong in the Transition Period

In the 1984 Sino-British agreement, China announced that after 1997 Hong Kong's economic system, legal system, and way of life would basically remain unchanged for fifty years. The Basic Law further confirmed these policies. However, after Hong Kong entered the transition period (1984–1997), development in the British colony became dynamic. Economically, Hong Kong continued its stable and rapid growth but politically, liberals appealed for radical reforms toward democracy. After 1990, their persistent advocacy of dramatic democratization became a challenge to the Basic Law, which stipulates a gradual reform. In addition, Britain and China perceived the transition period differently. As 1997 approached, the British government tried to promote further political reforms by establishing a more representative government; but the Chinese government did not favor any dramatic changes of the current system. China's policy in the transition period included (1) trying to make the British authorities cooperate in a smooth transition, (2) attempting to win the confidence and support of the people of Hong Kong, particularly the business community, and (3) using the Basic Law to influence Hong Kong's political reform.

The transition period can be divided into two parts: before 1990, when the Basic Law was enacted, and after 1990. Before 1990, the Chinese authorities mainly focused on the drafting and enactment of the Basic Law, but once that was accomplished their attention shifted to persuading the people of Hong Kong to accept the law and to using the law to affect Hong Kong's political reform. Previous chapters have discussed China's responses to events before 1990, such as Hong Kong liberals' appeals for radical political reform (Chapter 3) and London's proposal for Hong Kong citizens' right of abode in Great Britain (Chapter 5). This chapter will discuss China's policy in the transition period between 1984 and 1994, with emphasis on Beijing's responses to Hong Kong issues after 1990. After the passage of the Basic Law, China's Hong Kong policy focused on the three areas indicated above. An important part of this chapter will deal with Sino-British confrontation over Governor Christopher Patten's political reforms since 1992 as well as with the impact of Sino-British conflict on Hong Kong.

Sino-British Cooperation

The cooperation of the British authorities during the transition period was important to Chinese policy. Sino-British cooperation was mainly carried out through the channel of the Joint Liaison Group (JLG), which was regulated by the 1984 Joint Declaration. The JLG, consisting of five members from each side, was set up after the declaration was announced and will continue to work until January 1, 2000. The JLG is not an organ of power but only a channel for subsidiary negotiations and implementation of basic agreements, and therefore it does not and will not supervise the British Hong Kong government before 1997 nor the government of the SAR afterwards. The functions of the JLG are:

> (a) to conduct consultations on the implementation of the Joint Declaration;
> (b) to discuss matters relating to the smooth transfer of government in 1997;
> (c) to exchange information and conduct consultations on such subjects as may be agreed by the two sides.[1]

The JLG proved to be an efficient working group and settled a great number of issues related to the transfer of sovereignty, such as seamen's identity documents, border patrol activities, establishing the Court of Final Appeal in Hong Kong, and civil servants' pensions.[2] A subgroup on International Rights and Obligation under the JLG was established in 1986. This subgroup successfully made a large number of agreements on Hong Kong's direct and indirect participation in international organizations, including GATT and the International Monetary Fund (IMF).[3]

Two events—the planning of Hong Kong's new airport and Hong Kong's Court of Final Appeal agreement—demonstrate how China and Britain used the JLG to cooperate and solve differences in the transition period.

The New Airport Agreement

On October 11, 1989, Hong Kong governor Sir David Wilson reported in his annual address to the Legislative Council that the government had decided to build a new international airport at Chek Lap Kok. The new airport would have two runways and operate twenty-four hours a day. When this huge project, which also included a high-speed rail system and a six-lane highway, was completed, the airport would be able to handle eighty million passengers a year— over three times the capacity of the current Kai Tak airport. The first of the two runways would be open for operation by early 1997 and the entire project would be completed in 2006. In addition to the new airport and the transportation system necessary for it, a complete new port was also in the governor's plan. The whole project would cost HK$127 billion (US$16.3 billion).[4]

The Hong Kong community supported the airport project, perceiving that it would contribute to the economy in the next decades. Also, the announcement of the project came six months after the 1989 Tiananmen incident and therefore helped bolster the confidence of the Hong Kong people, which was greatly damaged at that time.

Nevertheless, the Chinese government did not entirely favor the governor's airport construction plan. The Beijing authorities expressed the view that the expense of the project would exhaust all the reserves of the Hong Kong government, and the future government of the SAR would be heavily burdened by it. The Chinese authorities agreed that Hong Kong needed a new airport, but stated that it should not necessitate new taxes for the people of Hong Kong.

The British colonial government seemed not to have expected China to intervene in the airport project. From the British perspective, though the project would not be completed by 1997, the Hong Kong government would pass the costs of construction to the SAR and not to China, based on China's policy of Hong Kong people ruling Hong Kong.[5]

The Chinese government's attitude was crucial to the success of the airport plan. Since the project would not be completed until 2006, bankers would not provide loans if they suspected their money might not be repaid after 1997. Therefore, London had to negotiate, and British foreign minister Douglas Hurd made a special trip to Beijing in January 1991. The disputes between the two countries on the airport issue aroused two other serious questions: Did the Chinese position mean that China had intervened in Hong Kong's internal affairs before 1997? Who had the right to represent the Hong Kong SAR when its interests were involved in the transition period? These questions had not been answered in the 1984 Sino-British Declaration. The Beijing authorities argued that China did not intend to intervene in Hong Kong's internal affairs before 1997. However, the airport project would not be completed until 2006, when Hong Kong would no longer be a British colony; therefore, the British side alone had no right to plan construction for the SAR, over which China would be sovereign. Beijing also stated that since the airport construction involved the interest of the SAR, which would not be established until 1997, it should be China, not Britain, who had the right to represent the future SAR in the transition period. The Chinese insisted that the differences between Beijing and London be solved according to one principle: China and Britain consult each other on all Hong Kong issues that straddle the year 1997.[6]

The British government, however, feared that China wanted to control Hong Kong even before 1997. The British also suspected that if the Chinese were allowed to participate in the airport decision, they would intervene in all of Hong Kong's internal affairs before 1997. In return, China made it clear that payment for airport loans incurred by the colonial government would not be guaranteed.[7]

In fact, the key difference between the two parties was over the financial reserves that the British colonial government would leave the government of the SAR. Chinese officials suspected that the British airport project might exhaust all the Hong Kong government reserves before Britain left the colony. Gordon Wu, an influential Hong Kong businessman and managing director of Hopewell Holdings of Hong Kong, which invested heavily in Guangdong's expressway construction, told Chinese officials that Hong Kong businesspeople could take over construction of the airport after 1997 if the British abandoned the plan. According to Wu, the whole project, including the proposed airport, port, and other infrastructures, would cost HK$70–80 billion, only half of what the British proposed.[8] Wu's suggestion might have increased Chinese suspicions of British colonial authorities.

However, though China and Britain disagreed over several aspects of the project, the two countries tried to compromise. Both recognized that a new airport was necessary to maintain Hong Kong's status as an international financial and shipping center. In addition, the abandonment of the British plan might result in the loss of investors' confidence in Hong Kong. As a result, after the colonial government made concessions on the figure of the reserve for the SAR and on China's authority on the airport, an agreement was reached on July 4, 1991. The airport agreement includes several provisions: First, China would be consulted about any Hong Kong government borrowing that exceeded HK$5 billion (US$641 million) and that was to be repaid after 1997. Second, there would be HK$25 billion in reserve when Britain passed its power to the government of the SAR. (This figure was a compromise between China's request for HK$50 billion and the British Hong Kong government's offer of HK$5 billion.) Third, a special airport committee under the JLG would be formed whose members would be appointed by Britain and approved by China. Finally, an Airport Consultant Committee would be established for local input on the project.[9] According to the budget proposed by the Hong Kong government, total cost of the airport project would be HK$98.6 billion in 1991 price terms.

The airport agreement was an important compromise and a step toward the transfer of sovereignty. In fact, the agreement established a new model for settling major Sino-British disputes on Hong Kong before 1997. That model was that China gained the right to speak for the SAR before 1997, and could propose any issue for discussion with Britain that Beijing believed would involve the SAR's interest. Britain accepted China's position in the airport issue, and as a result, China increased its influence over Hong Kong as 1997 approached.

The Court of Final Appeal Agreement

Hong Kong's Court of Final Appeal has always been the Privy Council in Britain. During the Sino-British negotiations on Hong Kong in the early 1980s, the Chinese authorities decided to grant the Hong Kong SAR a Court of Final Appeal, in accordance with the principle of Hong Kong people ruling Hong Kong that was enshrined in the joint declaration and the Basic Law. Though both the declaration and the Basic Law state that overseas judges may be invited to sit on the SAR's Court of Final Appeal, neither document clarified the ratio of judges from Hong Kong to judges from abroad, or the manner in which overseas judges would be recruited. After the 1984 agreement was made, acting on a proposal from the British side the JLG began to discuss establishing the court before 1997. The Chinese side agreed on the British proposal, because the Beijing authorities hoped to avoid radical change in the Hong Kong legal system after 1997. In September 1991, the JLG agreed that Hong Kong's Court of Final Appeal would be established in 1993. The court would be comprised of five judges, including the chief justice, three judges from Hong Kong, and a judge from overseas. The agreement also stated that the chief justice may not be a Hong Kong Chinese before 1997; he or she has the power to select the overseas judge; and he or she will be appointed by an independent judicial committee.[10]

Unexpectedly, the Court of Final Appeal agreement provoked a dispute in Hong Kong. On October 25, 1991, Hong Kong's Legco voted in favor of Simon Ip's motion that opposed the agreement. This occasion was the first time in history that the Legco had rebelled against its government. Among the forty-five legislative councillors present, thirty-eight voted for the motion that rejected the JLG's agreement, two voted against the motion, and five abstained. The overwhelming majority of the legislators wanted more overseas judges on the court. They also said that the appointment of overseas judges should be more flexible and the number of overseas judges should not be limited.[11]

The real issue involving the judge ratio was mistrust of the government in Beijing. Judges serving on the Court of Final Appeal would be appointed by the chief executive, whose final selection would be approved by the Central People's Government; and the dissenting Hong Kong legislators suspected that the four-to-one ratio arrangement would result in domination of the court by pro-Beijing judges. The majority of legislators wanted two or more overseas judges on the court as a counterpoise to judges appointed by the chief executive. Supporters of the Legco resolution argued that the matter was not a number or a ratio game, but a matter of defending Hong Kong's rights as guaranteed in the joint declaration and the Basic Law. These individuals feared that if the JLG's judge ratio were applied, the rights of the people of Hong Kong would not be protected.

Under pressure of criticism, British and Hong Kong officials seemed to want the JLG's agreement on the Court of Final Appeal to be amended. On October 26, the Hong Kong government's chief secretary, Sir David Ford, made the British position clearer: "We obviously have to find some compromise, some way forward, and now we will be thinking of how we can make some progress on this subject."[12] These remarks seemed to indicate two British positions: first, the Court of Final Appeal agreement might be amended; and second, agreements between London and Beijing on Hong Kong should be sanctioned by the colony's Legco.

The Chinese authorities rejected the Hong Kong Legco's resolution and any possibility of amending the JLG's agreement. Officials from all the Chinese departments dealing with Hong Kong affairs—including the Chinese foreign ministry, the state council's Hong Kong and Macao Affairs Office, the Xinhua News Agency, and the Chinese office of the JLG—openly ruled out any compromise on the agreement. A Chinese source hinted that if negotiations on the Court of Final Appeal agreement were to reopen, then other agreements reached by the JLG might also be renegotiated, disturbing the agenda of the JLG for matters to be resolved during the transition period.[13] For the Beijing authorities, the Court of Final Appeal issue related to Chinese sovereignty. Ji Penfei, former chair of the BLDC and currently Standing Committee member of the Central Advisory Commission of the Communist Party, said Hong Kong people ruling Hong Kong would be a general principle after 1997. "Neither people from the interior nor those from abroad will rule Hong Kong. Judiciary is a question of sovereignty rather than the number of overseas judges." Ji continued that a heavy participation of foreign judges in the Court of Final Appeal of the SAR would damage Chinese sovereignty, and concluded that because of sovereignty China would make no more concessions on the issue.[14] An editorial in the pro-China local newspaper *Wen Wei Pao* also argued:

> Only when Hong Kong judges are the majority in the Court of Final Appeal can the right of final appeal be put, and guaranteed to be in the hands of the Hong Kong SAR under China's sovereignty. This will safeguard China's sovereignty and put into effect the rule of Hong Kong by Hong Kong people.[15]

During his meeting with visiting Hong Kong lawyers, Lu Ping, director of the state council's Hong Kong and Macao Affairs Office, said that those who appealed for more foreign judges for the Court of Final Appeal of the SAR actually lacked confidence in Hong Kong's self-government and in themselves. Lu pointed out:

> Some people even said that the ratio of four local justices to one overseas justice in the Court of Final Appeal is in violation of the Basic Law and will affect judicial independence. Then, why would not a ratio of three to two also be in violation of the Basic Law and affect judicial independence? Such an argument is illogical.[16]

Another key issue in the Court of Final Appeal dispute related to the power of the Legco in the transition period. The Beijing authorities stressed that under the Letters Patent, the Legco is only an advisory body that cannot veto the government's decisions. The Chinese authorities perceived that the British intention to ask the Legco for approval of the Court of Final Appeal agreement was intended to increase the power of the Legco, giving it veto power over key issues in the transition period. One pro-Beijing commentary may represent the Chinese view: "The British authorities are trying to kill two birds with one stone, having the agreement changed and turning the Legco into a more powerful body."[17] Since the early 1980s, Beijing consistently had insisted that it dealt only with the British authorities and did not recognize the Legco as an independent body involved in all decisionmaking on 1997. Chinese officials had received delegations from Hong Kong's District Boards and Urban and Regional Councils, but accepted visits from Legco members only as individuals or members of special interest groups. By doing so, the Chinese regime tried to show that it did not recognize the Legco as the independent legislature of Hong Kong but rather as an advisory body to the governor. It is true, as discussed in Chapter 3, that the Letters Patent and Royal Instructions—Hong Kong's current constitution—provide that the Legco is only an advisory body to the governor and that most of the Legco members are appointed by him. China's position on the Legco indicated, however, that the Beijing authorities feared that the Legco would become a powerful independent body confronting China's Hong Kong policy. Guo Fengmin, Chinese chief representative in the JLG, asserted: "Legco is a British machine responsible for the administration of Hong Kong. Although some Legco seats are held by members elected in district elections since the beginning of this year, this does not change the nature of the Legco."[18]

As a result, the governments of London, Hong Kong, and Beijing agreed that they would ignore the Legco's resolution and that the Court of Final Appeal would be established as soon as possible. One reason for London's acceptance was that because it meant that the court would be established before 1997, it showed that the British government granted Hong Kong the power of final adjudication. However, for Hong Kong liberals, the result of the matter was much more significant, since the colony had not had its own Court of Final Appeal for 150 years.

The Bill of Rights

The British and the Chinese could not always compromise on disputed issues though negotiations. For example, Chapter 5 discussed the issue of right of abode in Great Britain, on which Beijing and London failed to compromise. Also, China and Britain did not make a compromise on the issue of the Bill of Rights.

Though there was no written Bill of Rights in the last decades the people of Hong Kong enjoyed political freedoms. In the 1984 Joint Declaration, the Chinese government pledged to "protect the rights and freedoms of inhabitants and other persons" in the SAR according to law and that the government of the SAR "shall maintain the rights and freedoms as provided for by the laws previously in force in Hong Kong."[19] The Basic Law confirmed this policy. Chapter 3 of the Basic Law, titled "Fundamental Rights and Duties of the Residents," explains these rights and freedoms in detail. According to Wang Shuwen, a Basic Law drafter from the mainland, the law delineated the following fifteen rights and freedoms of the people of Hong Kong:

1. the right of private ownership of property (BL 6);
2. the right to participate in the management of state affairs (BL 21);
3. the right to vote and the right to stand for election (BL 26, 45, 68);

4. political freedoms, including "freedoms of speech, of the press and publication, freedom of association, of assembly, of procession and of demonstration; and the right and freedom to form and join trade unions; and to strike" (BL 27);
    5. the freedom of person (BL 28);
    6. homes and premises are inviolable (BL 29);
    7. freedom and privacy of communication (BL 30);
    8. freedom of movement and emigration (BL 31);
    9. freedom of religion and conscience (BL 32);
    10. freedom of choice of occupation (BL 33);
    11. freedom to engage in academic research (BL 34);
    12. the right to gain an education (BL 136, 137);
    13. the right to gain access to a court (BL 35);
    14. the right to social welfare (BL 36);
    15. freedom of marriage (BL 37).[20]

From a legal perspective, these rights and freedoms are protected not only by the Basic Law and the Sino-British Joint Declaration, but also by two other international covenants—the International Covenant on Civil and Political Rights (ICCPR) and the International Covenant on Economic, Social, and Cultural Rights (ICESCR). Both the joint declaration and the Basic Law indicate that these two international covenants apply to the SAR.

However, the 1989 Tiananmen incident shocked the Hong Kong community, which was already suspicious of the Chinese government's promises in the Basic Law. In response to the request of Hong Kong liberals, the colonial government prepared a Bill of Rights Ordinance, which passed the Legco on June 8, 1991, and thereby became part of local laws in force. The new Bill of Rights was based on the two international conventions, the ICCPR and ICESCR. Though parts of the ICCPR had been extended to Hong Kong in 1976, the government's intention was to ensure that the principles enunciated in the two covenants finally became incorporated into local law. Because the Basic Law states that Hong Kong law will remain unchanged after 1997, the Bill of Rights will remain in force to protect the rights and freedoms of the Hong Kong people after the transfer of sovreignty. The Bill of Rights provides that anyone who believes that his or her political and civil rights have been violated will be able to seek court protection. However, the Bill of Rights also excluded important rights mentioned in the ICCPR, such as the right to have elected Executive and Legislative Councils.[21] These exclusions may have resulted from Hong Kong's actual circumstances: under the Letters Patent and the colonial system, the Exco and Legco are not elected. When the Hong Kong government began to prepare the Bill of Rights, the colonial authorities amended the Letters Patent so that the incorporation of the ICCPR into local laws would be constitutional. In the current Letters Patent, no reference is made to the application of the ICCPR and the ICESCR to Hong Kong.

A comparison of the rights and freedoms provided by the Basic Law and the Bill of Rights demonstrates that the differences between the two documents are small, because both were formulated on the principles of the ICCPR and

ICESCR. However, the Basic Law will be interpreted by the NPC, while the Bill of Rights will be interpreted only by Hong Kong courts. Supporters of the Bill of Rights believe that its interpretation by local courts will help prevent the central authorities' interference in cases involving the Hong Kong people's freedoms.

Chinese government officials were not happy when the Bill of Rights passed Hong Kong's Legco. They perceived that the introduction of the Bill of Rights by the colonial government was directed against the central authorities and the Basic Law. Duan Jin, the State Council's spokesman, said that provisions in the Basic Law give China the right to examine the laws currently in force in Hong Kong, including the Bill of Rights.[22] It is not clear how China will deal with Hong Kong's Bill of Rights after 1997. China may state that it will remain in force like other Hong Kong laws. It is also possible that China may reject the Bill of Rights on the grounds that the Basic Law itself already protects the rights and freedoms of the local people, or that one or more provisions contravene the Basic Law. The Hong Kong government's position is that all provisions of the Bill of Rights accord with the Basic Law. But if the rights and freedoms of the Hong Kong people cannot be protected by the Basic Law after 1997, neither can they be guaranteed by the Bill of Rights. The Basic Law indeed promises the same rights and freedoms to the local people as the Bill of Rights.

The key issue, however, does not concern whether China will recognize the Bill of Rights, but China's implementation of the Basic Law and the one country, two systems policy. If provisions about political and civil rights of the Hong Kong citizens provided by the Basic Law cannot be implemented, most probably the Bill of Rights would also become mere words on paper. The Basic Law authorizes the courts of the SAR to interpret almost all parts of the law itself, including its provisions about political and civil rights.

It would probably be difficult for the government of the SAR and the Beijing authorities to deny the Bill of Rights after 1997. After its adoption it was clear that the ordinance had already dissolved into the way of life in Hong Kong. The Bill of Rights has made a significant impact on Hong Kong's current legal system. For instance, each new bill introduced to the Legco has to be considered on the basis of whether the bill is compatible with the Bill of Rights. The operation of the Bill of Rights in the first year showed that its impact on the judicial system was even greater. The Hong Kong courts were flooded with Bill of Rights arguments, and about fifty different legislative provisions were changed.[23] The abandonment of the Bill of Rights after 1997 would mean a substantial change of the existing legal and judicial system in Hong Kong—a situation the Beijing authorities have consistently tried to avoid.

In conclusion, though China and Britain differed on Hong Kong citizens' right of abode in Great Britain and the Bill of Rights, generally they cooperated. From the 1980s to 1991, Hong Kong governor Wilson played an important role in that cooperation. Speaking at a London conference on business in Hong Kong on January 22, 1992, Wilson said:

> I believe that China can be trusted to honor its commitments under the Joint Declaration, which is based not only on the imaginative concept of two very different systems operating within one country, but also on a substantial degree of mutual self-interest. China has an impressive record of honoring its treaty obligations. And the simple fact is that Hong Kong is of immense economic value to China.[24]

Wilson assured the British business community that the change in sovereignty would not weaken Hong Kong's status as a world trade center. He expressed confidence that Hong Kong would "remain an internationally orientated city with a remarkable degree of energy and efficiency," and would continue to be "one of the best places in Asia in which and from which to do business."[25] Wilson's view greatly influenced Britain's China and Hong Kong policies by 1991.

However, after John Major replaced Margaret Thatcher as the prime minister, Wilson lost his influence on Britain's Hong Kong policymaking. London dramatically changed its Hong Kong policy; and Wilson lost his governorship, which he had wished to be renewed. A later part of this chapter will discuss Britain's new policy toward Hong Kong.

Influence on Hong Kong and Support from the Hong Kong People

According to a Hong Kong journal report, a secret party document revealed that the Chinese government planned to participate actively in Hong Kong's local affairs in the remaining years of the transition period. The purpose of the participation was to increase China's influence in the region, to win support from the Hong Kong people, and to prepare for resuming sovereignty. According to the report, China's participation was to be divided into four levels:

> First, participation in the diplomatic level. . . . Second, participation at the local government level. This is the focus of the participation. It is necessary to unite and win over civil servants in the Hong Kong Government and actively select and train the right personnel for governing Hong Kong so that they can be appointed to the leading posts in the special administrative region government. At the same time, it is necessary to extensively mobilize the patriotic masses to participate in the elections and operations of the Legislative Council, the Urban and Regional Councils, and the District Boards. Third, participation in various consultative organizations. Fourth, participation of mass organizations. It is necessary to rely on the broad patriotic masses and guide them to act in keeping with the arrangements of the central leadership. It is necessary to build up extensive social connections and establish a good and popular image among the masses, thus enabling the local masses to understand and accept what we are doing.[26]

The document also quoted Deng Xiaoping's directive in 1984 for the first time:

> What will be the focus in the next 13 years? Participation. . . . Since the sovereignty issue has been settled, if we do not settle the concrete issues, there will just be a hollow shell. It is certain that a heavy burden will be left to Hong Kong people and to the Chinese Hong Kong government in the future. So the key lies in participation.[27]

China's "participation" can be defined as increasing Beijng's influence on Hong Kong's local affairs, such as influencing Hong Kong's democratic process and intervening in the new airport project.

As a result of the participation directive, as 1997 approached China began to organize its supporters in Hong Kong. For instance, the Beijing authorities' announcement on January 23, 1992, to appoint Hong Kong citizens as their advisers on Hong Kong affairs before 1997 was significant participation. According to Lu Ping and Zhou Nan, these advisers were to solicit opinions from Hong Kong residents in order to help guarantee a smooth transition. The advisers would serve a two-year renewable term.[28] The first group of forty-four advisers included Hong Kong delegates to the NPC, such as Liu Yiu-chu, a lawyer and a Basic Law drafter, and Cheng Yiu-tong, chair of the Federation of Trade Unions; the Hong Kong delegates to the CPPCC, like Xu Ximin, publisher of *Mirror* [Ching Pao] magazine; and Ann Tse-kai, vice-chair of the BLDC and head of the One Country, Two Systems Economic Research Institute. Former Hong Kong government officials, such as Sir Chung Sze-yuen and Liao Poon-huai, were also invited as Beijing's advisers. Another group that served as Beijing's advisers were professionals, such as Albert Tong Yat-chu, executive director of the Construction Industry Training Association; Ng Chee-siong, chair of Sino Land; Li Fook-sean, a former judge of Hong Kong's High Court and also a Basic Law drafter; Shao You-bao, chair of the Bank of Tokyo; and Mun Kin-chok, dean of business administration at the Chinese University of Hong Kong. Businesspeople and industrialists accounted for the biggest proportion of the forty-four advisers. This group included Li Ka-sheng, Hong Kong's richest man and chair of Cheung Kong and also a Basic Law drafter; Henry Fok Ying-tung, a business tycoon who invested heavily in the mainland and was also a Basic Law drafter; Gordon Wu, managing director of Hopewell Holdings; and Li Kwok-po, chief executive of the Bank of East Asia, vice-chair of the BLDC, and also a member of the Legco. In addition, representatives of pro-China political groups were invited to be Beijing's advisers. These included Hu Fa-Kuang, chair of the Liberal Democratic Federation (LDF) and also a former Legco member; Maria Tam Wai-chu, a leading figure of the LDF and former councillor of the Exco and Legco; and Edgar Cheng Wai-chi, director of the One Country, Two Systems Economic Research Institute and Sir Pao Yue-Kong's son-in-law.[29] Fourteen among the group were former Basic Law drafters from

Hong Kong, and most supported China's Hong Kong policy. Radical liberals like Martin Lee were not included. In fact, as Liu Zhaojia, vice-dean of the Asian-Pacific Research Institute of Hong Kong Chinese University, pointed out, China's appointed local advisers had more functions than only consulting the people of Hong Kong: the local consultants would help improve understanding and cooperation between Beijing and Hong Kong and would unite Hong Kong's pro-Beijing elite. The advisers would work more efficiently for China in the local community, because they had official standing.[30]

The appointment of the advisers was announced at a time when the relationship between the Beijing authorities and the Hong Kong community had improved after the 1989 Tiananmen incident. Hong Kong was deeply involved in the development of Southern China as well as other regions of the mainland. In the spring of 1992, after Deng Xiaoping's travel in Southern China, the Chinese government launched new large-scale market-oriented reforms. The whole of China speeded up movement toward a market economy. The one country, two systems policy seemed assured. Given this background, China's appointment of local advisers should increase its influence on Hong Kong in the years up to 1997.

Beijing's appointment of advisers was also an appeal to the Hong Kong elites who supported the Basic Law and the one country, two systems policy. Responses to China's call in Hong Kong demonstrated that the appeal seemed powerful. A group of Hong Kong's China supporters announced in April 1992 that they would establish a new political party—the Democratic Association for the Betterment of Hong Kong (DABHK). It was formally established on July 10, 1992. DABHK included educators, businesspeople, bankers, industrialists, lawyers, engineers, and doctors. Some founders of DABHK were members of Hong Kong's Exco and Legco, and some were Hong Kong delegates to the NPC and the CPPCC. The DABHK elected Tsang Yok-sing, a schoolmaster, as its chair and Tam Yiu-chung, a workers' union leader, as its vice-chair. The manifesto of DABHK stated that its basic purpose was to support the return of Hong Kong to China, realize the concept of one country, two systems, and work to implement the Basic Law. In the inaugural meeting of this new political alliance, Chair Tsang said: "Our guidelines are to work to protect Hong Kong's overall interests, promote social stability, progress and development." The immediate task of DABHK was to help candidates who "love China and Hong Kong" to win the 1995 Legco election.[31]

After China's announcement of its Hong Kong affairs advisers, the Cooperative Resource Center (CRC), a conservative group representing the interests of the business and professional communities in the Legco, emerged. These conservative legislators were actually appointed by the governor. The convener of the CRC was Lee Peng-fei, a member in both the Exco and Legco. The major reason these conservative Legco members combined was to establish themselves as a counterpoise to the United Democrats of Hong Kong (UDHK). Founded in April 1990, when the Basic Law was adopted by the Chinese NPC, the UDHK was the first and biggest political party. Headed by Martin Lee and Szeto Wah, the UDHK advocated radical democratization, which would not be limited by the Basic Law. The CRC, on the other hand, favored China's policy of gradual democratization of Hong Kong. However, the CRC had not clearly expressed whether it would closely link with Beijing, though some members of the CRC were Basic Law drafters. Since the UDHK was the major local political party with an anti-Beijing and anti–Basic Law position and a stand for rapid democratization, the establishment of the CRC strengthened China's supporters in Hong Kong, particularly in the local Legco.

In the following months, it seemed that the CRC intended to act as an independent group. However, on political reform the CRC obviously favored China's position that changes before 1997 should converge with the Basic Law. In the Legco, the CRC and UDHK became adversaries of each other and their members voted along opposing party lines on major issues such as reforms of the current political system and the 1995 Legco election.

On February 28, 1993, almost one year after the CRC was founded, the CRC leaders announced that they would establish a formal political party, the Liberal Party. The forty-four members of the Preparatory Committee of the Liberal Party included fourteen CRC members and six local district members. Most of the committee members were influential businesspeople and professionals. Lee Peng-fei, convener of the CRC, was elected to be the president of the Liberal Party. According to President Lee, his party would not only be a party of businesspeople and professionals but also serve the interest of the entire Hong Kong community. The purpose of the party was to maintain Hong Kong's freedoms of person and of enterprise, which were considered to be the key factors for the region's success. President Lee also pointed out that the relationship between his party and Beijing would be one of mutual understanding, not confrontation, because no local party could be successful if it confronted the sovereign authorities. Currently, Lee continued, his party would run for the Legco election before 1997, and in future, for the chief executive and major governmental officials of the SAR.[32] Obviously, the Liberal Party can be expected to support China's Hong Kong policy, and the party will also be another adversary of Martin Lee's UDHK.[33]

China consistently stressed the importance of a capitalist Hong Kong to the mainland's modernization and the importance of the Hong Kong business community to the transfer of government. As is discussed in Chapter 6, Hong Kong has been China's biggest foreign investor and major trading partner. During his meeting with the principal members of the *Chingchi Taopao* [Economic Journal] delegation in Beijing on December 13, 1991, Jiang Zemin, general secretary of the CPC Central Committee, told his guests: "Hong Kong will keep its capitalist system. A prosperous capitalist Hong Kong is beneficial to China, while a stable socialist China is also beneficial to Hong Kong, hence the two need each other."[34] On January 23, 1992, Vice-Premier Zou Jiahua told a Hong Kong business delegation that Hong Kong was significant in China's foreign trade. Zou said: "The mainland and Hong Kong are inseparable. Hong Kong, as an international financial center, contributes enormously to the economic construction of the mainland."[35] In his report on a meeting on Hong Kong, Macao, and Taiwan affairs in January 1992, Chinese president Yang Shangkun stressed: "We should undoubtedly rely on Hong Kong's industrialists, businessmen, financiers, as well as on the businessmen and entrepreneurs of such foreign countries as Britain, the United States, and Japan." Yang also assured the businesspeople that the SAR government would fully guarantee their interests after 1997, and that the central authorities would "work . . . out concrete measures to ensure the attainment of this goal."[36]

China further expanded its political connections with leaders of the Hong Kong community after the Sino-British conflict over Governor Christopher Patten's reforms began in 1992. In February 1993, the Chinese authorities increased Hong Kong's deputies to the eighth NPC and the eighth CPPCC. In this new NPC, Hong Kong members increased to twenty-eight from the former eighteen. Thirteen of them were new members, and most of the new members were recruited from pro-Beijing political groups. For instance, four were members of the DABHK, and three were from the New Hong Kong Alliance. Their members included Wai Kee-shun, chair of the Alliance.[37] In the new CPPCC, Hong Kong's deputies were increased to seventy-nine from the former fifty-nine, while Macao's deputies increased to nineteen from seven. Of the seventy-nine Hong Kong members, thirteen, including Ann Tse-kai, Gordon Wu, and Henry Fok Ying-tung, were Beijing's advisers on Hong Kong affairs. Ann was also vice chair of the BLDC and chair of the BLCC. He had been a member of the Standing Committee of the seventh CPPCC. As mentioned previously, Wu was a well-known corporate executive. Henry Fok Ying-tung was chair of the Chinese General Chamber of Commerce of Hong Kong and had invested heavily in the mainland. He was also reelected as a deputy to the eighth NPC. The new CPPCC also recruited influential figures from pro-China political groups, such as Tsang Yok-sing, president of the DABHK, and Hu Faguang, president of the Association of Freedom and Democracy. A large number of CPPCC members were leading Hong Kong investors in the mainland. Also, some serving members of the Exco and Legco were recruited as CPPCC members.[38]

At the first session of the eighth CPPCC held in March 1993, Ann Tse-kai and Henry Fok Ying-tung as well as Ma Man-kei, chair of the Chinese General Chamber of Commerce of Macao, were elected to be vice-chairs of the CPPCC. The vice-chairship is an important position in Chinese national affairs, and the session marked the first time that Hong Kong and Macao deputies had held such important posts. Moreover, the terms of the eighth NPC and eighth CPPCC last through 1997. Therefore, it is clear that the Beijing regime expected these Hong Kong leaders to play important roles in supporting Beijing's Hong Kong policy and in the transfer of sovereignty.

Another Beijing target was the Hong Kong civil servants. The Chinese government has insisted, since the early 1980s, that the Hong Kong civil servants were important for the transfer of sovereignty and for the government of the SAR, because these civil servants were the backbone for the operation of a system with which the cadres of the mainland were not familiar. In both the Sino-British Joint Declaration and the Basic Law, the Chinese government promised to guarantee the interests of the civil servants and expressed the hope that they would stay after 1997. After the Basic Law was drafted, Chinese leaders continued to stress the importance of the civil servants. President Yang Shangkun said that civil servants' "existing welfare, remuneration, and promotion opportunities will not only remain unchanged after 1997, but may also be further improved."[39] During his inspection tour of China's southern cities in the spring of 1992, Deng Xiaoping praised the high efficiency of Hong Kong civil servants and maintained that the civil servants "will constitute a basic strength and work as backbones" in the future SAR government. Deng reiterated that the interests of the civil servants would be assured. "If conditions permit, they will be given more, not less, favorable treatment." He asked Chinese officials to pay attention to the opinions and concerns of civil servants and to have more meetings with them and "free their minds from misunderstandings and unnecessary worries."[40]

Political Reform Within the Scope of the Basic Law

As is described in Chapter 3, Hong Kong has political freedoms but no representative government under British rule. After the Basic Law was made, there were two options for reform policy between 1990 and 1997. One was to undertake reforms under the concept of "convergence," which meant that changes in the old colonial system would be designed to accord with the new system set forth by the Basic Law. This approach was favored by the Chinese government as well as by Hong Kong's business and professional communities. The other strategy, supported by the liberals, was to create a more democratic system more rapidly before 1997. Obviously, if during the Chinese attempt to link the old system with the new one a more democratic system were created that was not compatible with the Basic Law, the law would have to be amended. The only alternative would be for China to abandon the British-created system in 1997 for a new order established by the Basic Law. The Chinese government tried to avoid such a situation, because such dramatic changes would be likely to create instability. Therefore, the Beijing authorities opposed radical democratization before 1997. Governor Wilson's Hong Kong government agreed that the reforms before 1997 would converge with the Basic Law. The through train agreement was a typical example of the application of the concept of convergence.

Martin Lee's UDHK argued that the democratization process regulated by the Basic Law was too slow. According to the Basic Law, twenty of the sixty members of the SAR Legco will be elected directly in 1997. The democrats argued that the proportion of directly elected members was too small and that a more representative government should be in place before 1997. The UDHK's appeal was reinforced by its victory in the Legco election held on September 15, 1991. This contest was the first real election for the Legco since 1842, and eighteen of sixty members were elected directly by a universal constituency. While Lee's UDHK won twelve of the eighteen seats, none of the three China-backed candidates won. The 1989 Tiananmen incident may be an important factor in explaining the UDHK's gain in the election.

The election immediately raised two issues. First, who should take the Legco's appointed seats and who should be appointed in the Exco—Martin Lee's democrats, pro-Beijing, or pro-London members? Second, should the Legco's directly elected seats be increased to thirty (50 percent) in the following election in 1995, as the democrats proposed? Martin Lee argued that the UDHK and its allies had won the right to offer the governor their own list of candidates for eighteen appointed seats in the Legco and four seats in the Exco. Lee said, "We are entitled to say to the Government that as a matter of right we ought to form the majority in the Executive Council."[41] However, even before the election, China refused to deal with Martin Lee's party because of its strong anti-Beijing position. After the Legco election, Lu Ping told Governor Wilson that the Beijing authorities would not like to see the appointment of Martin Lee and Szeto Wah to the Exco.[42]

In the meantime, Hong Kong's business community disliked Lee's request for power and pressured the governor not to appoint UDHK members, because they would attempt to change the current system radically. Zhang Jianquan, chair of the Federation of Hong Kong Industries and a member of the Legco, stated that if investors, felt that its sound investment environment might be damaged by the UDHK, they might leave Hong Kong. Zhang also argued that before 1997, Hong Kong's political system was regulated by the Letters Patent and Royal Instructions and after 1997 by the Basic Law, and any change of this workable system would destroy Hong Kong's stability and prosperity. Liang Qinrong, president of the Chinese Manufacturers' Association of Hong Kong, stated that political reforms should be gradual.[43]

As a result, Governor Wilson rejected Martin Lee's request, stating that he would not make the appointments based on Lee's recommended list.[44] As a balance to the increased forces of directly elected democrats in the Legco, Wilson finally appointed pro-British or independent candidates (neither liberals nor conservatives) for both the Exco and the Legco seats.

The second disputed issue was the pace of Hong Kong's political reform and the question of amendment of the Basic Law. Before the 1991 election, the British government had proposed that acceleration of Hong Kong's democratization would be considered if the voting were supported by the people. The UDHK's appeal for direct election of half the Legco members in 1995 was a challenge to the Basic Law. The UDHK argued that the Basic Law should be amended before 1997 because the people supported the democrats' appeals, and when London announced Governor Wilson's retirement, members of Lee's UDHK thought that there might be an opportunity for a rapid democratization of Hong Kong. British politicians promised to reconsider the democrats' demand. After his visit to Hong Kong in May 1992, Alastair Goodlad, the newly appointed British Foreign Office minister responsible for Hong Kong, told the press that if the Hong Kong people wanted to increase the directly elected members in the Legco, China's NPC could amend the Basic Law.[45] Goodlad's talk was, in fact, a signal that London had changed its Hong Kong policy as directed by Governor Wilson. This policy change became clearer when Governor Patten announced his more radical political reform plan five months later.

China rejected any proposal to amend the Basic Law before 1997. For the Beijing regime, the Basic Law was a symbol of China's Hong Kong policy and Chinese sovereignty. The appeal to amend the Basic Law not only meant disarray for China's policy during the transition period, but also constituted a challenge to Beijing's authority. The Beijing regime emphasized its position that Hong Kong's political reforms should be within the scope of the Basic Law. In his meeting with a Hong Kong industrial and commercial delegation on October 10, 1991, Lu Ping stressed that amending the Basic Law should follow procedures stipulated by the law itself. These procedures included approval by the chief executive, support by two-thirds of the deputies to the NPC, and by two-thirds of the legislative councilors of the Hong Kong SAR.[46] Lu argued that since there would be no chief executive of the SAR before 1997, it would be impossible to amend the Basic Law by then.[47] Lu further pointed out:

> If the legislative councillors elected in the 1995 Legco election do not conform to the relevant provisions of the Basic Law, it would be impossible for them to "have direct access" to the first legislative organ of the SAR. Therefore, it is necessary to further strengthen the concept of linking the elections to the Basic Law during the later part of the transition period. Everyone should act according to law.[48]

While denying the possibility of changing the Basic Law before 1997, the Beijing authorities also tried to block the UDHK's access to power. Lu talked about the qualifications required of Legco members to take the through train.[49] These included support of the Basic Law and loyalty to the SAR. If councillors met those requirements, they could board the through train to the first Legco in 1997, but if not, members of the Legco chosen in 1995 might not qualify to board the through train.[50] Zhang Junsheng, vice-director of Xinhua News Agency's Hong Kong Branch, said that "it is impossible to get along with Martin Lee who is always aiming at overthrowing the Chinese government."[51] One *Wen Wei Pao* "Readers' View" said Martin Lee had burned the Basic Law, wanted to revise the Sino-British Joint Declaration, and aimed at overthrowing the legitimate government of China. The View also warned, "If Martin Lee does not thoroughly change this position, he himself should know . . . whether or not he will be able to take the 'through train' well beyond 1997."[52] China's criticism signaled that Lee and his followers might not be allowed to board the through train, even if elected as Legco members in 1995.

The Beijing authorities may have even prepared for the worst—that the PRC would be forced to take over Hong Kong before 1997. In September 1991, Ji Pengfei discussed the possibilities with the mainland officials:

> We have discussed and studied these issues. We are not willing to interfere or take over Hong Kong before the due date unless the following two circumstances occur in the transition period:
>
> First, the emergence of sustained chaos and political riots, which severely affect the people's livelihood and normal order in society, and the British Hong Kong Government's loss of effective control.
>
> Second, Taiwan authorities' involvement in Hong Kong by creating political incidents and turmoil, the occurrence of beating, smashing, looting, burning, and killing on a considerable scale; and the British Hong Kong Government's lack of control over the situation.[53]

Ji further said: "No matter what happens, either the first or the second scenario, we cannot sit idle, but will take over Hong Kong before the due date."[54] Obviously, the Chinese government was considering taking Hong Kong back before 1997 only on the condition that Britain had lost control over the colony and people's lives and property were threatened. At that moment, and only at that moment, Britain might ask China to intervene to maintain social order. However, it was most likely that this situation would not occur; the history of British rule over Hong Kong demonstrated that Britain had the ability to maintain social order of the colony. Also, the Chinese regime did not desire a state of uncontrolled disorder. A chaotic Hong Kong in which public order had collapsed was not in the Chinese interest.

No Concessions to Patten's Reforms

After John Major came to office, London's Hong Kong policy dramatically changed. This policy alteration can be explained in terms of several aspects. Internationally, the change of governments in the former Soviet Union and Eastern Europe and the 1989 Tiananmen incident convinced the Major administration that it should establish representative government before Hong Kong was returned to China, one of a few remaining Communist systems.[55] London might have expected that the Chinese Communist regime would also collapse soon. A quick step to place democracy in Hong Kong would not only change Hong Kong's political system but also influence the development of Chinese politics. Although China's socialist system survived the 1989 Tiananmen incident, the West placed sanctions on the country and the Beijing regime was temporarily weakened. In addition, London had promised that if the people supported the 1991 direct election the British government would accelerate Hong Kong's democratization. The victory of the UDHK further convinced the policymakers in London that a more democratic government could be established before 1997. There was no open official statement from London to demonstrate that its Hong Kong policy had been readjusted, but that policy change could be perceived in several connected events.

In 1991, London announced that Governor Wilson would be replaced in the next year when his term expired—an unusual decision[56] that showed London's dissatisfaction with Wilson's governorship. For years, Wilson was criticized as an appeasement policymaker who responded to China's pressure. In 1992, London appointed Christopher Patten, a former chair of the British Conservative Party and an influential supporter of John Major, to replace Wilson. In fact, Patten's mission as the new governor was to implement London's adjusted Hong Kong policy.

In October 1992, Governor Patten proposed, in his report to the Legco, a revolutionary reform of Hong Kong's current political system. Patten argued that his reform was intended to establish a more democratic system before 1997, so that the way of life of the colony could be continued after 1997. He said:

> My aim as governor is simple: it is to safeguard Hong Kong's way of life—the way of life set out in page after page of the Joint Declaration—its free economy, its rule of law; its sound administration. All the things that, together, underpin Hong Kong's prosperity and stability. . . . But if the continuation of Hong Kong's way of life is the best guarantee of Hong Kong's future prosperity, an integral part of that way of life is the participation of individual citizens in the conduct of Hong Kong's affairs. The ink of international agreements and the implacable realities of history, geography and economics shape and determine the way in which we can broaden that participation.[57]

The legal base of Patten's reform plan was the joint declaration. Patten further justified his reforms by arguing that "the people of Hong Kong . . . indicate they want a greater degree of democracy."[58] Patten stated that while his reform proposal was a response to the appeals of the Hong Kong people, it would still be within the scope of the Basic Law of the SAR, and would represent a new interpretation of both the agreement reached by Foreign Minister Douglas Hurd and his Chinese counterpart Qian Qichen in January 1990[59] and of the SAR's system as provided by the Basic Law. This new interpretation would differ from the Chinese one.

Major reforms in the governor's plan were several: (1) The Legco and the Exco should be separated, and no members of the Exco would also be members of the Legco. (2) All members of the Legco would be elected in 1995, and the governor would no longer appoint members of the Legco. (3) Most importantly, the way of filling the Legco seats returned by the Election Committee and the functional constituencies in the 1995 election would be rearranged, and those seats would be produced on a more open and democratic basis by a method of "one person, one vote." Patten's other proposals included reducing the voting age to eighteen from twenty-one and encouraging the development of political parties before the 1995 Legco election. In addition, the governor proposed that all members of the District Boards, the Urban Council, and the Regional Council would be elected directly in the 1994 and 1995 elections.[60]

In the perception of the Beijing authorities, Patten's plan totally dismantled the Sino-British arrangement for the transition of sovereignty based on the concept of the through train, under which the colony's last Legco produced in 1995 would continue to work through 1999. The Basic Law also confirmed this arrangement on the condition that the composition of the last Legco and its members met the requirements of the law. Patten's change of the manner of election of Legco members was a challenge to Beijing. Beijing had two options: to accept Patten's new arrangement for the transfer of sovereignty and to reinterpret the Basic Law, or to reject the governor's plan and establish the first government of the Hong Kong SAR based on the Basic Law without the through train. Beijing rejected Patten's plan immediately.

Some of Patten's proposals were promptly implemented. For instance, the new governor criticized the "double appointed system"—whereby under the Letters Patent some Legco members were also appointed to the Exco—and removed from the Exco all Wilson's appointees who simultaneously sat in the Legco. In this way he implemented his proposal of separating the executive from the legislature.[61] To gain international support, Patten visited several Western countries. The U.S., Canadian, and Australian governments did express their backing.

Since reform of the 1995–1999 Legco election constituted a major part of Patten's package and was central to the Sino-British confrontation, it is necessary to compare Patten's proposals with the Basic Law. According to the Basic Law, ten members of the 1995–1999 Legco would be returned by an Election Committee, which would comprise 800 people.[62] Patten proposed that the Election Committee be made up of the members of the District Boards, who themselves would not be appointed but would be elected directly by the people. In addition, the Basic Law stipulated that thirty members be elected by functional constituencies, which would be comprised of business and professional elites. In 1991, there were only 104,609 eligible voters in twenty-one functional constituencies.[63] Patten proposed that electors in the functional groups be expanded to include Hong Kong's entire working population of 2.7 million. Table 7.1 shows the differences between the Basic Law and the Patten proposal regarding Hong Kong's 1995–1999 Legislative Council.

The real difference between Patten and the Beijing authorities was that Beijing wanted to preserve the existing system, which it considered workable for Hong Kong, but Patten wanted to establish a representative government for the protection of the way of life of the Hong Kong people after 1997. The Chinese position was that the Basic Law's executive-led system, long in force under the Letters Patent and Royal Instructions, would be continued. Some members of the Legco would also be members of the Exco; within the executive, the

Table 7.1   Chinese-British Differences on Hong Kong's Legislative Council, 1995–1999

Sectors	Number of Seats	Returned by	
		Basic Law	Patten
Direct election	20	geographical constituencies	geographical constituencies
Election Committee	10	800 elite members	District Board members who are elected directly
Functional constituencies[a]	30	business and professional elites	entire working population of 2.7 million

Sources: White Paper: Representative Government in Hong Kong, February 1994; the Basic Law of the Hong Kong SAR.
Note: a. During the 1993 Sino-British negotiations on the 1994/1995 Hong Kong elections, China proposed that functional groups should be increased to thirty from the current twenty-one but the former election method for the functional constituencies should be continued. Under the former method, elections in constituencies such as the business and industrial sectors were conducted on the basis of corporate votes. Britain suggested a new method of "one person, one vote."

chief executive, like the British governor, would appoint, or dismiss, members of the Exco. Also, directly elected seats in the Legco would be increased gradually. Patten's position was that the current system should be reformed dramatically: the Executive and Legislative Councils should be separated completely, and no one would be a member of both. The governor would no longer appoint members of the Legco; and besides the directly elected seats in the Legco, other seats would also be elected by all eligible voters above eighteen years of age.

From Britain's perspective, under the 1984 agreement and the Hurd-Qian agreement the Chinese must respect British initiatives before 1997, because the Hurd-Qian agreement was not a final decision and the composition of the 1995–1999 Legco was still to be discussed. However, the Chinese government stated that Patten's plan violated the 1984 Joint Declaration and the Hurd-Qian agreement by attempting to change the current system, and that it was intended to force China to amend the Basic Law before it was in force. Zhou Nan asserted that the purpose of the governor's plan was to make Hong Kong independent or semi-independent and to continue British colonial rule after 1997.[64] The Beijing authorities asked the governor to abandon his reform plan and continue Sino-British cooperation as before. During his visit to London in November 1992, Chinese vice-premier Zhu Rongji stated that China wanted "cooperation, not confrontation, no one should expect confrontation to force us into concessions from our stand on the matter of principle."[65] For China, the Sino-British conflict on Patten's reform proposal related to these three major questions: Would the 1984 declaration and other agreements be implemented? Would the spirit of Sino-British cooperation from 1984 to 1991 be continued? Finally, would reforms undertaken before 1997 converge with the Basic Law?

The Hong Kong community was divided, although 59 percent of people surveyed by one newspaper in November 1992 said that they supported the governor's reform.[66] Martin Lee's UDHK strongly supported the governor, although the party argued that Patten's plan was not radical enough. The UDHK appealed to the people of Hong Kong to support Patten's proposal and asked for a referendum to decide whether that plan would be implemented. However, the business community, which supported China's Hong Kong policy and included a large portion of the Basic Law drafters from Hong Kong, announced that the governor's plan would destroy Hong Kong's stability and prosperity. In November 1992, the Business and Professionals Federation (BPF), comprised of more than 130 of Hong Kong's largest companies and trade and professional associations, declared in a position paper that it would fight against the governor's reform. The BPF's paper suggested that the current method of filling Legco seats by functional constituencies could not be changed and that seats whose members were chosen by the Election Committee should be filled according to procedures agreed to by Foreign Ministers Hurd and Qian early in 1990. Chair Vincent Lo of the BPF, who was also an adviser to China on Hong Kong affairs, asserted that Patten's reform plan was unacceptable and that any political change should converge with Basic Law. Lo continued: "Democracy is important, but it is not the only goal. A smooth transition is more important."[67]

Patten's reform plan and the Sino-British conflict about it indicated that the two countries' cooperation had ended and their conflict had begun. The Beijing authorities made it clear that China would establish the SAR's first government in 1997 based on the Basic Law, even if Patten's plan were practised. According to a report, China's hard line was adopted by its paramount leader Deng Xiaoping. In 1992, Deng instructed Chinese officials that if the British "overstep the line" once, "we will point this out"; if they do it twice, "we will warn" them; and if they do it a third time, "we will set up our own stove."[68] Deng's aphorism means that if disagreements continue unresolved, China alone will prepare for the establishment of the SAR's governmental system. In February 1993, Deng spoke again and said that Patten's reform was one conspiracy in a Western-initiated new Cold War against China. Deng connected the Sino-British dispute with his one country, two systems policy. He pointed out that China would have difficulties realizing reunification with Taiwan if China made any concessions on the Hong Kong issue. Deng instructed that China must force Patten to abandon his reform proposals; if the British were to continue their reforms, China would revoke its promises on Hong Kong.[69] Deng's talk may indicate that if the British fail to cooperate on the transfer of government China may not guarantee Britain's economic interests in Hong Kong after 1997.

In his interview with Hong Kong's magazine *Mirror* in February 1992, Zhou Nan said that one motive behind Patten's reform may be that the British expected China to follow the former Soviet Union and undergo similar changes. Thus, the British "are prepared to repudiate the Sino-British agreements, extend colonial rule in Hong Kong after 1997 through their agents, turn Hong Kong into a semi-independent political entity, and even attempt to influence the political situation in China." Zhou continued, "there are some forces in the world who do not want to see China realize reunification at an earlier date and become a stronger country. It seems that the question of Hong Kong is not accidental and isolated."[70] These remarks by Deng and Zhou demonstrated that China would not make concessions on Patten's reforms.

Economically, the Chinese government perceived that Patten's reform proposal was designed to create chaos in Hong Kong so as to hinder China's fast economic growth.[71] China and Hong Kong had been interdependent economically since the 1980s, and Chinese officials believed that the political instability that would result from Patten's reform would undermine the confidence of Hong Kong businesspeople for investing in China and Hong Kong.

Moreover, as the Hong Kong community debated Patten's reform proposal, an anti-Patten alliance emerged within the British colony. The anti-Patten forces included pro-China political groups such as the DAB, the New Hong Kong Alliance, and the CRC; Hong Kong deputies to the CPPCC and the NPC; Beijing's advisers on Hong Kong affairs; powerful business community members and professionals; trade union leaders; and District Board incumbents. These political groups and elites supported Beijing's position and asked the British governor to abandon his reform plan and return the Sino-British relationship to its pre-Patten days. Although there had been no particular organization established to coordinate their anti-Patten position, these groups and individuals demonstrated that there was a common ground on Patten's reforms.[72] For all these reasons, China stood firm and continued its hardline position on the issue.

On the British side, Patten persisted in his reforms for several reasons. Patten's reform proposals were not his personal idea. In fact, these proposals were London's new policy toward Hong Kong—that a more democratic system should be in place in the colony before 1997. In Hong Kong, although polls indicated that supporters of the governor had decreased and although the results of the polls varied greatly, they still showed that the governor had considerable backing. According to surveys conducted by a social science research institute of Hong Kong University, supporters of the governor's reform declined from over 40 percent in October 1992 to 35 percent in December 1992. Then, in the following months through mid-March 1993, the percentage of supporters of Patten's reforms remained at 30 to 40 percent. Only at the end of March 1993 did polls indicate that only 27 percent of those queried favored the governor's reforms.[73] Another poll, which was conducted in February 1993, investigated what issues most concerned the people of Hong Kong. Matters raised included Hong Kong's relationship with China, democratization, the governor's management, the Hong Kong economy, and the United States economy. Of 417 people polled, 40 percent thought Hong Kong's relations with China were most important and 20 percent viewed the Hong Kong economy as most important, while only 15 percent thought a democratic political system was most significant.[74]

In addition, as the colonial government planned, the governor's reform proposal was to be sent to the Legco for approval. In the Legco, support for the governor seemed strong, and when in November 1992 members of the Legco disputed the governor's plan, the majority favored it.[75] Martin Lee's UDHK was the major supporter of the governor in the Legco, and Lee asked the governor to send his proposals to the Legco as soon as possible. The governor was also backed by some British businesses located in Hong Kong, such as Jardine Matheson, whose president Henry Keswick had played an important role in former Governor Wilson's loss of his post.[76] For all these reasons, Patten was confident of his reforms.

Sino-British confrontation on Patten's reforms escalated when the governor published his bill for democratic reform in the official gazette on March 12, 1993. This first step in the colony's legislative process would be followed by Legco discussion and voting. The governor would sign it; and the new law would enter into force. For months after October 1992, the London and Beijing governments sought through diplomatic channels to resolve their differences on Patten's proposals. The two sides disagreed on two issues. One was whether the expected agreement between their governments would be sent to the colony's Legco for approval. The British insisted that because the Legco represented the interests of the local community its adoption of any new agreement was necessary. The Beijing authorities argued that the agreement would be reached between two sovereign governments and that under the Letters Patent the Legco was only an advisory body that had no right to veto such an agreement. The other point of difference was that Beijing refused to accept Hong Kong government officials as formal members of the British delegation participating in the negotiations, though the Chinese said that those officials could serve as advisers to British negotiators. However, despite these difficulties Patten could not tolerate that his reform schedule be further delayed.

The publishing of Patten's proposal occurred when China's eighth NPC and eighth CPPCC were to convene. Li Peng, the Chinese premier, revised his government work report to the NPC and included a strong criticism of Patten's plan, describing it as the British government's effort to create disorder and impede the smooth transfer of power. Li warned that Britain would be responsible for the consequences resulting from Patten's gazetting.[77]

From April to December of 1993, Britain and China held seventeen rounds of talks. Still no agreement was reached. Governor Patten could no longer wait for an agreement, and on December 15, 1993, he sent the first stage of his reform plan (a plan on the 1994 District Boards election) to the Legco for approval. For Patten, time was running out. He could no longer delay his reform schedule; but from China's perspective, Patten deliberately destroyed the talks, since China had warned before the talks began in April that the negotiations would be terminated if Patten submitted his plan to the Legco.

December 15, 1993, was the turning point for the Sino-British relationship in the transition period. Although to the Beijing authorities the announcement of the Patten proposal in October 1992 had been a serious challenge to Sino-British cooperation, they had tried to solve the differences between the two countries; but the December 15 event declared the end of any hope. As a result, Sino-British cooperation on Hong Kong's political reform was dead; and the through train arrangement that had developed for ten years was abandoned. Sino-British conflict was the result of differences between the two sovereign nations on the Hong Kong question and was due to their divergent cultures, histories, and political systems. The direct factor that resulted in the conflict was that Britain's new Hong Kong policy and Patten's plan challenged the Basic Law, which for Beijing was a masterpiece of China's long-term Hong Kong policy and a symbol of China's sovereignty. The end of Sino-British cooperation became predictable when Britain persisted in carrying out Patten's reforms. On February 24 and March 1, 1994, the British and Chinese governments each published a paper defending their positions on the 1994 negotiations.[78] The two papers fully disclosed the great differences between the two countries on Hong Kong's political reform.

For the remaining years up to 1997, the development of Hong Kong politics appears clear: Britain will build a more democratic system in Hong Kong by means of the 1994 and 1995 elections, based on Patten's plan. In February and July of 1994, the Legco passed Patten's two proposals for reforms on elections to the District Boards and to the Urban and Regional Councils and the Legco. Patten finally completed his legislative reform process. In September 1994, all the members of the District Boards were elected and in March 1995 members of the Urban and Regional Councils will also be elected under the new election law. Most importantly, a new Legco will be produced in September 1995 under Patten's plan. However, members of the 1995 Legco will not take the through train and Patten's election procedures will be terminated on July 1, 1997. In September 1994, China's NPC unanimously passed a resolution that the new political structure based on Patten's reforms would be abolished and China would establish the Hong Kong SAR's system based on the Basic Law. In fact, China had begun to prepare for the first government of the Hong Kong SAR.

Preparations for the First Government of the SAR

According to the Basic Law, during the year 1996 the NPC was to establish a Preparatory Committee responsible for organizing the first government and first Legco of the SAR. The Preparatory Committee was to be composed of mainland and Hong Kong members with those from Hong Kong constituting more than 50 percent of its membership.

A few days after Governor Patten gazetted his reform proposal in February 1993, the NPC formally adopted a motion, proposed by the Guangdong Province Delegation, that the NPC Standing Committee should be authorized to establish the Preparatory Committee for the first government of the Hong Kong SAR. The Chinese officials explained that the mission of the Preparatory Committee was to set up a "new kitchen"—the administrative and legislative structure for Hong Kong after 1997 in accordance with the Basic Law. In a discussion of whether the Preparatory Committee would be established in 1996, as stipulated in the Basic Law, or earlier, the majority of NPC members argued that if the British adopted a noncooperative policy the one-year preparatory period would be too short.[79]

On July 16, 1993, a Preliminary Working Committee (PWC) for the Preparatory Committee of the Hong Kong SAR was set up by the NPC Standing Committee. According to Vice-Premier and Foreign Minister Qian Qichen, who was also head of the PWC, the tasks of the PWC included studying issues and offering ideas regarding the establishment of the Hong Kong SAR as well as conducting preliminary exploration of the work of the future Preparatory Committee. Qian said:

> Specifically, it will consider and study specific methods for constituting the region's first government and Legislature, and make suggestions for reference purpose after the preparatory committee's formation. It will promote and publicize the Basic Law, offer ideas on dealing with Hong Kong's current statutory clauses that contradict the Basic Law, and study and offer ideas on issues that extend beyond 1997 and may greatly affect the Hong Kong SAR's interests.[80]

As a subcommittee of the NPC Standing Committee, the PWC would provide reference to the Standing Committee, the State Council, and the Preparatory Committee to be created in 1996. The PWC would cease its work once the Preparatory Committee was set up in 1996. Of the fifty-seven members of the PWC, thirty were from Hong Kong, all of whom supported China's policy toward the 1997 issue. Some of the Hong Kong members were former Basic Law drafters. The PWC set up five ad hoc groups for political, economic, legal, cultural, and social affairs.

To fight against Patten's reforms and to prepare for the transfer of sovereignty without British cooperation, Beijing tried to get more local support. On March 29, 1993, the Hong Kong and Macao Office of the State Council and the Xinhua News Agency Hong Kong Branch jointly announced the names of a second group of forty-nine Hong Kong citizens as advisers to Beijing on Hong Kong affairs to replace the advisers appointed in January 1992. Fourteen of the forty-nine were businessmen, and several were famous tycoons who had invested heavily in the mainland. They were Peter Kwong Ching Woo, son-in-law of the late Sir Pao Yue-kong and chair of the Wharf Holdings Limited of Hong Kong; Lee Shau-kee, chair of Henderson Land Development; Kwok Ping-sheng, chair of Sun Hung Kai Properties; Cheng Yiu-tung, chair of New World Development; and Charles Lee, chair of the Hong Kong Stock Exchange. At that point, almost all Hong Kong's billionaires and the majority of the local business leaders had been recruited as Beijing's advisers. No British business-people were tapped, however.

Fourteen of this group of advisers were from local political parties or groups: Five were the DABHK members, including Chair Tsang Yok-sing and Vice-Chair Tam Yiu-chung, and four were current legislative councillors, including Lee Peng-fei, chair of the Liberal Pary. Advisers from political groups also included members from New Hong Kong Alliances, the BPF, and the One Country, Two Systems Economic Research Institute. These political parties and groups clearly supported China's Hong Kong policies. Once again leading democrats were not invited, an exclusion that probably resulted from the democrats' disagreement with the concept of convergence with the Basic Law and their support of Governor Patten's reforms.

The most impressive members in this second group of Hong Kong advisers were fourteen academic and professional personalities. Only three from these sectors had been in the first group appointed one year earlier. Among those named in 1993 were Kao Kuen, president of Hong Kong Chinese University; Woo Hia-wai, president of Hong Kong Science and Technology University; Xie Zhiwei, president of Hong Kong Baptist College; and Zhang Youqi, vice-president of Hong Kong University. Some influential university faculty members and lawyers were also appointed. Moreover, three former Hong Kong government officials and four Hong Kong District Board leaders were in the second group of advisers.[81]

Including the first group of forty-four, altogether ninety-three local leaders were appointed as Chinese advisers on Hong Kong affairs. Zhou Nan said that China would announce the third group of advisers before 1997. Obviously, these influential counselors will help the Chinese government establish the first government and legislature of the SAR, and they may also be expected to play an important role in the SAR's political, economic, and social affairs after 1997.

On March 4, 1994, China's Xinhua News Agency Hong Kong Branch announced that it had invited Hong Kong residents to be its advisors on the affairs of the District Boards. Of the 247 advisors, forty-three were from the DABHK. Some members of prodemocracy parties, such as Meeting Point, were also on the list of China's advisers, but once again no member from the anti-China Democratic Party was invited. This recruiting of advisers on Hong Kong's district affairs was designed to strengthen China's supporting forces at the grassroots level.

The effects of the Sino-British conflict on Patten's reforms were felt on economic issues and other affairs related to the transfer of sovereignty, such as the airport issue and the transfer of property from British troops stationed in Hong Kong to a future PLA unit. In 1994, when it was clear that the two countries would not be cooperating on the political through train system, Beijing again adopted a pragmatic policy for an economic through train—China was willing to work with Britain on economic and other issues that straddled the year 1997. In the long run, Beijing's willingness to compromise with Britain on nonpolitical matters was in the best interests of the Hong Kong SAR and China.

The July 1994 Sino-British agreement on the transfer of land and facilities of the British forces stationed in Hong Kong to the Chinese forces that will be stationed in the SAR was the first step in their new cooperation on nonpolitical matters. Currently the British forces in Hong Kong employ thirty-nine military sites with more than 2,800 hectares (28 square kilometers) of land, the market value of which exceeds HK$100 billion. Initially, China's military insisted that all the land and facilities owned by British forces in Hong Kong be handed over to the future PLA unit stationed in the SAR. However, China finally made concessions on the issue and agreed that only part of the property and facilities of the British forces would be transferred to the PLA in 1997. The remaining land and other properties would be sold by the colonial government for commercial development.

The most significant new cooperative agreement reached by the two countries concerned the airport. Although they had concurred on this issue in July 1991, as is discussed earlier in this chapter, they disagreed on the budget for the new airport proposed by the Hong Kong government in March 1992. According to this new proposal, the cost of the whole airport project would rise to HK$112.2 billion from the earlier estimate of HK$98.6 billion, an increase of 13.8 percent. Also, total loans to the Hong Kong government would increase to HK$73 billion from HK$5 billion set in the 1991 agreement. Additional government borrowing of HK$22.5 billion would be necessary if such things as a delay of the project, an increase of the cost, or a diminishment of profits occurred.[82] China insisted that the airport budget should be within the scope of the 1991 agreement. After Patten became governor, the airport budget negotiations were influenced by the dispute over Hong Kong's political reform. Patten took a strong position on the issue: if it could not get China's approval, the Hong Kong government alone would make the decision. China stated in turn that it would not be responsible for the extra debt that the Hong Kong government might incur and that the Land Commission would not allocate the land needed. Also, Beijing stated that if the colonial government planned to complete parts of the project without China's approval, as Patten had said, airplanes landing at the new airport would not be allowed to enter China's airspace.[83]

According to a report, the dispute between China and Britain on the airport issue was exacerbated by Hong Kong governmental favoritism toward British companies in contracting airport and container projects. Of forty-eight contracts for consulting, projected to be worth US$22 billion, thirty-five had been awarded to British companies rather than to U.S. and Hong Kong Chinese corporations. British-controlled Jardine Matheson received contracts, signed on November 11, 1992, for the construction and operation of the terminal, a decision that was made by the Hong Kong government at the cost of Li Ka-shing's Cheung Kong and the late Sir Pao Yue-kong's Wharf Holdings. The Chinese government declared that Jardine Matheson did not compete for those jobs and criticized the Patten government for failing to award contracts by open bidding.[84]

For the Beijing authorities, the airport contracts were expressions of Britain's new Hong Kong policy and Patten's political reforms. The official Xinhua News Agency made the accusation that the Jardine Matheson corporation "grew along with colonial dictatorship" but was "yelling about democracy." The Xinhua commentary continued, "In the course of Governor Chris Patten's promotion of his constitutional reforms, it [Jardine] has further actively helped, in front of and behind the scenes in London and Hong Kong."[85] The Xinhua commentary did not actually name the Jardine Matheson company, but the article referred to an old British conglomerate that had sold opium to China, making clear the reference. The Chinese article also commented that Jardine tried to shake the confidence of Hong Kong by moving the corporation's legal domicile to Bermuda in 1984 and changing the location of the stock market on which the company's offerings were primarily traded to London in 1992.[86] This criticism also said that British companies like Jardine had no real interest in Hong Kong and created instability by supporting the governor's reform—a position that might have been expressed in part to gain favor with pro-Chinese Hong Kong business rivals of Jardine.

China and Britain did not settle the airport dispute until November 3, 1994, when the two countries reached a second airport agreement. The whole airport, which involved ten infrastructure projects, including tunnels, bridges, and a railway, would cost HK$158.2 billion, the biggest civil engineering project in the world. Under the new agreement, the Hong Kong government would inject no less than HK$60.3 billion (US$7.8 billion) into the key portion of the project—the airport itself and the railway connecting it with the rest of the city. A total borrowing limit of HK$23 billion was set for the two subprojects. The total cost of the project increased to HK$158.2 billion from HK$98.6 billion set by the 1991 agreement; total loans, which would be paid by the future SAR government, increased to HK$23 billion from the previous limit of HK$5 billion. Obviously, China had made substantial concessions to secure the agreement, but nevertheless the colonial government promised that most portions of the airport and airport railway projects would be completed before June 30, 1997.[87]

The 1994 airport agreement was a clear signal that after their conflict over Hong Kong's political reform, Britain and China were again ready to compromise on nonpolitical issues. Sino-British cooperation on nonpolitical matters is important for the maintenance of investor confidence and economic growth. A prosperous Hong Kong is in the interest of both countries.

Conclusion

Securing the cooperation of the British government was an important Chinese goal during the transition period. From 1984 to 1991, Sino-British cooperation was orchestrated through the Joint Liaison Group. Britain and China reached agreements on several matters related to 1997, most significantly the construction of Hong Kong's new airport and the establishment of Hong Kong's Court of Final Appeal, even though they disagreed on the British proposal of right of abode in Britain and the colonial government's introduction of a Bill of Rights. As a result of the efforts of the JLG, Hong Kong participated in GATT and IMF and many other international organizations.

Before 1991, Beijing and London also had reached agreements on the introduction of representative democracy before and after 1997. The concepts of the through train and convergence with the Basic Law were products of Sino-British cooperation in political matters. Guided by these concepts, the two countries consulted each other on alterations to Hong Kong's existing governmental system and agreed that this system, with mutually accepted reforms, would remain unchanged after 1997. The adoption of the Basic Law in 1990 demonstrated this cooperative arrangement and stipulated that the last Legco members as well as the Legco component pattern would take the through train and work through 1999. Under the Thatcher government, Governor David Wilson was the key figure in implementing British cooperation with China.

However, the collapse of communist regimes in Eastern Europe and the Soviet Union as well as the prodemocracy demonstration of Beijing students in 1989 greatly affected Britain's Hong Kong policy. These events convinced the new administration under John Major that a more representative system should be established in Hong Kong before 1997. Chris Patten was chosen as the new governor to carry out Britain's revised China and Hong Kong policies, and not unexpectedly, Patten's reforms resulted in Sino-British confrontation. After seventeen rounds of talks, the two countries failed to reach an agreement on Hong Kong's political reform and the through train arrangement was abandoned. Britain was determined to continue with Patten's reforms. China pledged to dismantle the systems created by Patten and to establish the first government and Legco of the SAR according to the Basic Law. Although Britain showed the world that it could build a representative system in Hong Kong in the last three years of a 155-year colonial rule, this new system will be removed after just a few years of functioning. Actually, Britain is the real loser: it will have little impact on the formation of the SAR's systems before and after 1997. On the grounds that Britain refused to compromise on the 1993 talks, Beijing has made it clear that it will not accept any of Britain's suggestions on the SAR's political system. Beijing established the PWC to prepare for the SAR's government as well as for matters of transfer of government. The British actions apparently undermined their ability to contribute to long-term development of democracy in Hong Kong, as well as limited their immediate opportunities for input to the Chinese government.

The Sino-British conflict over Hong Kong's political reform can be attributed to one major issue—how the one country, two systems and Hong Kong people ruling Hong Kong policies, set out in the 1984 Joint Declaration and the Basic Law, should be interpreted. The British and the Chinese governments both demonstrated that they perceived themselves to have the real authority to interpret the declaration and the law, and that they would not make concessions on their stands.

Throughout this period of conflict, China's influence on Hong Kong increased. Beijing strengthened its ties with the Hong Kong business and professional communities, which Chinese officials believed were essential to a smooth transition, and invited ninety-three local community leaders, most of whom were business and professional persons, to be its advisers on Hong Kong affairs. Beijing's advisers also included individuals from political parties and groups, current Legco members, and former Hong Kong government officials. By establishing this advisory model, Beijing intended to organize its local supporters and weaken local opponents in the Sino-British confrontation, and in fact, the naming of local advisers greatly increased Beijing's influence in Hong Kong.

In 1993, Beijing also increased the number of Hong Kong deputies to the NPC and the CPPCC. The election of Henry Fok Ying-tung, Ann Tse-kai, and Ma Man-kei, leading Hong Kong and Macao businessmen, to be vice-chairs of the CPPCC demonstrated Beijing's confidence in local leaders.

In the remaining days up to 1997, the projection for Hong Kong politics seems clear: Governor Patten will continue his reform as planned, while China will be busy with preparations for the first government and Legco of the SAR as well as with other matters related to resuming sovereignty. Nevertheless, the two countries may cooperate again on nonpolitical matters. In his speech to the opening session of the 1994/95 Legco on October 5, 1994, Governor Patten demonstrated his willingness to cooperate with the Chinese government on the transfer of sovereignty over the remaining thousand days. The governor offered to provide every support and help to the Preparatory Committee that would be set up in 1996, the first chief executive, members of the Executive Council and principal officials of the first SAR, the Chinese military stationed in the SAR, and also with the joint ceremonies marking the transfer of sovereignty. The governor also spoke of his willingness to build up relationships between departments of the Hong Kong government and their Chinese counterparts in order to deal jointly with issues such as cross-border crime and security, transportation, security markets, and financial reserves for the SAR government and the 1997–1998 budget.[88] After his temporary victory in battling China over Hong Kong's democratic reform, Patten appeared to be ready to cooperate with the Chinese on matters concerning the transfer of sovereignty. Therefore, although the mutual distrust that resulted from Patten's reforms has made it unlikely that the two countries will restore their cooperation to the level prior to 1991, it is possible for them to cooperate on nonpolitical matters in the remaining days before 1997.

Notes

1. See the 1984 Sino-British Joint Declaration, Annex II.

2. Davies, *Hong Kong to 1994*, 67.

3. Ibid., 67–68; and Lane, *Sovereignty and the Status Quo*, 143. With the agreement of the JLG, Hong Kong also joined many other international organizations, including the Multi-Fiber Arrangement (MFA); the Asia-Pacific Telecommunity (APT); the Economics and Social Commission for Asia and the Pacific (ESCAP); the International Atomic Energy Agency (IAEA); the International Bank for Reconstruction and Development (IBRD); the International Development Association (IDA); the International Finance Cooperation (IFC); the International Hydrographic Organization (IHO); the International Labor Organization (ILO); the International Maritime Organization (IMO); the International Telecommunications Union (ITU); Interpol; the Universal Postal Union (UPU); the United Nations Commission on Narcotic Drugs (UNCND); the United Nations Conference on Trade and Development (UNCTAD); the United Nations Food and Agriculture Organization (FAO); and the World Health Organization (WHO). See Davies, *Hong Kong to 1994*, 67–68.

4. David Wilson, "A Vision of the Future: Annual Address to the Legislative Council on October 11, 1989," in David Roberts, ed., *Hong Kong 1990* (Hong Kong: The Government Printer, 1990), 17–19.

5. "Hong Kong's Governor Looks Ahead," *The China Business Review* 17, no. 1 (January–February, 1990): 53.

6. "Airport Issue Can Be Solved in Accordance with Sino-British Joint Declaration, Says 'Bauhinia,'" *Zhongguo Xinwen She*, 1 July 1991, in FBIS, 2 July 1991, 68.

7. Zhang Ping, "Positive Proposal Offered on HK Airport," *China Daily*, 24 May 1991, 1.

8. Liu Jianzhi, "Gangfu Ruo Gezhi Xin Jichang Jihua, Chuang Zhonggong Tongyi You Siren Caituan Jieshou" [China Will Ask Private Financial Groups to Build the New Airport if the Hong Kong Government Abandons Its Plan], *Zhongyang Ribao* [*Central Daily News*], 28 May 1991, 4.

9. Stacy Mosher, "Creeping Intervention: Britain Concedes China's Demands in Airport Deal," *FEER*, 18 July 1991, 10; "Great Significance of Lu Ping's Meetings with Hong Kong Governor," *Wen Wei Pao*, 27 July 1991, 2, in FBIS, 2 August 1991, 59.

10. Stacy Mosher, "Local Justice: Concern over Make-up of Future Court of Final Appeal," *FEER*, 10 October 1991, 11–12.

11. Doreen Cheung, "Councillors Question Agreement," *South China Morning Post*, 26 October 1991, 4, in FBIS, 30 October 1991, 68.

12. Stanley Leung, "'Collision' Feared over Appeal Court Controversy," *The Standard*, 1 November 1991, D8, in FBIS, 5 November 1991, 57.

13. "Beijing Rules Out Compromise," *The Standard*, 5 November 1991, pp, A1, 3, in FBIS, 5 November 1991, 58.

14. Chen Chien-ping, "Ji Pengfei Comments on Hong Kong Court of Final Appeal," *Wen Wei Pao*, 23 October 1991, 2, in FBIS, 30 October 1991, 69.

15. "Defend Solemnity of Agreement on the Final Court of Appeal," *Wen Wei Pao*, 25 October 1991, 2, in FBIS, 30 October 1991, 71.

16. Duo Duo, "Lu Ping Says Criticism of Setup of Court of Final Appeal Reflects Lack of Confidence in Hong Kong People's Self-Government," *Zhongguo Xinwen She*, 5 November 1991, in FBIS, 7 November 1991, 74.

17. Stanley Leung, "'Collision' Feared over Appeal Court Controversy," *The Standard*, 1 November 1991, D8, in FBIS, 5 November 1991, 57.

18. "China, Britain, Reaffirm Implementation of Agreement on Court of Final Appeal," *Ta Kung Pao*, 7 December 1991, 2, in FBIS, 10 December 1991, 74.

19. Appendix I, XIII.

20. Wang, *Xianggang Tebie Xingzhengqu Jibenfa Daolun*, 143–155.

21. Stacy Mosher, "Uncertain Rights," *FEER*, 4 July 1991, 16.

22. Zhang Ping, "Beijing Regrets 'Bill of Rights'," *China Daily*, 7 June 1991, 1. The Basic Law states: "The laws previously in Hong Kong, that is, the common law, rules of equity, ordinances, subordinate legislation and customary law shall be maintained, except for any that contravene this law, and subject to any amendment by the legislature of the Hong Kong Special Administrative Region" (BL 8).

23. Johannes M. M. Chan, "The Legal System," in Cheng and Kwong, *The Other Hong Kong Report 1992*, 17.

24. "Governor Wilson Says 'China Can Be Trusted,'" *Xinhua*, 22 January 1992, in FBIS, 23 January 1992, 60.

25. Ibid.

26. He Po-shih, "Five Major Tasks Are Aimed at Control," *Tangtai* [Contemporary], no. 7 (15 October 1991): 14–15, in FBIS, 14 November 1991, 72–74.

27. Ibid.

28. "China Set to Appoint Hong Kong Affairs Advisers," *Xinhua*, 29 February 1992, in FBIS, 2 March 1992, 81.

29. "Hong Kong Figures to Form PRC Advisers Panel," *South China Sunday Morning Post*, 8 March 1992, 1, 4, in FBIS, 9 March 1992, 83–84. Concerning Beijing's appointment of Hong Kong affairs advisers, also see Stacy Mosher, "Shadow of China: Peking to Appoint New Local Advisory Group," *FEER*, 6 February 1992, 18; and id., "Gang of Forty-four: China's New Panel of Advisers Raises Misgivings," *FEER*, 26 March 1992, 13.

30. Wei Yanan and Huang Jichang, "Fanying Gefang Yiyuan, Kuoda Zhijie Goutong" [Reflect All-circles' Will and Increase Direct Communications], *Renmin Ribao: Haiwai Ban*, 13 March 1992, 5.

31. "Canyu Zhi Gang Dashi, Quebao Pingwen Guodu" [Participate in Administering Hong Kong and Ensure a Stable Transition], *Renmin Ribao: Haiwai Ban*, 22 May 1992, 5; and "New Political Group Announces Establishment," FBIS, 13 July 1992, 70.

32. "QiLuan Cui Sheng, Ziyoudang Chouweihui Chengli" [Initiated by the CRC, the Preparatory Committee of the Liberal Party Is Established], *Shijie Ribao*, 1 March 1993, 4.

33. Here it is necessary to distinguish Hong Kong liberals, headed by Martin Lee, from Liberal Party members. For the purposes of discussion in this book, liberals are individuals who oppose Beijing's interpretation of the one country, two systems policy and the gradual political reform process in the Basic Law, and appeal for direct election of the Legco and for establishment of a more democratic system before 1997. Obviously, the manifesto of the Liberal Party demonstrates that its members are not liberals. To distinguish them from Liberal Party members the term "democrats" is given to Martin Lee's liberals because they favor establishing a representative system through direct election.

34. "Notes on Beijing Activities on Occasion of *Ching Chi Tao Pao*'s 45th Anniversary," *Ching Chi Tao Pao*, 1 January 1992, 12–14, in FBIS, 21 January 1992, 72.

35. Chris Yeung, "Wang Qiren, Zou Jiahua Reassure Businessmen," *South China Morning Post*, 23 January 1992, 1, in FBIS, 23 January 1992, 60.

36. Chen Wei-Min, "Yang Shangkun Reassures Hong Kong People," *Ching Pao*, 5 January 1992, 11, in FBIS, 21 January 1992, 73.

37. Chen Tianquan, "Jin Ban Xinren Gangqu Daibiao Ju Qinzhong Beijing" [Almost Half of Hong Kong's New Deputies to the NPC Have a Pro-China Background], *Shijie Ribao*, 2 February 1993, 4.

38. "Zhonggong Ba Jie Zhengxie Gang'ao Weiyuan 110 Ronghuo Weiren" [110 Hong Kong and Macao Deputies Were Appointed to the Eighth CPPCC], *Shijie Ribao*, 20 February 1993, 4.

39. Chen Wei-Min, "Yang Shangkun Reassures Hong Kong People," *Ching Pao*, 5 January 1992, 11, in FBIS, 21 January 1992, 73.

40. Chen Wei-ming, "Deng Xiaoping Praises Hong Kong's Civil Servants," *Ching Pao*, 5 May 1992, 11, in FBIS, 17 March 1992, 72–73.

41. Barbara Basler, "Democracy Backers in Hong Kong Win Election Landslide," *The New York Times*, 16 September 1991, A4.

42. Stacy Mosher, "Liberal Landslide: Election Result Puts China on the Spot," *FEER*, 26 September 1991, 19.

43. "Zhang Jianquan: Gangtongmeng Le Hunle Tounao" [Zhang Jiaquan Says: The UDHK Was Blinded for Over Enjoying Its Victory], *Shijie Ribao*, 20 September 1991, 5; and "Gongshangjie Dui Minzhupai 'Xingdong' Bu'an," [Business Community Was Disturbed by the Democrats], *Shijie Ribao*, 23 September 1991, 5.

44. Stacy Mosher, "The Governor's Men: Low-Key Professionals Named to Legislative Council," *FEER*, 3 October 1991, 11–13; and id., "Out of the Club: Liberals Excluded from Executive Council," *FEER*, 7 November 1991, 12.

45. Stacy Mosher, "Basic Flaw: Britain, China Argue Over Pace of Democratization," *FEER*, 11 June 1992, 18.

46. See Article 159.

47. Chen Chien-ping, "Lu Ping Stresses Basic Law Cannot Be Amended Before 1997," *Wen Wei Pao*, 9 October 1991, 2, in FBIS, 11 October 1991, 68–69.

48. He Wei-Tzu, "Lu Ping on Direct Election of Hong Kong Legislative Council," *Wen Wei Pao*, 20 September 1991, 2, in FBIS, 20 September 1991, 82.

49. Concerning the concept of through train, see Chapter 3.

50. Chen Chien-ping, "Lu Ping Stresses Basic Law Cannot Be Amended Before 1997," *Wen Wei Pao*, 9 October 1991, 2, in FBIS, 11 October 1991, 68–69.

51. Christine Chan, "Xinhua Official Criticizes Martin Lee," *The Standard*, 10 October 1991, A3, in FBIS, 10 October 1991, 87.

52. Chen Wen, "Martin Lee Quibbles Again," *Wen Wei Pao*, 4 October 1991, 11, in FBIS, 5 October 1991, 80–81.

53. Lo Ping, "Notes on Northern Journey: Possible Takeover of Hong Kong by Communist China before Due Date," *Cheng Ming*, 1 November 1991, 6–8, in FBIS, 15 November 1991, 89.

54. Ibid.

55. Frank Ching, "Hong Kong: Boxed in a Corner," *FEER*, 17 December 1992, 17.

56. London usually announced a new governorship when the term of the incumbent governor expired. However, this time the announcement was made one year before Wilson left his office, weakening Wilson's power during his last year. In fact, Wilson expected that his governorship would be renewed. See Philip Bowring and Stacy Mosher, "Lord Without Manor: News of Governor's Exit Suggests Disarray and Confusion," *FEER*, 16 January 1992, 10–11.

57. "Hopes for Hong Kong: Chris Patten on His Plans to Safeguard a Way of Life," *The Times*, 8 October 1992, 14.

58. Ibid.

59. See Chapter 3.

60. "Hopes for Hong Kong: Chris Patten on His Plans to Safeguard a Way of Life," *The Times*, 8 October 1992, 14; Michael Binyon and James Pringle, "Patten Move to Broaden Democracy Angers China," *The Times*, 8 October 1992, 11; Jesse Wong, "Hong Kong Governor's Speech Raises Hackles in Beijing with Proposals for More Democracy," *The Asian Wall Street Journal Weekly* 24, no. 41 (12 October 1992): 5, 12; and Frank Ching, "Hong Kong: Cleared for Action," *FEER*, 22 October 1992, 20–21. Concerning the current system for the selection of members of the Legco, see Chapter 3.

61. Frank Ching, "Past Imperfect," *FEER*, 29 October 1992, 23.

62. Concerning the composition of the Election Committee, see Chapter 3; or see the Basic Law, Annex I: "Methods for the Selection of the Chief Executive of the Hong Kong Special Administrative Region."

63. Stacy Mosher, "Selective Suffrage: Electoral System Remains Firmly Titled in Favour of Vested Interest," *FEER*, 29 August 1991, 16–18. In the 1991–1995 Legco, the twenty-one functional constituency seats were allocated as follows: commercial, industrial, financial, labor, and medical constituencies produced two seats each; and social services, teaching, legal, engineering, architectural, accountancy, real estate and construction, tourism, Urban Council, Regional Council, and rural constituencies elected one representative each. See Norman Miners, *The Government and Politics of Hong Kong*, 5th ed. (Hong Kong: Oxford University, 1991), 116–117.

64. Yi Feng, "Zhou Nan Zhichu: Zhongguo Zhengfu Juebu Na Yuanze Zuo Jiaoyi" [Zhou Nan Indicated That China Would Never Barter Away Principle], *Renmin Ribao: Haiwai Ban*, 7 November 1992, 3.

65. Tai Ming Cheung, "Hong Kong Embattled Governor," *FEER*, 26 November 1992, 10.

66. Steven Strasser, "The 'God of Democracy': Hong Kong's British Governor Defies Beijing and Pushes for Reform," *Newsweek*, 23 November 1992, 43. As will be shown later, other polls indicated that only 40 percent of the polled supported Patten's reforms.

67. Tai Ming Cheung, "Hong Kong: Embattled Governor," *FEER*, 26 November 1992, 10.

68. Frank Ching, "Hong Kong: Boxed in a Corner," *FEER*, 17 December 1992, 17.

69. "Deng Xiaoping Shuo: Gangdu Bu Chexiao Zhenggai, Zhonggong Hui Shouhui Chengnuo" [Deng Xiaoping Says: China Would Revoke Its Promises on Hong Kong if the Hong Kong Governor Would Not Abandon His Reforms], *Shijie Ribao*, 19 February 1993, 1.

70. "China Firm on Sovereignty over Hong Kong," *Beijing Review* 36, no. 7 (15 February 1993): 10.

71. Frank Ching, "Hong Kong: Boxed in a Corner," *FEER*, 17 December 1992, 17.

72. Tai Ming Cheung, "Common Front: Extremists Influential in Pro-China Lobby," *FEER*, 17 December 1992, 19–20.

73. "Jin Sanchengwu Shoufangzhe Zhichi Pengdu Fang'an" [About 35 Percent Polled Supported Patten's Package], *Shijie Ribao*, 24 February 1993, 4; and "Zhengcao Kandeng Xianbao, Gangdu Shengwang Hualuo" [Governor Patten's Popularity Dropped Because His Reform Proposals Were Gazetted], *Shijie Ribao*, 27 March 1993, 4.

74. "Gangren Guanzhu Zhonggang Guanxi Chaoguo Zhenggai" [Hong Kong People Concerned Hong Kong's Relationship with China More than Hong Kong's Political Reform], *Shijie Ribao*, 10 February 1993, 4.

75. "Liju Bianlun Zhengzhi Fazhan, Yiyuan Lichang Xianming" [The Legco Debated over the Political Reforms and the Councillors Take Distinct Stand], *Shijie Ribao*, 12 November 1992, 4.

76. Philip Bowring and Stacy Mosher, "Lord Without Manor: News of Governor's Exit Suggests Disarray and Confusion," *FEER*, 16 January 1992, 12.

77. Jonathan Karp, "Through Train Slows Down: China Hits Back as Patten Gazettes His Reforms," *FEER*, 25 March 1993, 12.

78. *White Paper: Representative Government in Hong Kong* (Hong Kong: The Government Printer, February 1994); and "Zhong Ying Guanyu Xianggang 1994/95 Nian Xuanju Anpai Huitanzhong Jige Zhuyao Wentide Zhenxiang" [The Real Facts of the Major Issues about the China-Britain Talks on Hong Kong's 1994/95 Elections], *Renmin Ribao: Haiwai Ban*, 1 March 1994, 3, 5.

79. Chang Hong, "NPC Considers Motion to Set to HK Group," *China Daily*, 25 March 1993, 1.

80. Li Zehong and Gao Jianxin, "Qian Qichen Addresses Preliminary Group Meeting," *Xinhua Domestic Service*, 16 July 1993, in FBIS, 19 July 1993, 62.

81. "Diyi, Di'er Jie Gangshi Guwen Zong Mingdan" [Lists of the First and Second Groups of Hong Kong Affairs Advisers], *Shijie Ribao*, 30 March 1993, 4; and Ming Cheung, "The Class of 49: China Selects Another Group of Local Advisers," *FEER*, 8 April 1993, 13.

82. Zhao Jiemin and Feng Xiuju, "Jianku Cuoshangde Chengguo" [Accomplishment Resulted from Difficult Negotiations], *Renmin Ribao: Haiwai Ban*, 5 November 1994, 3.

83. "Zhengzhi Fang'an Zhengyi Dian, Gangdu Fang Jing Bairehua" [Dispute Over the Governor's Political Reform Plan Became White-Hot When the Governor Visited Beijing], *Shijie Ribao*, 28 October 1992, 4.

84. Criton M. Zoakos, "Hong Kong's Money War," *The New York Times*, 9 January 1993, Y15.

85. "China Restarts Opium Wars with Giant Hong Kong Firm," *The Guardian*, 12 December 1992, 12.

86. Ibid.

87. "Britain, China Sign Pact on Financing of New Airport," *The Asian Wall Street Journal Weekly* 16, no. 45 (7 November 1994): 8; "Hong Kong: Fasten Your Seat Belts," *The Economist*, 12 November 1994, 44–45.

88. Christopher Patten, *Hong Kong: A Thousand Days and Beyond* (Hong Kong: The Government Printer, October 1994).

8

China's Policy on the
1997 Issue: A Pragmatic View

This book examines China's one country, two systems policy toward Hong Kong—why the Chinese government created that policy, the development of the policy in the 1984 Sino-British Joint Declaration and the Basic Law of the Hong Kong SAR, and the way it has informed Chinese decisionmaking during the transition period. In this concluding chapter, it is necessary to summarize propositions made in the previous chapters.

Chinese Policy Toward Hong Kong 1997: A Summary

The Hong Kong 1997 transfer of sovereignty issue was a great challenge to policymakers in Beijing in the early 1980s. The issue had been on Beijing's agenda ever since the radical change in China's politics caused by the Great Proletarian Cultural Revolution (1966–1976). After Deng Xiaoping regained power in 1978, his regime abandoned Mao's theory of class struggle and launched the new "four modernizations" drive. Economic reconstruction became the first priority of Deng's China. The change in Chinese domestic politics and China's adoption of the open door policy immediately highlighted the significance of Hong Kong's role in the PRC's modernizations.

In the late 1970s and early 1980s, several factors determined the importance of Hong Kong for China: the nations of the West had continued their economic sanctions against the People's Republic because of the Cold War; during the 1970s, Hong Kong had become one of the financial and trading centers of the world; and more importantly, Hong Kong had become China's major trading partner and was in a position to play a unique role in aiding China's modernization. Hong Kong's capital, management skills, and connections with the Western industrial nations became important resources for China in realizing its economic reforms and gaining access to the world market. By 1982, the change in political life on the mainland brought about by Deng's economic reforms and open door policy had already encouraged Hong Kong business-men to invest in the mainland—particularly in Shenzhen and other SEZs. By that point, it was clear that any damage to the confidence of the people of Hong Kong resulting from the 1997 issue would not be in the Chinese interest.

When the Hong Kong 1997 issue became significant in Beijing's agenda in the early 1980s, Chinese leaders had few alternatives on the issue of sover-eignty. International factors affecting the Chinese position on sovereignty in-cluded the origin of the Hong Kong question, the concept of sovereignty in international politics, and decolonization by the British Empire. Chinese do-mestic politics also determined the regime's decision on the 1997 issue. For a hundred years, generations of Chinese—the reformers of 1898 under the Qing Dynasty, Sun Yat-sen's and Chiang Kai-shek's Nationalists, and Mao Zedong's Communists—had pledged to abolish the unequal treaties and struggled for national independence. The emergence of the People's Republic as a military power further strengthened the Chinese negotiating position on the 1997 issue. The pressure of all these external and internal circumstances made it all but impossible for the Chinese leaders to concede on sovereignty in the 1980s. In a move to regain sovereignty and maintain Hong Kong's prosperity as well, the Beijing regime announced its Hong Kong policy of one country, two systems, which stated that after 1997 mainland China would continue its socialist sys-tem while Hong Kong's existing capitalism would remain unchanged for fifty years. The major considerations mandating the one country, two systems for-mula were the already established differences between the mainland and Hong Kong in social, economic, and political systems. Beijing's purpose in practic-ing two systems in one country was to maintain Hong Kong's existing systems and prosperity under Chinese sovereignty.

In fact, the one country, two systems policy was originally designed to settle the Taiwan issue. Between 1979 and 1981, the Beijing regime appealed to the Taiwan authorities for peaceful reunification under the concept of one country, two systems. In early 1982, when the 1997 issue was actually being considered, the Chinese leaders proposed that the Hong Kong and Macao ques-tions might also be settled under the one county, two systems formula. By the time of British Prime Minister Margaret Thatcher's historic Beijing visit in Sep-tember 1982, the planning on application of this policy to Hong Kong was well developed. Maintenance of Hong Kong's existing social and economic systems and way of life after 1997 became an important issue strengthening the Chinese negotiating position. By 1982, the coexistence of two different social systems in China had become Beijing's reunification policy for settling the Hong Kong, Macao, and Taiwan questions, and it was written into the 1982 amended consti-tution of the People's Republic. The Chinese formula for Hong Kong was ac-ceptable to Britain, and in the 1984 Sino-British agreement it was developed in detail.

According to Deng Xiaoping, a major contributor to the thinking about one country, two systems, the core of the theory was the mainland's socialist system and modernizations. On the one hand, the mainland's socialism would be politically dominant in the anticipated unified China. On the other hand, the pledge to maintain capitalism in Hong Kong and Macao for fifty years was based on the assumption that within that period the mainland economy would catch up with those regions.

From 1985 to 1990, development of China's Hong Kong policy was concentrated in the drafting of the Basic Law, which was the constitution of the SAR. During the drafting process, the two most controversial issues were the development of representative government in Hong Kong and the relationship between the central authorities and the autonomous SAR. Several factors affected the introduction of representative democracy to the political system of the SAR. The first factor was the existing colonial system. Under the Letters Patent and Royal Instructions, which served as the constitution of the British colony, the governor of Hong Kong was appointed by the British Crown and maintained exclusive powers over the Executive and Legislative Councils, which were only advisory bodies to the governor. By 1984, when the Sino-British Joint Declaration was announced, except for ex officio members all members of the two councils were appointed by the governor. For over 140 years, the British government failed to introduce a representative government to Hong Kong. The first direct election of the Legco was held in 1991, one year after the Basic Law was formally adopted by the NPC. However, the Chinese authorities believed that Hong Kong's economic success from the 1950s to the 1980s had proved that an authoritarian government was efficient and appropriate, and that the SAR should maintain this executive-led political structure.

During the Basic Law drafting process, the Hong Kong community was divided on the introduction of representative government. The business and professional communities argued that the current system was successful and direct election of the Legco should be introduced gradually, while the liberals headed by Martin Lee and Szeto Wah insisted that representative democracy should be in place by 1997.

In January 1990, the British and Chinese foreign ministers reached an accord on direct election to the Legco between 1991 and 2007. The Chinese also accepted the British through train proposal as conditioned by the "Luohu solution," according to which the last Legco established under British rule would automatically became the first Legco of the SAR through 1999, if the composition of the British Legco accorded with the Basic Law. Generally, the development of representative democracy under the Basic Law seemed to satisfy conservative businesspeople and professionals rather than prodemocracy liberals.

Another controversial issue during the Basic Law drafting process was the relationship between sovereign China and the autonomous SAR. A comparison of the autonomy accorded to the Hong Kong SAR with other regional autonomous practices in the world demonstrates that the Hong Kong SAR will have a high degree of autonomy. The Hong Kong SAR will be a special case, in which local government will have tremendous powers in economic, financial, and monetary matters, and also in the conduct of the region's external economic and cultural affairs. The SAR's autonomous powers in those areas can be seen as a continuation of Hong Kong's existing autonomy under British rule.

While granting the Hong Kong SAR independent powers in economy and finance, the central authorities reserved their sovereign powers over the SAR in political areas. This central political authority is formulated in several aspects of the Basic Law: Foreigners will no longer take major government posts in the SAR, though foreign citizens who reside permanently in Hong Kong will be allowed to participate in the government of the SAR. The Central People's Government will appoint the chief executive and major government officials based on local selection. The NPC will interpret and amend the Basic Law. In addition, the PLA will be stationed in Hong Kong as a symbol of China's sovereignty over the region. It was over the political relationship between the central authorities and the SAR that the mainland Basic Law drafters and Hong Kong democrats differed. Democrats argued that the SAR should have stronger powers in the selection of its own chief executive and in interpretation of the Basic Law, while the mainland drafters maintained that because the SAR would be only an autonomous region, the reservation of those powers by the central authorities was necessary.

The guiding principle for the Beijing authorities in drafting the Basic Law was the maintenance of Hong Kong's current political, economic, and legal systems except in the area of sovereignty. Deng Xiaoping, who directed China's Hong Kong policy, believed that under its current systems Hong Kong could both maintain its economic prosperity and serve China's modernizations, and that therefore dramatic changes were undesirable. Alterations in the political system were related mainly to the transfer of sovereignty. Hong Kong's colonial systems, including the colony's constitution—the Letters Patent and Royal Instructions—would be terminated; as would the British government's appointment of the governor and major officials and the Privy Council as Hong Kong's Court of Final Appeal.

Under the Basic Law, the chief executive, like the British governor, is to be the key figure of the SAR, though the range of his or her power will be less than the British governor's. The chief executive will be appointed by the Chinese central authorities on the basis of local consultation and election, but the governor is appointed by the British government in London directly. Also, the chief executive will be responsible to both the local Legco and the Central People's Government, but the governor is responsible only to London. In addition, the chief executive will have a limited role in the legislature; but the governor has been the president of the Legco, which is only his advisory body.

In conclusion, the Beijing authorities tried to maintain Hong Kong's current executive-led system of government, and to avoid the rapid development of direct election of the Legco that would strengthen its democratic role and change the current structure. Under the Basic Law, Hong Kong's existing executive-led system will be maintained, though the role of the executive will be gradually weakened as the number of directly elected members in the Legco increases.

China's Policy Toward the 1997 Issues: Challenges and Promises

Ever since it was initiated as mainland China's policy on reunification with Taiwan in the early 1980s, the concept of one country, two systems has been in a process of development. In 1982, the Beijing authorities decided to apply the formula to the Hong Kong question, and the 1984 Sino-British Joint Declaration was the first document to clearly describe a concrete Chinese policy toward Hong Kong under the formula's rubric. From 1985 to 1990, the one country, two systems policy was further defined in terms of the relationship between the central authorities and the SAR as well as within the SAR's governing system. After 1990, new issues emerged that challenged the Basic Law and necessitated new elaboration and interpretation of the formula. These challenges came from shifts in the international power structure after the Cold War; the development of democracy in Hong Kong; and the great changes in China that resulted from Deng Xiaoping's reforms and open door policy.

The first challenge to the one country, two systems formula came from Deng's economic reforms and open door policy, which altered China's state-planned economic system and encouraged private ownership and marketization. In 1992—after Deng's historic visit to prosperous Southern China, where a market-oriented economy had been well developed—the Chinese government decided to establish a socialist market economy throughout the country. The proposed socialist market economy was to continue current market-oriented reform and ultimately to establish, under the socialist political system, a market system similar to those operating in Hong Kong and Taiwan. In March 1993, the amended Chinese constitution confirmed this significant policy change, which seemed likely to be continued.

China's changing economic system has naturally altered the interpretation of the concept of one country, two systems. For instance, in 1984 Deng Xiaoping explained that the core of that policy was the dominance of the mainland's socialism, with "socialism" defined as the mainland's political system under the leadership of the Communist Party as well as its economic system with the state's planned sector as the main body. The market sector was still very limited at that point. Therefore, the "two systems" of the mainland and Hong Kong were interpreted as two different political as well as economic systems. However, by 1994 the mainland had developed dramatically toward a market economy, and it is expected that after 1997 the mainland and Hong Kong will have many fewer differences in terms of economic systems. As a result, the "two systems" should be reinterpreted as mainly two different political systems between the mainland and Hong Kong. It is expected that the mainland and

Hong Kong economies will become further interdependent as the differences between their economic systems diminish, and that the development of the market system on the mainland will be helpful in maintaining Hong Kong's capitalism and prosperity.

Second, political parties have emerged in Hong Kong. Deng Xiaoping stated that Western political party politics would not be appropriate in the Hong Kong SAR, but after the announcement of the 1984 Sino-British Joint Declaration, the British colonial government began to introduce representative democracy. As a result, since 1990 political parties and groups have emerged and offered candidates for the Legco and even for the Exco. The most influential political party was the UDHK headed by Martin Lee. The UDHK not only appealed for establishment of representative democracy—a system that is not provided in the Basic Law—before 1997, but also questioned the legitimacy of the Chinese government under the leadership of the Communist Party. The success of the democrats in elections to the Legco in 1991 and to District Boards in 1994 further challenged Beijing's position on party politics in Hong Kong. In 1994, the UDHK and Meeting Point, another democratic group, merged to become the Democratic Party (DP). It is expected that the DP will continue to be the biggest opposition party in Hong Kong.

To strengthen Beijing's support in Hong Kong, the central authorities recognized the establishment of political parties and groups that supported China's policy and the Basic Law. These political parties and groups included the DABHK, which claimed for itself the motto "love China, love Hong Kong," and the CRC, a conservative political group in the Legco that represented the interest of the business and professional communities and later developed into the Liberal Party. Though not as closely tied with Beijing as the DABHK, the LP clearly stated that its relationship with Beijing would be one of mutual understanding and cooperation. Chinese officials received delegations from the DABHK, the CRC, the LP, and other pro-China local political groups such as the New Hong Kong Alliance, and recruited the leaders of these political groups as deputies to the NPC and the CPPCC. The leading figures of the DABHK and the LP were also invited to serve as Beijing's advisers on Hong Kong affairs.

The change in Beijing's position on the development of the political parties in Hong Kong indicated that party politics would be a new aspect in Hong Kong's political system in the future. Probably the Beijing authorities will have to support, through political parties, their favored candidates in order to win elections in the Hong Kong SAR. After 1997, it is possible that two different party politics will coexist in the People's Republic: on the mainland, the Communist Party will continue to dominate Chinese politics and opposition political parties will not be allowed; but in the Hong Kong SAR, opposition parties will continue to exist, even though the Beijng authorities may not favor their development.

Third, and finally, the greatest challenge to the Chinese arrangement for the transfer of government came from the change in Britain's Hong Kong policy since 1992. From 1982 to 1984, when China and Britain negotiated on Hong Kong, their differences were focused on two issues. One was sovereignty, and the other was how to maintain Hong Kong's stability and prosperity. The two issues were closely related. London asserted that only if British systems were continued under the formula of "divided sovereignty" would Hong Kong's prosperity be secure—that without a British administration, the Hong Kong economy would collapse. The Chinese argued, however, that sovereignty was non-negotiable and that Hong Kong's prosperity could be maintained under the one country, two systems formula.[1]

After the 1984 agreement was made, the British and Chinese governments pledged to cooperate in the transition period, both sides agreeing that the political system established before 1997 would be continued by the Hong Kong SAR. As a result, the post-1997 political system as defined in the Basic Law was framed according to the current system. The concepts of the through train (Hong Kong's 1995 Legco would become the first Legco of the SAR and would work through 1997) and of convergence (the political reforms undertaken before 1997 would converge with the Basic Law) were typical examples of Sino-British cooperation.

However, the collapse of Communist regimes in Eastern Europe and the Soviet Union as well as the 1989 Tiananmen incident convinced the British administration under Prime Minister John Major that a representative government should be in place in Hong Kong before 1997. If the Chinese Communist government proved to be unstable, it might not be able to execute the transfer of sovereignty without disrupting the political and economic freedoms of the people of Hong Kong. During the Sino-British negotiations from 1982 to 1984, the British government stressed that its goal was to maintain Hong Kong's prosperity and way of life. In these later negotiations, prosperity was no longer mentioned, perhaps because Hong Kong had continued its stable economic growth after 1984. In addition, the success of China's reforms toward a market economy and the economic interdependence between the mainland and Hong Kong seemed to be contributing to Hong Kong's prosperity.

Chris Patten, the new governor of Hong Kong, was chosen to implement this new British policy of representative government for Hong Kong. Patten proposed to weaken the current executive-led system and to increase the role of the Legco—a change that would be produced through direct election. The Chinese authorities viewed Patten's reforms as violations of Sino-British arrangements for the transfer of sovereignty in the 1984 Joint Declaration, the 1990 Hurd-Qian accord, and the Basic Law. The Chinese government rejected Patten's proposal; and the Sino-British conflict began. The NPC adopted a resolution that the political procedures that were created by Governor Patten for Hong Kong would end on July 1, 1997, and that China would establish the first government and Legco of the SAR based on the Basic Law.

Economically, Hong Kong has achieved remarkable progress between 1984, when the joint declaration was announced, and 1994. As Governor Patten reported for this period, Hong Kong's GDP grew by 79 percent in real terms; the value of foreign trade increased by 350 percent; and earnings grew by 66 percent.[2] In the years to come, Hong Kong's economy will continue to grow and the city will prosper for the following reasons: First, Hong Kong will continue to benefit from China's economic boom, and in fact economic interdependence between Hong Kong and the mainland will be the major source of Hong Kong's prosperity. Second, China's one country, two systems policy and the Basic Law will serve to maintain the confidence of Hong Kong's business and professional community. Third, because Beijing's policy is supported by the business community, when the governmental system created by Governor Patten ends in 1997 there will be little impact on Hong Kong's economy. Of all the factors that will affect Hong Kong in the following decades, it will not be Hong Kong's internal political development but rather the development of China's modernization that will be the most significant.

Conclusion

Although the Chinese government did reinterpret some policies toward Hong Kong during the transition period, the core one country, two systems policy remained unchanged and is likely to be practised after the People's Republic resumes sovereignty in 1997. In fact, because of changes occurring in Hong Kong and the mainland, policies were reinterpreted in such a way as to become more flexible toward Hong Kong.

Today, many differences between China's and Hong Kong's political systems exist. The PRC remains under Communist rule, and permits no competitive political parties or anticommunist activities. The people of Hong Kong, however, although still ruled by an authoritarian British colonial government, now enjoy freedom of speech, the press, religion, and assembly. When competitive political parties emerged in the 1990s and party candidates began to run for Legco seats through direct election, the Beijing authorities changed their former position and acquiesced to party politics in Hong Kong. Furthermore, the Basic Law provides that the number of Legco members elected directly will continue to increase, so although the Beijing officials do not expect any radical change in Hong Kong's political system after 1997, it is possible that Hong Kong citizens may keep their political freedoms while the mainland remains socialist.

Differences between the mainland and Hong Kong in economic systems have diminished. The mainland government dramatically introduced market mechanisms, and the PRC's determination and progress in establishing a market economy are impressive. Since Hong Kong continues its active participation in China's modernization drive, economic interdependence between the mainland and Hong Kong will continue and differences between the two economic systems will probably be reduced even more in the years ahead. It is most likely that because of the importance of Hong Kong in China's economic development and of the Hong Kong model in China's reunification strategy, the authoritarian Communist government in Beijing will allow "two systems" to coexist in the mainland and Hong Kong after 1997.

Notes

1. In June 1984, Deng Xiaoping said: "We should have faith in the people of Hongkong. The notion that Chinese cannot manage Hongkong affairs satisfactorily is a left-over from the old colonial mentality. . . . The Chinese in Hongkong . . . have the ability to run the affairs of Hongkong well and they should be confident of this. The prosperity of Hongkong has been achieved mainly by Hongkong residents, most of whom are Chinese. Chinese are no less intelligent than foreigners and are by no means less talented. It is not true that only foreigners can be good administrators. We Chinese are just as capable." See Deng Xiaoping, "One Country, Two Systems," in *Speeches and Writings* (New York: Pergamon Press, 1987), 93.

2. Patten, *Hong Kong: A Thousand Days and Beyond*, 8.

Bibliography

References in English

Books

Aristotle. *The Politics.* Book 3. Baltimore, Md.: Penguin, 1966.

Bodin, Jean. *Six Books of the Commonwealth.* Rev. ed. M. J. Tooley, trans. and ed. Oxford: Basil Blackwell, 1962.

Bonavia, David. *Hong Kong 1997: The Final Settlement.* Hong Kong: South China Morning Post, 1985.

Brierly, J. L. *The Law of Nations: An Introduction to the International Law and Peace.* 6th ed. New York: Oxford University Press, 1963.

Brownlie, Ian. *Principles of Public International Law.* New York: Oxford University Press, 1990.

Chan, Ming K., and David J. Clark. *The Hong Kong Basic Law: Blueprint for "Stability and Prosperity" under Chinese Sovereignty?* Armonk, N. Y.: M. E. Sharpe, 1991.

Chen, Lung-Fong. *State Succession Relating to Unequal Treaties.* Hamden, Conn.: Archon, 1974.

Cheng, Joseph Y. S., ed. *Hong Kong: In Search of a Future.* Hong Kong: Oxford University Press, 1984.

———, ed. *Hong Kong in Transition.* Hong Kong: Oxford University Press, 1986.

———, ed. *China: Modernization in the 1980s.* Hong Kong: The Chinese University Press, 1989.

———, and Par C. K. Kwong, eds. *The Other Hong Kong Report 1992.* Hong Kong: The Chinese University Press, 1992.

Chiang, Kai-shek. *China's Destiny and Chinese Economic Theory.* New York: Roy Publishers, 1947.

Chinese Ministry of Information. *The Collected Wartime Messages of Generalissimo Chiang Kai-shek, 1937–1945.* New York: John Day, 1946.

Chiu, Hungdah, Y. C. Jao, and Yuanli Wu, eds. *The Future of Hong Kong: Toward 1997 and Beyond.* New York: Quorum Books, 1986.

Cohen, J. A., and Hungdah Chiu, eds. *People's China and International Law: A Documentary Study.* Vol. 1. Princeton, N. J.: Princeton University Press, 1974.

Darvin, John. *Britain and Decolonization: The Retreat from Empire in the Post-War World.* New York: St. Martin's Press, 1980.

Davies, Ken. *Hong Kong to 1994: A Question of Confidence.* London: The Economic Intelligence Unit Limited, 1990.

Deng, Xiaoping. *Speeches and Writings.* 2nd ed. Oxford: Pergamon Press, 1987.

Dikshit, Ramesh Dutta. *The Political Geography of Federalism: An Inquiry into Origins and Stability.* New York: John Wiley & Sons, 1975.

Dinstein, Yoram, ed. *Models of Autonomy.* Brunswick, N. J.: Transaction Books, 1981.

Endacott, G. B. *Government and People in Hong Kong 1841–1962: A Constitutional History.* Hong Kong: Hong Kong University Press, 1964.

———. *A History of Hong Kong.* 2nd ed. Hong Kong: Oxford University Press, 1977.

Endicott, Stephen Lyon. *Diplomacy and Enterprise: British China Policy, 1933–1937.* Vancouver: University of British Columbia, 1975.

FEER, ed. *Asian Yearbook, 1980.* Hong Kong: FEER, 1980.

Fishel, Wesley R. *The End of Extraterritoriality in China.* New York: Octagon Books, 1974.

Gilpin, Robert. *War and Change in World Politics.* New York: Cambridge University Press, 1981.

Hartland-Thunberg, Penelope. *China, Hong Kong, Taiwan and the World Trading System.* London: Macmillan, 1990.

Hinsley, F. H. *Sovereignty.* New York: Cambridge University Press, 1968.

Hobbes, Thomas. *The Leviathan.* Michael Oakeshott, ed. Oxford: Basil Blackwell, 1960.

Hu, Sheng. *Imperialism and Chinese Politics.* Beijing: Foreign Language Press, 1955; reprint, Westport, Conn.: Hyperion Press, 1973.

Issacs, Harold R. *The Tragedy of the Chinese Revolution.* 2nd ed. Stanford, California: Stanford University Press, 1961.

Jain, J. P. *China in World Politics: A Study of Sino-British Relations, 1949–1975.* New Delhi: Radiant Publishers, 1976.

Kau, Michael Y. M., and Jogh K. Leung, eds. *The Writings of Mao Zedong 1949–1976.* Vol. 1. Armonk, N. Y.: M. E. Sharpe, 1986.

Keeton, George. *The Development of Extraterritoriality in China.* New York: Howard Fertig, 1969.

Kelley, Ian. *Hong Kong: A Political-Geographic Analysis.* Honolulu: University of Hawaii Press, 1986.

Keohane, Robert O., and Joseph S. Nye. *Power and Interdependence: World Politics in Transition.* Boston: Little, Brown, 1977.

Kraus, Willy. *Private Business in China: Revival Between Ideology and Pragmatism.* Erich Holz, trans. Honolulu: University of Hawaii Press, 1991.

Kulessa, Manfred., ed. *The Newly Industrializing Economies of Asia: Prospects of Cooperation.* Berlin: Spring-Verlag, 1990.

Lane, Kevin P. *Sovereignty and the Status Quo: The Historical Roots of China's Hong Kong Policy.* Boulder, Colo.: Westview Press, 1990.

Lardy, Nicholas R. *China in the World Economy.* Washington, D. C.: Institute for International Economics, 1994.

Lenin, V. I. *State and Revolution.* New York: International Publishers, 1968.

Liao, Kuang-sheng. *Antiforeignism and Modernization in China, 1860–1980: Linkage Between Domestic Politics and Foreign Policy.* New York: St. Martin's Press, 1984.

Locke, John. *The Second Treatise of Government.* J. W. Gough, ed. Oxford: Basil Blackwell, 1976.

Merriam, Jr., C. E. *History of the Theory of Sovereignty Since Rousseau.* New York: Cambridge University Press, 1986.

McGurn, William, ed. *Basic Law, Basic Questions.* Hong Kong: Review Publishing Company, 1988.

Miners, Norman. *The Government and Politics of Hong Kong.* 2nd ed. Hong Kong: Oxford University Press, 1977.

———. *The Government and Politics of Hong Kong.* 4th ed. Hong Kong: Oxford University Press, 1986.

————. *Hong Kong Under Imperial Rule, 1912–1941.* Hong Kong: Oxford University Press, 1987.

————. *The Government and Politics of Hong Kong.* 5th ed. Hong Kong: Oxford University Press, 1991.

Moon, Parker Thomas. *Imperialism and World Politics.* New York: Macmillan, 1939.

Morgenthau, Hans J. *Politics Among Nations: The Struggle for Power and Peace.* New York: Alfred A. Knopf, 1962.

North, Henry Kittredge. *China and the Powers.* New York: John Day, 1927.

North, Robert C. *The Foreign Relations of China.* North Scituate, Mass.: Duxbury Press, 1978.

Nozari, Fariborz. *Unequal Treaties in International Law.* Stockholm, Sweden: S-Byran Sundt, 1971.

Perkins, Dwight H., ed. *China's Modern Economy in Historical Perspective.* Stanford: Stanford University Press, 1980.

Rabushka, Alvin. *The New China: Comparative Economic Development in Mainland China, Taiwan, and Hong Kong.* Boulder, Colo.: Westview Press, 1987.

Rafferty, Kevin. *City on the Rocks: Hong Kong's Uncertain Future.* New York: Viking, 1990.

Reed, Steven R. *Japanese Prefectures and Policymaking.* Pittsburgh, Penn.: University of Pittsburgh Press, 1986.

Review Publishing Company. *Asian 1990 Yearbook.* Hong Kong: Review Publishing Company, 1990.

Riker, William H. *Federalism: Origin, Operation, Significance.* Boston: Little, Brown, 1964.

Roberts, David, ed. *Hong Kong 1990.* Hong Kong: The Government Printer, 1990.

Rosenau, James N. *Linkage Politics.* New York: Free Press, 1969.

Rousseau, Jean Jacques. *The Social Contract.* Charles Frankel, trans. and ed. New York: Hafner Publishing, 1947.

Scott, Ian. *Political Change and the Crisis of Legitimacy in Hong Kong.* London: Hurst & Company, 1989.

Snow, Donald N. *National Security: Enduring Problems of U.S. Defense Policy.* New York: St. Martin's Press, 1987.

Sorensen, Max. *Manual of Public International Law.* New York: St. Martin's Press, 1968.

Sun, Yat-sen. *San Min Chu I: The Three Principles of the People.* Frank W. Price, trans. Taipei, Taiwan: China Publishing, n.d.

Sung, Yun-wing. *The China-Hong Kong Connection: The Key to China's Open-Door Policy.* New York: Cambridge University Press, 1991.

Tsang, Steven Yui-sang. *Democracy Shelved: Great Britain, China, and Attempts at Constitutional Reform in Hong Kong, 1945–1952.* Hong Kong: Oxford University Press, 1988.

Tung, William L. *China and the Foreign Powers: The Impact of and Reaction to Unequal Treaties.* Dobbs Ferry, N. Y.: Oceana Publications, 1970.

United Nations Industrial Development Organization. *China: Towards Sustainable Industrial Growth.* Cambridge, Mass.: Blackwell Publishers, 1992.

Vincent, John Carter. *The Extraterritorial System in China: Final Phase.* Cambridge: Harvard University Press, 1970.

Walker, R. B. J., and Saul H. Mendlovitz, eds. *Contending Sovereignties: Redefining Political Community.* Boulder, Colo.: Lynne Rienner Publishers, 1990.

Wesley-Smith, Peter. *Unequal Treaty 1898–1997: China, Great Britain and Hong Kong's New Territories.* Hong Kong: Oxford University Press, 1980.

————, and Albert H. K. Chen, eds. *The Basic Law and Hong Kong's Future.* Hong Kong: Butterworths, 1988.

Wheare, K. C. *Federal Government.* 4th ed. New York: Oxford University Press, 1964.
Woetzel, Jonathan R. *China's Economic Opening to the Outside World.* New York: Praeger, 1989.
Youngson, A. J., ed. *China and Hong Kong: The Economic Nexus.* Hong Kong: Oxford University Press, 1983.

Documents, Reports, Articles, and Other Sources

"AFP: PRC Confirms Intent to Regain Hong Kong." FBIS, 23 September 1982, G4.
"Airport Issue Can Be Solved in Accordance with Sino-British Joint Declaration Says 'Bauhinia'." *Zhongguo Xinwen She,* 1 July 1991, in FBIS, 2 July 1991, 68.
"An Example of Mainland–Hong Kong–Taiwan Economic Cooperation." *GNT,* 5 January 1988, in FBIS, 9 January 1989, 71.
"An Unacceptable Accord." *The Times,* 16 February 1990, 13.
An, Zhiguo. "Regional Autonomy for Minorities." *Beijing Review* 27, no. 24 (11 June 1984): 4–5.
Asherford, Douglas E. "Are Britain and France 'Unitary'?" *Comparative Politics* 9, no. 4 (July 1977): 483–499.
"A Significant Concept." *Beijing Review* 27, no. 44 (29 October 1984): 16–17.
Baldinger, Pamela. "Guangdong's Rockfeller." *The China Business Review* 20, no. 1 (January–February 1993): 38–41.
Basic Law of the Hong Kong Special Administrative Region of the People's Republic of China, 1990.
Basler, Barbara. "Democracy Backers in Hong Kong Win Election Landslide." *The New York Times,* 16 September 1991, A4.
Baum, Julian. "The Narrowing Strait: Taipei and Peking Prepare for Unofficial Talks." *FEER,* 29 April 1993, 13.
———. "The Stumbling Block: Investment Guarantees a Hurdle at Singapore Talks." *FEER,* 6 May 1993, 11–12.
———. " Divided Nations." *FEER,* 16 September 1993, 10.
———. "A Difficult Age: Taiwan Struggles to Engineer Sustainable Growth." *FEER,* 30 June 1994, 56.
———. "Ready When You Are." *FEER,* 15 September 1994, 62.
———, John McBeth, and Rodney Tasker. "In His Private Capacity: President Lee Scores Points in Holiday Diplomacy." *FEER,* 24 February 1994, 18–19.
"Beijing Calling." *The Economist,* 18 April 1992, 31–32.
"Beijing Rules Out Compromise." *The Standard,* 5 November 1991, A1, 3, in FBIS, 5 November 1991, 58.
Bernhardt, Rudolph. "Federalism and Autonomy." In *Models and Autonomy,* Yoram Dinstein, ed., 23–28. Brunswick, N. J.: Transaction Books, 1981.
Binyon, Michael, and James Pringle. "Patten Move to Broaden Democracy Angers China." *The Times,* 8 October 1992, 11.
Blaustein, Albert P., ed. *Fundamental Legal Documents of Communist China.* South Hackensack, N. J., 1962.
Bonavia, David. "Get Back in Step: Deng Blasts Two Colleagues Who Said PLA Troops Will Not Be Stationed in Hong Kong." *FEER,* 7 June 1984, 13–14.
Bowring, Philip. "Down in the Dumps." *FEER,* 29 September 1983, 146–147.
———, and Stacy Mosher. "Lord Without Manor: News of Governor's Exit Suggests Disarray and Confusion." *FEER,* 16 January 1992, 10–12.
Braude, Jonathan. "Campaigners Give Hurd's Plan a Guarded Welcome." *The Times,* 21 December 1991, 6.

————, and Catherine Sampson. "Deal with Peking on Hong Kong Is Branded a Sell-Out." *The Times*, 16 February 1990, 8.

"Britain, China Reveal 'Secret Deal' Letters." *South China Morning Post,* 30 October 1992, 1.

"Britain, China Sign Pact on Financing of New Airport." *The Asian Wall Street Journal Weekly* 16, No. 45 (7 November 1994): 8.

"Britain's Argument Is Untenable." *Beijing Review* 26, no. 41 (10 October 1983): 10–11.

Broadfoot, Robert. "Wither Hong Kong Investment: All Eyes on the Japanese." *The China Business Review* 18, no. 1 (January–February 1991): 26–29.

"Building Better Relations." *Free China Review* 43, no. 2 (February 1993): 4–15.

"Can China Reach Its Economic Targets by 2000?" *Beijing Review* 25, no. 40 (4 October 1982): 16–18.

Cao, Yong. "Billion-dollar Deal for Shanghai Port." *China Daily,* 4 September 1992, 1.

"Chairman Ye Jianyng's Elaborations on Policy Concerning the Return of Taiwan to Motherland and Peaceful Reunification." *Beijing Review* 24, no. 40 (5 October 1981): 10–11.

Chan, Christine. "Xinhua Officials Criticize Martin Lee." *The Standard,* 10 October 1991, A3, in FBIS, 10 October 1991, 87.

Chen, Albert H. K. "The Relationship Between the Central Government and the SAR." In *The Basic Law and Hong Kong's Future,* Peter Wesley-Smith and Albert H. Y. Chen, eds., 107–140. Hong Kong: Butterworths, 1988.

Chen, Adward K. Y. "The Hong Kong Economy in a Changing International Economic Environment." In *The Newly Industrializing Economies of Asian,* Manfred Kulessa, ed., 97–110. Berlin, 1990.

Chen, Chien-ping. "Lu Ping Stresses Basic Law Cannot Be Amended Before 1997." *Wen Wei Pao,* 9 October 1991, 2, in FBIS, 11 October 1991, 68–69.

————. "Ji Pengfei Comments on Hong Kong Court of Final Appeal." *Wen Wei Pao,* 23 October 1991, 2, in FBIS, 30 October 1991, 69.

Chen, Chu-yuan. "Peking's Economic Reform and Open Door Policy After the Tiananmen Incident." *Issues and Studies* 26, no. 10 (October 1990): 43–64.

Chen, Qiuping. "Guangdong, A Latent Dragon." *Beijing Review* 35, no. 21 (25 May 1992): 7–9.

Chen, Wei-Min. "Yang Shangkun Reassures Hong Kong People." *Ching Pao,* 5 January 1992, 11, in FBIS, 21 January 1992, 72–73.

————. "Deng Xiaoping Praises Hong Kong's Civil Servants." *Ching Pao,* 5 May 1992, 11, in FBIS, 17 March 1992, 72–73.

Chen, Wen. "Martin Lee Quibbles Again." *Wen Wei Pao,* 4 October 1991, 11, in FBIS, 5 October 1991, 80–81.

Cheng, Denis. "Toward a Jurisprudence of the Third Kind—One Country, Two Systems." *Case Western Reserve Journal of International Law* 20, no. 1 (Winter, 1988): 105.

Cheng, Elizabeth. "The East Is Red: China Unveils New Development Direction." *FEER,* 31 May 1990, 57–58.

————. "China's Changing Tide: Coastal Cities Rush to Offer Land After Peking Policy Shift." *FEER,* 28 June 1990, 68–69.

————. "Small Leap Forward: Shenzhen Bourse Opens with a Whimper." *FEER,* 18 July 1991, 69–70.

————. "Through the Roof: Shenzhen to Curb Property Speculation." *FEER,* 24 October 1991, 75–76.

————, and Stacy Mosher. "Free for All: Economic Strategy by Hongkong." *FEER,* 14 May 1992, 26–30.

————, and Michael Taylor. "Delta Force: Pearl River Cities in a Partnership with Hong Kong." *FEER,* 16 May 1991, 64–68.

Cheng, Joseph Y. "The Future of Hong Kong: A Hong Kong 'Belonger's' View." *International Affairs* 58 (Summer, 1982): 476–488.

————. "The 1985 District Board Elections in Hong Kong." In *Hong Kong in Transition.* Joseph Cheng, ed., 67–87. Hong Kong: Oxford University Press, 1986.

————. "Political System." In *The Basic Law and Hong Kong's Future,* Peter Wesley-Smith and Albert H. K. Chen, eds., 141–171. Hong Kong: Butterworths, 1988.

Cheng, Terry. "China Leaking Lease Plans." *The Standard,* 11 August 1982, 1, 16, in FBIS, 11 August 1982, W4.

Cheung, Doreen. "Councillors Question Agreement." *South China Morning Post,* 26 October 1991, in FBIS, 30 October 1991, 68–69.

Cheung, Tai Ming. "Clogged Arteries: Shanghai's Revival Hinges on Better Transport." *FEER,* 4 October 1990, 68–69.

————. "Hong Kong: Embattled Governor." *FEER,* 26 November 1992, 10–11.

————. "Common Front: Extremists Influential in Pro-China Lobby." *FEER,* 17 December 1992, 19–20.

————. "The Class of 49: China Selects Another Group of Local Advisers." *FEER,* 8 April 1993, 13.

Chiang, Ching-kuo. "Bitter Lessons and a Solemn Mission." In *Mainland China, Taiwan, and U.S. Policy,* Hung-mao Tien, ed., 241–245. Cambridge, Mass.: Oelgeschager, Gunn & Hain, 1983.

Chien, Fredrick F. "UN Should Welcome Taiwan." *FEER,* 5 August 1993, 23.

"China, Britain, Reaffirm Implementation of Agreement on Court of Final Appeal." *Ta Kung Pao,* 7 December 1991, 2, in FBIS, 10 December 1991, 74–75.

"China Firm on Sovereignty over Hong Kong." *Beijing Review* 36, no. 7 (15 February 1993): 9–10.

"China Regrets HK Decision by London." *China Daily,* 30 July 1990, 1.

"China Restarts Opium Wars with Giant Hong Kong Firm." *The Guardian,* 12 December 1992, 12.

"China Set to Appoint Hong Kong Affairs Advisers." *Xinhua,* 29 February 1992, in FBIS, 2 March 1992, 81.

"China's Constitution to be Amended." *Beijing Review* 36, no. 9 (1 March 1993): 4.

"China's Stand on Hong Kong Issue Is Solemn and Just." *NCNA,* 30 September 1982, in FBIS, 1 October 1982, E1.

"China's 1992 GDP Increases by 12 Percent." *Beijing Review* 36, no. 2 (11 January 1993): 5.

Ching, Frank. "Hong Kong: Cleared for Action." *FEER,* 22 October 1992, 20–21.

————. "Past Imperfect." *FEER,* 29 October 1992, 23.

————. "Hong Kong: Boxed in a Corner." *FEER,* 17 December 1992, 16–18.

————. "An About-Turn by Taiwan." *FEER,* 4 August 1994, 30.

Chiou, C. L. "China's Reunification Policy: No 'Mousetrapping' of Taiwan." In *China: Modernization in the 1980s,* Joseph Y. S. Cheng, ed., 203–229. Hong Kong: The Chinese University Press, 1989.

Clark, David J. "The Basic Law: One Document, Two Systems." In *The Hong Kong Basic Law: Blueprint for "Stability and Prosperity" Under Chinese Sovereignty?* Ming K. Chan and David J. Clark, eds., 37–60. Armonk, N. Y.: M. E. Sharpe, 1991.

"Commentator on Reaction to Basic Law Proposal." *Ta Kong Pao,* 1 December 1988, 16, in FBIS, 1 December 1988, 42–43.

Constitution of People's Republic of China of 1982.

"Council's S. Y. Chung Opposes Political Reform." *South China Morning Post,* 4 May 1987, 1, in FBIS, 5 May 1987, W3–4.

"CPPCC Delegate Gives Deng's Views on Hong Kong." *AFP,* 27 June 1983, in FBIS, 28 June 1983, E1.

Dai, Yannian. "Yangpu: China's Largest Development Zone." *Beijing Review* 35, 23 (1 June 1992): 18–21.

"Defend Solemnity of Agreement on the Final Court of Appeal." *Wen Wei Pao,* 25 October 1991, 2, in FBIS, 30 October 1991, 70–73.

"Delegation of Industrialists, Businessmen Asks About Hong Kong's Prospects; Gu Mu Says Its Prosperity Will Continue." *Wen Wei Pao,* 12 August 1982, 1, 2, in FBIS, 12 August 1982, W1.

Delfs, Robert. "Hongkong: 1997 and All That." *FEER,* 16 July 1982, 15–16.

"Deng Congress Speech Hints Hong Kong Reunification." *The Standard,* 4 September 1982, in FBIS, 7 September 1982, W3–4.

Deng, Xiaoping. "Our Basic Position on the Hong Kong Question." *Beijing Review* 36, no. 41 (4 October 1993): 7–8.

———. "Gift of Speeches Made in Wuchang, Shenzhen, Zhuhai and Shanghai." *Beijing Review* 37, no. 7 (7 February 1994): 9–20.

"Development in Shanghai's Pudong Area Viewed." *Xinhua,* 9 July 1993, in FBIS, 9 July 1993, 47.

Dicks, Anthony. "Treaty, Grant, Usage or Sufferance? Some Legal Aspects of the Status of Hong Kong." *China Quarterly* 95 (September 1983): 427–455.

Dinstein, Yoram. "Autonomy." In *Examples of Autonomy,* Yoram Dinstein, ed., 191–303. New Brunswick, N. J.: Transaction Books, 1981.

The Draft Basic Law of the Hong Kong Special Administrative Region. In *The Basic Law and Hong Kong's Future,* Peter Wesley-Smith and Albert H. Y. Chen, eds., 329–369. Hong Kong: Butterworths, 1988.

Duo, Duo. "Lu Ping Says Criticism of Setup of Court of Final Appeal Reflects Lack of Confidence in Hong Kong People's Self-Government." *Zhongguo Xinwen She,* 5 November 1991, in FBIS, 7 November 1991, 74.

Fang, Sheng. "Economic Co-operation between Mainland, Taiwan and Hong Kong." *Beijing Review* 34, no. 46 (25 November 1991): 28–30.

Fei, Xiaotong. "Turning Shanghai into a 'Mainland Hong Kong'." *Beijing Review* 33, no. 43 (22 October 1990): 25–27.

Foreign Relations of the United States, 1928. vol. 2. Washington, D. C.: U.S. Government Printing Office.

"Free Trade Zone Opened in Tianjin." *Beijing Review* 34, no. 43 (October 1991): 37–38.

"Free Trade Zones Multiplying." *Beijing Review* 36, no. 30 (26 July 1993): 5.

"Fuzhou Free Trade Zone Set Up." *Beijing Review* 35, no. 50 (12 December 1992): 38.

Gao, Shangquan. "China's Economy Vital for Asia-Pacific." *Beijing Review* 38, no. 3 (16 January 1995): 17–19.

Gibney, Frank, Jr. "China's Renegade Province: Guangdong Does Fine Without Either Marx or Mao." *Newsweek,* 17 February 1991, 35–38.

"Gives Inaugural Speech." FBIS, 21 May 1990, 61–63.

Goldstein, Carl. "Stranglehold Loosens: Hongkong's Li Ka-shing Boosts Shanghai Port." *FEER,* 60–61.

"Governor Wilson Says 'China Can Be Trusted.'" *Xinhua,* 22 January 1992, in FBIS, 23 January 1992, 60.

"Governor's Banquets." *AFP,* 29 March 1979, in FBIS, 30 March 1979, E7.

"Great Significance of Lu Ping's Meeting with Hong Kong Governor." *Wen Wei Pao,* 27 July 1991, 2, in FBIS, 2 August 1991, 59.

Green Paper: The Further Development of Representative Government in Hong Kong. Hong Kong: Government Printer, July 1984.

Green Paper: The 1987 Review of Developments in Representative Government. Hong Kong: Government Printer, May 1987.

Greenhouse, Steven. "New Tally of World's Economies Catapults China into Third Place." *The New York Times,* 20 May 1993, A1, A6.

Han, Guojian. "Stock Exchange Adds Wings to SEZ." *Beijing Review* 34, no. 25 (24 June 1991): 11.

Hannum, Hurst, and Richard B. Lillich. "The Concept of Autonomy in International Law," *The American Journal of International Law* 74 (1980): 858–889.

He, Po-shih. "Five Major Tasks Are Aimed at Control." *Tangtai* [Contemporary], no. 7 (15 October 1991): 14–15, in FBIS, 14 November 1991, 72–74.

He, Sui-i. "Allied Economic Relations between Guangdong and Hong Kong—An Interview with Wu Mingyu, Deputy Director of the State Economic Development Research Center." *Ta Kung Pao,* 15 May 1992, 2, in FBIS, 27 May 1992, 41–42.

He, Wei-Tzu. "Lu Ping on Direct Election of Hong Kong Legislative Council." *Wen Wei Pao,* 20 September 1991, 2, in FBIS, 20 September 1991, 82–83.

"Hong Kong and Foreign Business Increases Investment in Mainland China." *Zhongguo Tongxun She,* 17 February 1992, in FBIS, 28 February 1992, 83–84.

"Hong Kong Figures to Form PRC Advisers Panel." *South China Sunday Morning Post,* 8 March 1992, 1, 4, in FBIS, 9 March 1992, 83–85.

"Hong Kong Gets Same Status as Macao After 1997." *AFP,* 7 July 1983, in FBIS, 8 July 1983, E1.

Hong Kong Government Industry Department, *Hong Kong Works,* Spring 1994.

"Hong Kong Newspaper President Visits Beijing: Meets Deng Xiaoping." *Xinhua,* 18 July 1981, in FBIS, 22 July 1981, E5.

"Hong Kong's Governor Looks Ahead." *The China Business Review* 17, no. 1 (January–February, 1990): 53–54.

"Hopes for Hong Kong: Chris Patten on His Plans to Safeguard a Way of Life." *The Times,* 8 October 1992, 14.

Hu, Yaobang. "Create a New Situation in All Fields of Socialist Modernization—Report to the 12th National Congress of the Communist Party (September 1, 1982)." *Beijing Review* 25, no. 37 (13 September 1982): 11–40.

Huang, Taihe. "Development of China's SEZ." *Beijing Review* 32, no. 26 (8 April 1991): 20–26.

"Hurd Accused of Cave-in on Hong Kong." *The Times,* 17 February 1990, 4.

Jao, Y. C. "Hong Kong's Economic Prospects after the Sino-British Agreement: A Preliminary Assessment." In *The Future of Hong Kong,* Hungdah Chiu, Y. C. Jao, and Yuan-li Wu, eds., 57–94. New York: Quorum Books, 1987.

———. "Hong Kong's Role in Financing China's Modernization." In *China and Hong Kong: The Economic Nexus,* A. J. Youngson, ed., 12–76. Hong Kong: Oxford University Press, 1983.

Jiang, Zemin. "China on Its March Toward the 21st Century." *Beijing Review* 34, no. 21 (27 May 1991): 11–16.

Jin, Fu. "China's Recovery of Xianggang (Hongkong) Area Fully Accords with International Law." *Beijing Review* 26, no. 39 (26 September 1983): 14–19, 25.

Jin, Mingjun. "Competition No, Emulation Yes." *Beijing Review* 23, no. 22 (2 June 1980): 20–21.

Jing, Bian. "Pudong: An Open Policy Showcase." *Beijing Review* 33, no. 29 (16 July 1990): 27–30.

Joint Declaration of the Government of the Kingdom of Great Britain and Northern Ireland and the Government of the People's Republic of China on the Question of Hong Kong, 1984.

Kao, Lang. "One Country, Two Systems: Its Theory, Practice, and Feasibility." Ph.D. diss., University of Maryland, 1988.

———. "A New Relationship Across the Taiwan Strait." *Issues and Studies* 27, no. 4 (April 1991): 44–68.

Kaye, Lincoln. "Reformists' Attempted Comeback Is Reflected in Media." *FEER,* 13 February 1992, 10–11.

Kristoff, Nicholas D. "Chinese Communism's Secret Aim: Capitalism." *The New York Times,* 19 October 1992, A4.

———. "Starting to Build Their First Bridge, China and Taiwan Sign 4 Pacts." *The New York Times,* 30 April 1993, A7.

Lau, Emily. "Hong Kong: A Question of Semantics." *FEER,* 23 August 1984, 16–17.

———. "The Grey Paper: Policy on Political Reform Falls Short of Promises." *FEER,* 18 February 1988, 14.

———. "The Early History of the Drafting Process." In *The Basic Law and Hong Kong's Future,* Peter Wesley-Smith and Albert H. K. Chen, eds., 90–104. Hong Kong: Butterworths, 1988.

———. "Skimming the Cream." *FEER,* 4 January 1990, 9.

———. "Fog and Drizzle: Britain Hesitates on Political Development." *FEER,* 25 January 1990, 17.

Lee, Martin C. M. "How Much Autonomy?" In *Basic Law, Basic Questions,* William McGurn, ed., 37–52. Hong Kong: Review Publishing Company, 1988.

———. "A Tale of Two Articles." In *The Basic Law and Hong Kong's Future,* Peter Wesley-Smith and Albert H. Y. Chen, eds., 309–325. Hong Kong: Butterworths, 1988.

Lee, Tung-Ming. "The Sino-British Joint Declaration on the Question of Hong Kong: Political and Legal Perspectives." Ph.D. diss., Norman: University of Oklahoma, 1985.

Leung, Stanley. "Businesses Oppose Elections," *South China Morning Post,* 29 September 1987, 2, in FBIS, 29 September 1987, 37.

———. "'Collision' Feared Over Appeal Court Controversy." *The Standard,* 1 November 1991, D8, in FBIS, 5 November 1991, 57.

Leung, Stanley, and C. K. Lau. "Li Hou Discusses Party Politics." *South China Morning Post,* 3 June 1986, 14, in FBIS, 4 June 1986, W5–7.

Li, Haibo. "Party Congress Introduces Market Economy." *Beijing Review* 35, no. 42 (19 October 1992): 9–10.

Li, Janquan. "Mainland and Taiwan: Formula for China's Reunification." *Beijing Review* 29, no. 5 (3 February 1986): 18–24.

———. "Mainland-Taiwan Trade: Look Back and into Future." *Beijing Review* 34, no. 4 (28 January 1991): 26–29.

Li, Peng. "Report on the Outline of the Ten-Year Programme and of the Eighth Five-Year Plan for National Economic and Social Development." *Beijing Review* 34, no. 23 (15 April 1991): II.

Li, Ping. "Tianjin Profile (I): A Future Free Trade Port in North China." *Beijing Review* 34, no. 33 (19 August 1991): 14–15.

Li, Rongxia. "Fledgling Free Trade Zone in Tianjin." *Beijing Review* 36, no. 31 (2 August 1993): 19–21.

———. "Free Trade Zones in China." *Beijing Review* 36, no. 31 (2 August 1993): 14–19.

———. "Tianjin Zone Lures Foreign Investors." *Beijing Review* 37, no. 10 (7 March 1994): 11–15.

Li, Zehong, and Gao Jianxin. "Qian Qichen Addresses Preliminary Group Meeting." *Xinhua Domestic Service,* 16 July 1993, in FBIS, 19 July 1993, 62.

Li, Zhai. "Shanghai Takes a Big Leap Forward." *Beijing Review* 34, no. 24 (17 June 1991): 22–27.

Liang, Yu-ying. "Peking's Hong Kong Policy after Tiananmen" *Issues and Studies* 26, no. 12 (December 1990): 71–84.

Liu, Philip. "Golf Diplomacy." *Free China Review* 44, no. 5 (May 1994): 30–37.

Lo, Ping. "CPC Brain Trust's Plans for Post-1997 Hong Kong." *Cheng Ming,* 1 September 1982, 14–15, in FBIS, 7 September 1882, W2–3.

———. "Notes on Northern Journey: Possible Takeover of Hong Kong by Communist China before Due Date." *Cheng Ming,* 1 November 1991, 6–8, in FBIS, 15 November 1991, 88–90.

Lo, Shiu-hing. "Democratization in Hong Kong: Reasons, Phases and Limits," *Issues and Studies* 26, no. 5 (May 1990): 100–117.

"Lu Ping Views Hong Kong Law, Election." *Hsin Wan Pao,* 2 July 1986, 2, in FBIS, 9 July 1986, W5.

Luo, Ping. "Hu Yaobang on the Hong Kong–Macao Policy." *Cheng Ming,* no. 58 (1 August 1982): 8–11, in FBIS, 5 August 1982, W6.

Ma, Teresa. "No News Is Bad News." *FEER,* 6 October 1983, 18–20.

"Majority Favor Links with Mainland." *China Post,* 10 October 1990, 12.

"Manifesto of the National People's Convention Concerning the Abrogation of Unequal Treaties." *The Chinese Social and Political Science Review,* vol. 15, supplement (1931–1932): 461–465.

Mao, Zedong. "The Chinese Revolution and the Chinese Communist Party." In *Selected Works of Mao Tse-Tung* [Mao Zedong],vol. 3. London: Lawrence & Wishart, 1954.

———. "On the Correct Handling of Contradictions Among the People." *Selected Works,* vol. 5. Beijing: Renming Chubanshe, 1965.

———. "On the Outrages by British Warships—Statement by the Spokesman of the General Headquarters of the Chinese People's Liberation Army." *Selected Works,* vol. 5. New York: International Publishers, n.d.

Mark, Jeremy. "Taiwan and China Fail to Resolve Investment Dispute." *The Wall Street Journal,* 29 April 1993, A10.

Montalla, Denda. "Li Chiang: Hong Kong Can Assist in Modernization." *South China Morning Post,* 20 December 1978, 1, in FBIS, 20 December 1978, A27.

Mosher, Stacy. "Uncertain Rights." *FEER,* 4 July 1991, 16–17.

———. "Creeping Intervention: Britain Concedes China's Demands in Airport Deal." *FEER,* 18 July 1991, 10–11.

———. "Selected Suffrage: Electoral System Remains Firmly Titled in Favour of Vested Interest." *FEER,* 29 August 1991, 16–18.

———. "Liberal Landslide: Election Result Puts China on Spot." *FEER,* 26 September 1991, 19–20.

———. "The Governor's Men: Low-Key Professionals Named to Legislative Council." *FEER,* 3 October 1991, 11–13.

———. "Local Justice: Concern over Make-up of Future Court of Final Appeal" *FEER,* 10 October 1991, 11–12.

———. "Out of the Club: Liberals Excluded from Executive Council." *FEER,* 7 November 1991, 12.

———. "Shadow of China: Peking to Appoint New Local Advisory Group." *FEER,* 6 February 1992, 18.

———. "Gang of Forty-Four: China's New Panel of Advisers Raises Misgivings." *FEER,* 26 March 1992, 13.

———. "Basic Flaw: Britain, China Argue over Pace of Democratization." *FEER,* 11 June 1992, 18.

"New Political Group Announces Establishment." FBIS, 13 July 1992, 70.

Ng, Norman Y. T. "From Special Economic Zones to the Coastal Open Cities: A Strategy for Modernization of China." In *China: Modernization in the 1980s,* Joseph Y. S. Cheng, ed., 445–459. Hong Kong: Chinese University Press, 1989.

Ngawang Jigme, Ngawang. "Explaining Regional Autonomy." *Beijing Review* 27, no. 26 (25 June 1984): 17–19.

"Notes on Beijing Activities on Occasion of *Ching Chi Tao Pao's* 45th Anniversary." *Ching Chi Tao Pao,* 1 January 1992, 12–14, in FBIS, 21 January 1992, 72.

"NPC Considers Motion to Set Up HK Group." *China Daily,* 25 March 1993, 1.

NPC Standing Committee. "Message to Compatriots in Taiwan." *Beijing Review* 22, no. 1 (5 January 1979): 16–17.

"Number of Free Trade Zones Increasing." *Xinhua,* 10 July 1993, in FBIS, 13 July 1993, 42.

Oakley, Robin. "Passports Scheme Is a Delicate Balancing Act." *The Times,* 21 December 1989, 6.

"'One Country, Two Systems' Born of Reality." *Beijing Review* 28, no. 5 (4 February 1985): 15.

PAIL Institute. *The Theory and Practice of Governmental Autonomy.* 2 vols. Washington, D. C.: Libraries of the American Society of International Law and PAIL Institution, 1980.

Patten, Christopher. *Hong Kong: A Thousand Days and Beyond.* Hong Kong: The Government Printer, October 1994.

"Peng Says PRC Policy on Hong Kong Unchanged." *Xinhua,* 25 June 1983, in FBIS, 6 July 1983, E1.

Peng, Zhen. "Report on the Draft of the Revised Constitution of the People's Republic of China." *Beijing Review* 25, no. 50 (13 December 1982): 9–23.

"PRC Forms Committee to Study 1997 Question." *South China Morning Post,* 10 July 1982, 1, in FBIS, 21 July 1982, W5.

"PRC Vice Foreign Minister Stresses Importance of Hong Kong, Macao." FBIS, 27 November 1978, A14.

"Premier Hua Guofeng Holds Press Conference." *Beijing Review* 22, no. 41 (12 October 1979): 8–11.

"Premier Reiterates to Talk with PRC." *Taipei International Service,* 10 October 1981, in FBIS, 13 October 1981, V2.

"Prime Minister Thatcher Holds Press Conference." *Hong Kong Television Broadcasts,* 27 September 1982, in FBIS, 28 September 1982, W4, W6.

"Private Economy Maintains Growth Momentum." *Xinhua,* 21 August 1993, in FBIS, 23 August 1993, 50.

"Private Economy to Continue Booming." *Beijing Review* 36, no. 7 (15 February 1993): 4.

Ren, Luosun. "Changes in China's Economic Management." *Beijing Review* 23, no. 5 (4 February 1980): 21–22.

Ren, Tao, and Zheng Jingsheng. "Why a Change in Emphasis?" *Beijing Review* 26, no. 1 (3 January 1983): 14–18.

"Republic of China on Taiwan in the Global Community," *Foreign Affairs* 73, no. 5 (September/October 1994): Advertising Section.

Riker, William H. "Six Books in Search of a Subject or Does Federalism Exist and Does It Matter?" *Comparative Politics* 2, no. 1 (October 1969): 135–146.

Rosario, Louise do. "Port of Convenience: Taipei to Keep Using Hong Kong as China Gateway." *FEER,* 1 September 1994, 22.

Sampson, Catherine. "Britain Accepts Peking Formula on HongKong." *The Times,* 15 February 1990, 10.

Sbragia, Alberta May. "Urban Autonomy Within the Unitary State: A Case Study of Public Housing in Milan, Italy." Ph.D. diss., University of Wisconsin, Madison, 1974.

"Self-Rule 'To Be Assured.'" *South China Morning Post,* 15 October 1983, 1, 8, in FBIS, 17 October 1983, W1–2.

Sender, Hanny. "Companies: China Savvy." *FEER,* 22 April 1993, 64–67.

"Shantou SEZ (I): Establishment, Progress and Planning." *Beijing Review* 34, no. 42 (21 October 1991): 16–20.

Shaw, Yu-ming. "An ROC View of the Hong Kong Issue." *Issues and Studies* 22, no. 6 (June 1986): 13–30.

"Shenzhen to Be Given Legislative Rights." *Beijing Review* 35, no. 27 (6 July 1992): 13.

Shih, Chuan. "New Trend in Investment in Mainland by Hong Kong Businessmen." *Zhongguo Tongxun She,* 14 February 1992, in FBIS, 28 February 1992, 83.

Skisdelski, Robert, and Felix Patrikeeff. "Trumping the China Cards." *The Times,* 21 September 1983, 12.

Sohn, Louis B. "Models of Autonomy Within the United Nations Framework." In *Models of Autonomy,* Yoram Dinstein, ed., 5–28. New Brunswick, N. J.: Transaction Books, 1981.

"The South China Miracle: A Great Leap Forward." *The Economist,* 5 October 1991, 19–22.

"*South China Morning Post* on Sovereignty Question." FBIS, 18 May 1983, W3–4.

"Spokesman Comments on CCP 'Peace Offensive.'" *Taipei CNA,* 10 October 1981, in FBIS, 13 October 1981, V2–3.

State Statistical Bureau. "Economic Progress in 14 Coastal Cities." *Beijing Review* 30, no. 13 (30 March 1987): 31–33.

Strasser, Steven. "The 'God of Democracy': Hong Kong's British Governor Defies Beijing and Pushes for Reform." *Newsweek,* 23 November 1992, 43.

Taiwan Affairs Office and Information Office State Council, "The Taiwan Question and Reunification of China," *Beijing Review* 36, no. 36 (6 September 1993): I–VIII.

"Taiwan: The Outsider." *The Economist,* 2 July 1994, 17–19.

Tanzer, Andrew. "The Mountains Are High, the Emperor Is Far Away." *Forbes,* 5 August 1991, 70–76.

———. "Cantonese Conquistadores." *Forbes,* 2 March 1992, 56–57.

"Tasks in the 80s." *Beijing Review* 23, no. 2 (14 January 1980): 5–6.

"Three Great Missions for 1980s." *NCNA,* 1 September 1982, 1.

Tsai, Wenhui. "Convergence and Divergence between Mainland China and Taiwan: The Future of Unification." *Issues and Studies* 27, no. 12 (December 1991): 1–28.

"Turn Shanghai into a Trade Center." *Beijing Review* 33, no. 35 (27 August 1990): 9.

"12th National Party Congress Opens." *Beijing Review* 25, no. 36 (6 September 1982): 4–6.

Webster, Philip. "Hong Kong Told of Citizenship by Points." *The Times,* 5 April 1990, 2.

———. "Tory and Labor Attack Bill: Points to Win Passports in Hong Kong." *The Times,* 15 April 1990, 1.

Wei, Jing. "Notes on a Trip to Shenzhen (1): Fruit of the Open Policy." *Beijing Review* 32, no. 33 (21 August 1989): 11–13.

———. "Notes on a Trip to Shenzhen (2): Progress and Problem in Attracting Foreign Capital." *Beijing Review* 32, no. 34 (28 August 1989): 27–31.

———. "Notes on a Trip to Shenzhen (3): Establishing an Export-Oriented Economy." *Beijing Review* 32, no. 35 (4 September 1989): 29–31.

———. "Notes on a Trip to Shenzhen: A Glimpse of the Science and Technology Industrial Park." *Beijing Review* 32, no. 36 (11 September 1989): 27–31.

Weng, Byron S. "The Hong Kong Model of 'One Country, Two Systems': Promises and Problems." In *The Basic Law and Hong Kong's Future,* Peter Wesley-Smith and Albert H. K. Chen, eds., 73–89. Hong Kong: Butterworths, 1988.

White Paper: The Further Development of Representative Government in Hong Kong. Hong Kong: The Government Printer, November 1984.

White Paper: The Development of Representative Government: The Way Forward. Hong Kong: The Government Printer, February 1988.

White Paper: Representative Government in Hong Kong. Hong Kong: The Government Printer, February 1994.

Wilson, David. "A Vision of the Future: Annual Address to the Legislative Council on October 11, 1989." In *Hong Kong 1990,* David Roberts, ed., 4–22. Hong Kong: Government Printer, 1990.

Wong, Jesse. "Hong Kong Governor's Speech Raises Hackles in Beijing with Proposals for More Democracy." *The Asian Wall Street Journal Weekly* 24, no. 41 (12 October 1992): 5, 12.

Worthy, Ford S. "Where Capitalism Thrives in China." *Fortune,* 9 March 1992, 71–75.

Wu, An-chia. "'One Country, Two Systems': A Model for Taiwan?" *Issues and Studies* 21, no. 7 (July 1985): 33–59.

Wu, Tongguang. "Yes, There Is Competition." *Beijing Review* 23, no. 22 (2 June 1980): 19–20.

Xie, Liangjun. "Rapport Is Reached at Historic Meeting." *China Daily,* 28 April 1993, 1.

———. "'Historic' Strait Agreements Signed." *China Daily,* 30 April 1993, 1.

Xu, Bing. "The Necessity and Feasibility of 'One Country, Two Systems' from the Perspective of Economic Development." *Zhongguo Fazhi Bao* [China Legal News], 25 January 1985, in FBIS, 4 February 1985, E3.

Xu, Dixin. "China's Special Economic Zones." *Beijing Review* 24, no. 50 (14 December 1981): 14–17.

"Xu Jiatun Hong Kong Remarks." *Ta Kung Pao,* 28 November 1985, in FBIS, 3 December 1985, W1–4.

Xue, Muqiao. "On Reforming the Economic Management System (II)." *Beijing Review* 23, no. 12 (24 March 1980): 21–25.

Yang, Yi. "'Controversy' Over Hong Kong's Draft Basic Law." *China Daily,* 18 June 1988, 4, in FBIS, 22 June 1988, 30.

Yao, Jianguo. "Yangtze River Valley: A Soaring Dragon." *Beijing Review* 36, no. 7 (15 February 1993): 14–16.

Yen, Tzung-ta. "Taiwan Investment in Mainland China and Its Impact on Taiwan's Industries." *Issues and Studies* 27, no. 5 (May 1991): 10–42.

Yeung, Chris. "Two Law Drafters Claim Majority Wishes Ignored." *South China Morning Post,* 21 November 1988, 1, 6, in FBIS, 23 November 1988, 71–72.

———. "Wang Qiren, Zou Jiahua Reassure Businessmen." *South China Morning Post,* 23 January 1992, 1, in FBIS 1992, 60.

Yu, Lulu. "Basic Law Body: Businessmen Propose 'Blueprint.'" *South China Morning Post,* 22 August 1986, 2, in FBIS, 25 August 1986, W3–5.

Yuan, Yvonne. "A Pragmatic Vision." *Free China Review* 43, no. 2 (February 1993): 16–20.

Zhang, Ping. "Positive Proposal Offered on HK Airport." *China Daily,* 24 May 1991, 1.

———. "Beijing Regrets 'Bill of Rights.'" *China Daily,* 7 June 1991, 1.

Zhang, Zeyu, and Weng Xiaoqing. "Shantou SEZ (II): Why More Foreign Investment?" *Beijing Review* 34, no. 42 (21 October 1991): 21–24.

Zhang, Zeyu, and Huang Yuxin. "Shantou SEZ (III): A Report on State-run Corporations." *Beijing Review* 34, no. 42 (21 October 1991): 24–27.

Zhao, Yuangguang. "'Mainstream Program,' Drawbacks Discussed." *Zhongguo Tongxun She,* 28 December 1988, in FBIS, 28 December 1988, 74.

Zhou, Enlai. "Some Questions on Policy Towards Nationalities (1)." *Beijing Review* 23, no. 9 (3 March 1980): 14–23.

———. "Some Questions on Policy Towards Nationalities (2)." *Beijng Review* 23, no. 10 (10 March 1980): 18–23.

Zhong, Shiyou. "Fresh Impetus from Deng's Message." *Beijing Review* 35, no. 15 (13 April 1992): 4–6.

Zhu, Jiaming. "Competition Means Progress." *Beijing Review* 23, no. 22 (2 June 1980): 21–22.
Zoakos, Criton M. "Hong Kong's Money War." *The New York Times*, 9 January 1993, Y15.

References in Chinese

"Canyu Zhi Gang Dashi, Quebao Pingwen Guodu." [Participate in Administering Hong Kong, and Ensure a Stable Transition.] *Renmin Ribao: Haiwai Ban* [People's Daily: Overseas Edition], 22 May 1992, 5.
Che, Shuming. "Zhongguo Geti Gongshanghu Shuliang Chuang Jilu." [Number of Private Businesses in China Set a Record.] *Renmin Ribao: Haiwai Ban,* 30 October 1992, 1.
Chen, Tianquan. "Jin Ban Xin Ren Gangqu Daibiao Ju Qinzhong Beijing." [Almost Half of Hong Kong's New Deputies to the NPC Have a Pro-China Background.] *Shijie Ribao* [World Journal], 2 February 1993, 4.
Deng, Xiaoping. *Deng Xiaoping Wenxuan, 1975–1982.* [Selected Works of Deng Xiaoping, 1975–1982.] Beijing: Renmin Chubanshe, 1983.
"Deng Xiaoping Shuo: Gangdu Bu Chexiao Zhenggai, Zhonggong Hui Shouhui Chengnuo." [Deng Xiaoping Says: China Will Revoke Its Promises on Hong Kong If the Hong Kong Governor Will Not Abandon His Reforms.] *Shijie Ribao,* 19 February 1993, 1.
"Diyi, Di'er Jie Gangshi Guwen Zong Mingdan." [Lists of the First and Second Groups of Hong Kong Affairs Advisers.] *Shijie Ribao,* 30 March 1993, 4.
"Gangren Guanzhu Zhonggang Guanxi Chaoguo Zhenggai." [Hong Kong People More Concerned with Hong Kong's Relationship with China than with Hong Kong's Political Reform.] *Shijie Ribao,* 10 February 1993, 4.
"Gongshangjie Dui Minzhupai 'Xingdong' Bu'an." [The Business Community Was Disturbed by the Democrats.] *Shijie Ribao,* 23 September 1991, 5.
"Haixia Liang'an Zhuankou Maoyi Qunian Tupo 80 Yi Maiyuan." [Indirect Trade Across the Taiwan Strait Topped US$8 Billion Last Year.] *Renmin Ribao: Haiwai Ban,* 8 January 1993, 5.
He, Chunlin. "Jingji Tequ: Tansuo he Fazhan de Shi Nian." [Special Economic Zone: Ten Years of Exploration and Development.] *Liaowang* [Outlook], no. 35 (27 August 1990): 4–6.
He, Guanghuai. "Shenzhen: Chongman Huolide Jingji Yunxing Jizhi." [Shenzhen: Economic Mechanism Runs with Full Vitality.] *Liaowang,* no. 34 (20 August 1990): 9–10.
Hua, Guofeng. "Zai Diwu Jie Quanguo Renmin Daibiao Dahui Di'er Ci Huiyishangde Gongzuo Baogao." [Report on the Work of the Government Presented at the Second Session of the Fifth National People's Congress.] *Hongqi* [Red Flag], no. 7 (3 July 1979): 24–32.
Jibenfa de Dansheng. [The Birth of Basic Law.] Hong Kong: Wen Wei Publishing, 1990.
"Jin Sanchengwu Shoufangzhe Zhichi Pengdu Fang'an." [About 35 Percent Polled Supported Patten's Package.] *Shijie Ribao,* 24 February 1993, 4.
Li, Shuzhong, and He Guanghuai. "Shenzhen, Zhanqi Laile." [Shenzhen Has Stood Up.] *Liaowang,* no 34 (20 August 1990): 6–8.
Li, Xian. "Tequ Shi Shehuizhuyide." [The Special Economic Zone Is Socialist.] *Liaowang,* no. 35 (27 August 1990): 7.
"Liju Bianlun Zhengzhi Fazhan, Yiyuan Lichang Xianming." [The Legco Debated over the Political Reforms and the Councillors Take Distinct Stand.] *Shijie Ribao,* 12 November 1992, 4.

Liu, Jianzhi. "Gangfu Ruo Gezhi Xin Jichang Jihua, Chuang Zhonggong Tongyi You Siren Caituan Jieshou." [China Will Ask Private Financial Groups to Build the New Airport If the Hong Kong Government Abandons Its Plan.] *Zhongyang Ribao* [Central Daily News], 28 May 1991, 4.

"Neidi Daju Touzi Xianggang Aomen, Qunian Zijin Yu Erbai Yi Meiyuan." [The Mainland Has Invested in Hong Kong and Macao Dramatically, and Total Investment Exceeded US$20 Billion Last Year.] *Renmin Ribao: Haiwai Ban*, 10 February 1993, 1.

"Qiluan Cui Sheng, Ziyoudang Chouweihui Chengli." [Initiated by the CRC, the Preparatory Committee of the Liberal Party Is Established.] *Shijie Ribao*, 1 March 1993, 4.

"Taishang Zai Dalu Touzi Qunian Zengjia." [Taiwanese Businessmen's Investment in the Mainland Increased Last Year.] *Renmin Ribao: Haiwai Ban*, 27 March 1992, 5.

Tao, Beichuan, "Jianli Zhonghua Gongtongti, Micheng Gouhe Shen Mou Tongyi." [On the Establishment of the Chinese Commonwealth and Ending the Dispute for Reunification.] *Zhongyang Ribao*, 24 October 1991, 1.

Wang, Shuwen. *Xianggang Tebie Xingzhengqu Jibenfa Daolun*. [A Guide to the Basic Law of Hong Kong Special Administrative Region.] Beijing: Zhonggong Zhongyang Dangxiao Chubanshe, 1990.

Wang, Yanbin. "Zhongguo Xiangzhen Qiye Honghong Huohuo, Qunian Chanzhi Tupo Yiwan Yi Yuan." [China's Rural Industry Is Prosperous and Its Output Topped 1000 Billion Yuan Last Year.] *Renmin Ribao: Haiwai Ban*, 5 January 1993, 1.

Wei, Yanan, and Huang Jichang. "Fanying Gefang Yiyuan, Kuoda Zhijie Goutong." [Reflect All-Circles' Will and Increase Direct Communications.] *Renmin Ribao: Haiwai Ban*, 13 March 1992, 5.

Xianggang Tebie Xingzhengqu Jibenfa Qicao Weiyuanhui Mishuchu [Secretariat of the Basic Law Drafting Committee of the Hong Kong Special Administrative Region], ed. *Guanyu Zhonghua Renmin Gongheguo Xianggang Tebie Xingzhengqu Jibenfa de Zhongyao Wenjian*. [Important Documents about the Basic Law of the Hong Kong Special Administrative Region of the People's Republic of China.] Beijing: Renmin Chubanshe, 1990.

Xiao, Weiyuen. *Yiguo liangzhi Yu Xianggang Jiben Falu Zhidu*. [One Country, Two Systems and Basic Legal System of Hong Kong.] Beijing: Beijing Daxue Chubanshe, 1990.

Yi, Feng. "Zhou Nan Zhichu: Zhongguo Zhengfu Juebu Na Yuanze Zuo Jiaoyi." [Zhou Nan Indicated That China Would Never Barter Away Principle.] *Renmin Ribao: Haiwai Ban*, 7 November 1992, 3.

"Zhang Jianquan: Guangtongmeng Le Hunle Tounao." [Zhang Jianquan Says: The UDHK Was Blinded for over-Enjoying its Victory.] *Shijie Ribao*, 20 September 1991, 5.

Zhao, Jian. "Haiwai Hua Shang Touzi Zhongguo Xin Qushi." [New Trend in Investment in China by Overseas Chinese Businessmen.] *Renmin Ribao: Haiwai Ban*, 12 January 1993, 5.

"Zhengzhi Fang'an Zhengyi Dian, Gangdu Fang Jing Bairehua." [Dispute Over the Governor's Political Reform Plan Became White-Hot When the Governor Visited Beijing.] *Shijie Ribao*, 28 October 1992, 4.

"Zhonggong Ba Jie Zhengxie Gang'ao Weiyuan 110 Ronghuo Weiren." [110 Hong Kong and Macao Deputies Were Appointed to the Eighth CPPCC.] *Shijie Ribao*, 20 February 1993, 4.

"Zhonggong Chengwei Xianggang Zuida Touzi Guo." [China Has Become Hong Kong's Biggest Foreign Investor.] *Shijie Ribao*, 18 July 1991, 6.

"Zhongguo Dalu de Baiwan Fuweng." [Mainland China's Millionaires.] *Shijie Ribao*, 17 June 1992, 11.

Zhonghua Renmin Gongheguo Xianggang Tebie Xingzhengqu Jibenfa Zixun Weiyuanhui [The Consultative Committee of the Basic Law of the Hong Kong Special Administrative Region of the People's Republic of China], ed. *Zixun Baogao.* [Consultative Report.] Vols. 1–5. Hong Kong: Zhonghua Shangwu Caise Yinshua Youxian Gongsi, 1988 and 1989.

"Zhong Ying Guanyu Xianggang 1994/95 Nian Xuanju Anpai Huitanzhong Jige Zhuyao Wentide Zhenxiang." [The Real Facts of the Major Issues About the China-Britain Talks on Hong Kong's 1994/95 Elections.] *Renmin Ribao: Haiwai Ban,* 1 March 1994, 3, 5.

"Zhong Ying Shuangfang Guanyu Xianggang Wentide Qige Wenjian." [Sino-British Seven Documents About the Hong Kong Question.] *Renmin Ribao: Haiwai Ban,* 29 October 1992, 3.

Zhou, Nan. "Zhongguo Yu Xianggang de Hudong Jingji Guanxi." [The Economic Interdependence Between China and Hong Kong.] *Renmin Ribao: Haiwai Ban,* 26 March 1992, 5.

Index

About the Book and Author

Thoroughly researched and well documented, this accessible book looks at the past, present, and future of Hong Kong.

Wang examines China's policy toward the Hong Kong transition in general—including the "one country, two systems" formula, the 1984 Sino-British agreement, and the Basic Law of the Hong Kong Special Administrative Region (SAR)—and also addresses two controversial issues: the democratization, or political reform, of Hong Kong and the relationship between China's sovereignty and the SAR's autonomy. Interpreting China's Hong Kong policy from the perspective of Beijing's overall reform measures, he illuminates the link between the PRC's modernization programs and the intended reunification with Hong Kong, Taiwan, and Macao.

The book concludes with a look beyond 1997—when China may or may not have a leadership that continues Deng's reforms—honestly assessing Hong Kong's chances of maintained capitalism and prosperity.

Enbao Wang is assistant professor of political science at Lewis-Clark State College in Lewiston, Idaho.